What they said about Thomas Myler's previous books

New York Fight Nights

Thomas Myler has served up another collection of gripping boxing stories. The author packs such a punch with his masterful storytelling that you will feel you were ringside inhaling the sizzling atmosphere at each clash of the titans. A must for boxing fans.

Ireland's Own

There are few more authoritative voices in boxing than Thomas Myler and this is another wonderfully evocative addition to his growing body of work.

Irish Independent

Another great book from the pen of the prolific Thomas Myler.

RTE, Ireland's national broadcaster

The Mad and the Bad

Another storytelling gem from Thomas Myler, pouring light into the shadows surrounding some of boxing's most colourful characters.

Irish Independent

The best boxing book of the year from a top writer.

Daily Mail

Boxing's Greatest Upsets: Fights That Shook The World

A respected writer, Myler has compiled a worthy volume on the most sensational and talked-about upsets of the glove era, drawing on interviews, archive footage and worldwide contacts.

Yorkshire Evening Post

Fight fans will glory in this offbeat history of boxing's biggest shocks, from Gentleman Jim's knockout of John L. Sullivan in 1892 to the modern era. A must for your bookshelf.

Hull Daily Mail

Boxing's Hall of Shame

Boxing scribe Thomas Myler shares with the reader a ringside seat for the sport's most controversial fights. It's an engaging read, one that feeds our fascination with the darker side of the sport.

Bert Sugar, US author and broadcaster

Well written and thoroughly researched by one of the best boxing writers in these islands, Myler has a keen eye for the story behind the story. A must read for all fight fans.

Yorkshire Post

Close Encounters with the Gloves Off
Reading like a beautiful love letter to the fight game's glorious past, there's not a better boxing book on the shelves – anywhere.

Irish Independent

Admired and respected around the world, Thomas Myler has surpassed himself with this latest offering.

Dublin Herald

Book of the Month

Lonsdale Sports

Myler's ability to dig deep, gather plenty of background information, coupled with his easy-flowing style of writing, paints a fascinating scene building up to the contests. We urge you to add this book to your collection.

Boxing News

Myler doesn't just deal with what happened inside the ropes but also provides a balanced overview of the controversies, personalities and historical contexts that make these fights worth reading about.

Ring

Ringside with the Celtic Warriors
The offering from this highly respected boxing writer is well up to the standard we expect from him.

Boxing News

Thomas Myler has come up with another gem. His credentials and easy, readable style make this a must book for fight fans.

The Sun

As a ring historian, Thomas Myler has few peers.

Belfast Telegraph

JOE LOUIS

JOE LOUIS

THOMAS MYLER

JOE LOUIS

The Rise and Fall of the
BROWN BOMBER

First published by Pitch Publishing, 2019

Pitch Publishing
A2 Yeoman Gate
Yeoman Way
Worthing
Sussex
BN13 3QZ
www.pitchpublishing.co.uk
info@pitchpublishing.co.uk

A CIP catalogue record is available for this book
from the British Library.

ISBN 978 1 78531 536 7

Typesetting and origination by Pitch Publishing
Printed and bound in India by Replika Press Pvt. Ltd.

Contents

Dedication

To six real champions
Betty, Jacqueline, Sinead,
Ciaran, Colin and Vivian,
always in my corner

About the author

Thomas Myler is a well-known boxing historian, journalist, author and broadcaster. This is his tenth book, his ninth on boxing, the most recent being the best-selling *The Mad and the Bad*, published by Pitch. Myler was described by the late, great American boxing scribe and best-selling author George Kimble as 'one of the best boxing writers in the world'. He has spent a lifetime in the business, meeting boxers, promoters, managers, trainers, matchmakers and publicists, and has interviewed many of the sport's greats. His work has appeared in many magazines and newspapers. He lives in Dublin.

Acknowledgements

This book would not have been possible without the help of so many people too numerous to mention. But special note must be made of *Boxing News* and *Independent News and Media* for their always-helpful assistance as well as their fine writers, including Matt Christie, Tris Dixon, John Jarrett, Claude Abrams, Bob Mee and Vincent Hogan, all good friends and true experts in the noble art. What they don't know about boxing is not worth knowing. Also of immense help was the invaluable *International Boxing Research Organization* journal and Patrick Myler. My own family, too, were always by my side, Jacqueline, Sinead, Ciaran, Colin and Vivian. My wonderful late wife Betty also deserves mention.

Photographs are by kind permission of Getty Images, with some from the Thomas Myler Collection. Last but certainly not least, credit must go to Pitch Publishing for having the foresight, dedication and care to get the book into print. Credit here must go to publishing executives Paul and Jane Camillin and their excellent team.

Thank you all.

That's what boxing is,
the sweet science.

A. J. Liebling, master storyteller
on the *New Yorker*

Prologue

As a youngster growing up in the 1940s, it is not difficult to recall that Joe Louis was the number one boxer during the war years. His name was on everybody's lips. Louis, the famous 'Brown Bomber', was heavyweight champion of the world and master of all he surveyed. Hadn't he beaten the best that the division had to offer?

His lone defeat, against Max Schmeling in 1936, was well and truly avenged two years later. There seemed nobody who could take the title from Louis after he won it from a game James J. Braddock in 1937. Many tried and failed, some narrowly.

Billy Conn, an ambitious Irish-American from Pittsburgh, almost succeeded with a points lead after 12 rounds in 1941, but Louis knocked him out in the 13th. At the tail end of his career in 1947, Louis won an unpopular points decision over the veteran Jersey Joe Walcott. The referee voted for Walcott but the two judges opted for Louis, allowing him to keep his title. In a return bout six months later, Louis knocked out his man in 11 rounds. Even in the closing years of his career, 1950–1951, he beat top contenders.

It is often hard to point out to modern boxing people how great Louis was, or the powerful influence he had on the fight game. He transcended the sport. He was world heavyweight champion for 11 years and eight months, and put his title on the line no fewer than 25 times, feats that no previous heavyweight champion had ever achieved. It was also more than the combined total of defences by Louis' nine immediate predecessors going back 32 years. Moreover, if there were any doubts or controversies surrounding any defence, Louis would give the challenger a second shot.

Louis also helped to smash the despicable colour bar that denied many great boxers in the heavyweight division an opportunity to fight for the title. John L. Sullivan, the first world heavyweight champion under the Queensberry Rules in the late 1880s, refused to put his title on the line against a black challenger. In the 1920s, Jack Dempsey never took on his number one contender Harry Wills, the 'Black Panther'.

In the first half-century of the heavyweight championship, only one black boxer, Jack Johnson, managed to win the title – and the big Texan only got his deserved chance by following Tommy Burns across three continents before catching up with him in Australia.

At Rushcutter's Bay Arena in Sydney on 26 December 1908, Johnson made the French-Canadian pay for every ounce of anger, frustration and discrimination he had endured over the years. Taunting and tormenting the outclassed champion, Johnson won when the police at ringside mercifully instructed the referee to stop the one-sided fight in the 14th round.

Johnson lost his title seven years later to a white boxer, Jess Willard, on a controversial knockout in the 26th round. There would not be another black heavyweight champion for 22 years until Louis came along in 1937.

Louis helped to open the way for many other great non-white boxers to compete on level terms. He gave black contenders a chance at the title, an opportunity they would have been denied in the past. In the modern age, black champions seem the norm in any division, which is only right and proper.

This writer was fortunate to have met Louis – thankfully outside the ring – when he was on a promotional tour of the UK and Ireland in 1970. For well over an hour of fascinating chat over lunch in a Dublin hotel, the boxing legend proved to be a charming and pleasant individual.

In between fans coming over to our table for an autograph or just to say hello, the 'Brown Bomber' was always open and frank, revealing many stories never told before. He offered insights into his big fights and supplied many quotes. Where appropriate, the author has used some of this information in the following pages.

On the downside, Louis was not without his faults, inside and outside the roped square. In the ring, despite his powerful blows, underrated boxing skill and resilience, he was open to a right-hand punch, even though he was beaten inside the distance on just two occasions in 67 fights.

Outside the ring, Louis was a serial womaniser and had a string of lady friends, including many celebrities, all through his three marriages. A notoriously big spender but a decidedly poor businessman, he was forever plagued by income tax demands and in his closing years was ravaged by ill health. It was a sad end to one of the greatest ever boxing champions.

Whenever or wherever Louis' name comes up for discussion, one big question will surely linger. Was he the best of all the heavyweight kings? Would he have beaten Jack Johnson, or Jack Dempsey, or Rocky Marciano in their primes? What of Muhammad Ali? Could he have landed his powerful punches on the fleet-footed 'Louisville Lip'? Who can tell? Different eras, different situations, different rules. The answers will never be satisfactorily found but speculation certainly makes for lively discussion.

In *The 100 Greatest Boxers* published by *Boxing News* in 2017, Louis is ranked fourth, directly behind Sugar Ray Robinson,

Ali and Henry Armstrong, the incredible fighter who held three world titles simultaneously – featherweight, lightweight and welterweight – in the days when there were only eight divisions in the whole of boxing, flyweight to heavyweight.

You could name the eight champions then at a moment's notice. The world champion was what he claimed to be, the best boxer in the world. America's two main controlling bodies, the National Boxing Association and the New York State Athletic Commission, often disagreed but generally came together and recognised one official champion in each division. The British Boxing Board of Control and the European Boxing Union usually came on board too.

All that changed drastically from the 1960s when new boxing organisations started popping up like flowers in springtime, each setting up their own 'world' champions. By the 1980s, more had come on the scene. Today, there are no fewer than 17 weight divisions, from minimumweight to heavyweight, and conceivably 17 'world' champions. Can you name the 17? Very unlikely. And the 17 does not even include today's 'super' champions.

There are at least seven 'world' organisations around the world. The four main ones are the World Boxing Association, the World Boxing Council, the International Boxing Federation and the World Boxing Organisation. They are recognised by their initials, the WBA, the WBC, the IBF and the WBO, and are collectively known as the alphabet boys, or alphabet soup. On this subject, the WBA, once a very respected organisation, now lists 29 'world' champions across the 17 divisions. Where will it all end? Maybe Sir Walter Scott had something when he said, 'Oh what a tangled web we weave when first we practise to deceive.'

Meanwhile, enjoy the journey through simpler if turbulent times in the following pages.

Life on the plantation

In a ramshackle, unpainted dwelling in Chambers County, Alabama, about 12 miles from the little village of Lafayette in the Buckalew mountain region, a seventh child was born to Munroe and Lillie Reese-Barrow on 13 May 1914. He was named Joseph Louis Barrow. Munroe did not experience any great joy at the arrival of his new son. He was a sharecropper, which meant that he farmed his own piece of land but had to share the crop with the landowner. In addition, the sharecropper also had to buy or rent a horse, a plough, fertiliser and other essentials from the owner.

Living in the Buckalew region was tough and hard, and Munroe could not foresee a life for his new son that would be different from the one he had always known himself, filled as it was with work and worry, toiling on the land. It was a precarious existence, not far removed from the slavery that preceded it.

Indeed, both Munroe's parents had been slaves, taking the name 'Barrow' from the owner of the plantation on which they worked. Munroe, who was known as Mun, was predominantly African-American while Lillie had Native American blood traced back to the Cherokee tribe. The morning Joseph Louis was born, Susan Radford, a midwife, attended to Lillie while

Munroe and the children worked on the plantation, a regular occurrence from sunrise to sunset. The wheat, cotton and vegetables that Mun raised with Lillie's help were not enough to support their large family in the way they would have liked.

The Barrows were hungry most of the time. They were often shoeless and were dressed in rags. Their home was basically a shack that stood on a 120-acre tract of stubborn, rocky soil they had rented just four years previously. It had been much too small for a family of six children, now seven. Eventually, there would be eight in total.

'He weighed about 11lb when he was born, and except for an earache when he was little, he was never sick a day in his life,' Lillie would recall of Joseph in later years. 'He's always been healthy and strong because I would feed him plenty of collard greens, fat pack and corn pone, all good nourishing food. He didn't talk until he was six and he always liked to sleep too much. It was worth my life to get him out of that bed.'

Louis' own recollections matched his mother's memory of a slow-developing child. 'Mom always told me I was a worse cry-baby than my brothers and sisters,' he said. 'I hollered louder than the others. I took a long time to walk, too. I think it was almost a year before I could get around. I was stubborn in school and my teacher used to make me say words over and over again. I didn't like that because the other kids in class didn't have to do it. Maybe that's why, when I was coming up in boxing, I never liked to talk too much. Still don't. If a man has something to say, he can say it in a couple of words. He doesn't need all week to make his point.'

Louis grew up to be a big, strong boy who never had a day's illness. Sadly, Mun was not so fortunate. From 1906 onwards, he spent short spells in the Searcy State Hospital for the Criminally Insane at Mount Vernon in Mobile, Alabama. A melancholy man of 6ft and weighing close to 200lb, the long years of strain, hard work on the plantation and struggle to rear a large family were becoming too much. In 1916, when Louis was two, Mun was led away to Searcy, where he would spend the rest of his life.

The hospital, built in 1828 and today nothing more than a decaying tourist attraction, was Mun's haven. As a result, Louis knew very little of his biological father. By the time of Mun's death on 27 November 1938, aged 59, he knew nothing of his famous son's accomplishments in the boxing ring or outside it, which had made him the best-known African-American in the land.

Louis felt the loss of the father. He wished he could have shared with Mun some of his earnings, which in 1938 totalled more than a million dollars. He showed his love in the only way he knew, by providing a costly funeral. Relatives from Detroit joined those from the Buckalew region to hear the minister's oration and watch the ornate metal casket being lowered into the ground. The little burial ground at the foot of Buckalew mountain claimed as a hero the man who had lived in obscurity.

Back in 1920, Lillie had received information from a hospital official that Mun had died and made arrangements for 'a decent burial'. She would not be in attendance, preferring to remember him as he was: big and strong. It was only in later years that Lillie, having remarried, discovered that she had been given the wrong information and that Mun was still alive, though still institutionalised. She would still visit him in Searcy, though he would not know who she was.

'When momma had the time, she was a great teacher,' recalled Louis. 'Time for her was hard to come by. When daddy was taken away, she was left with eight children to raise on a back-breaking piece of land. She worked as hard, and many times harder, than any man around. She could plough a good straight furrow, plant and pick with the best of them, cut cord wood like a lumberjack, then leave the fields an hour earlier than anyone else and fix a meal for her family. God, I loved that woman.

'Don't get me wrong, though. Momma could mix it up, tough and tender. If you stepped out of line with her, she'd put your head between your knees and whip you with a strap. One thing, though. Nobody around could say that the Barrow children were wild or bad or didn't have any manners.'

When Louis was six years old, the family moved to Mount Sinai, a hamlet deeper in the Buckalew mountains. By this time, his mother, working on the assumption that Mun was dead, was keeping company with Patrick Brooks, a slender, fair-haired widower with five children of his own. They would soon marry. According to Louis' younger sister Vunies, Brooks 'worked for the richest man in Alabama, at least that's what he said. His boss apparently was a white man who had something to do with building bridges. Because of our stepdad, our situation improved. It was certainly better than we had known.'

At the same time, life was not ideal. With 13 children now in the household, the family would sleep three in a bed. Louis, more than the others, would rebel against this form of crowding. What he remembered most was how cold it was in the mountains. The kids did not wear shoes and were required to save their good clothes for Sundays. By then, Louis was in school and his sister, Eulalia, would escort him and Vunies to the Mount Sinai Baptist Church on Sundays.

Louis would remember that his mother was very religious and that despite being so busy at work, she would make sure that all her children had clean clothes before going to church for a day of worship. He recalled that she always made sure they did the right thing, made the right decisions and that each and every one of her children took pride in themselves. He would say that she always said that a good name was more important than money.

'When I was a little boy, I always wanted my momma to smile on me,' Louis recalled. 'Sometimes I'd run off and try to sneak away from my chores and play games, but lots of times I'd scrub all the floors in the house. When momma would come home and see what I had done, she would grab me and give me a big kiss for it. Then I could have floated clear up to the sky.'

Louis' most pleasant memories of Alabama revolved around Saturday trips to the town of Camp Hill in nearby Tallapoosa County. His stepfather would take all the children there in his Model T Ford. They would look forward to these trips because Camp Hill had a lot of stores on the main street and it would be fun just to sit in the car and observe the busy scene as their stepfather did his business.

On his return, he would have cheese and crackers for 'a little party, a kind of holiday'. Louis would remember that real holidays like Easter and Christmas would be celebrated with egg hunts and the Christmas stocking at the end of the bed. This would be filled with apples, oranges and red peppermint sweets.

Such meagre pleasures were the order of the day. America then was still primarily rural and heavily agricultural. It was not until 1920, around the time the Barrow and Brooks families combined forces, that the official US census finally showed more Americans living in towns and cities than on farms. If not exactly blissful, life in the Alabama countryside was necessarily simple. Kerosene lamps, not electricity, provided light. Water for bathing, washing and cooking was brought in from outside. Wood needed to be chopped to feed the large cast-iron stove.

Though it was not fancy, nor even plentiful, it was varied. Fish, bacon, chicken, corn and potatoes found their way to the table and were devoured by the hard-working family. They were early risers. By the time the sun came up in the morning, the family were already back in the fields, toiling to keep the cotton growing, bending their backs to assure themselves of a reasonable share of the proceeds after the landlord took his portion. They seldom came home before sundown.

'We played lots of games, like hide and seek in a tree until the fellow called the leader found you,' Louis remembered. 'Sometimes we would just swing in the trees like little Tarzans. It was good for the development of shoulders and arms. One time near a tree, I found half a bottle of White Lightning, a strong cider. Of course, I drank it, out of curiosity more than anything else, and naturally got drunk. I wandered around stumbling until I fell asleep under the tree. Momma came looking for me and found me, still asleep. She didn't spank me but did give me a lecture on the evils of drink. It was many decades before I touched a drink of alcohol, and then only rarely and very little.'

Louis was not aware of any racial tension at the time. Not once, he insisted, did he hear talk of lynching or the difficulties of being a black man in the Alabama of his youth. In his adult years, people would often ask him about life then, and if the Ku Klux Klan ever bothered his family. 'To tell the absolute truth, there didn't seem to be anything bad between blacks and whites in Lafayette, but you have to remember I was a little boy,' he said.

'There were other things that I did not take a hold on. I remember black people getting together and talking about how much white blood they had, and how much Indian blood they had, but hardly anybody talked about how much black blood they had.

'I didn't know too much but I could easily see that all those white-blooded, Indian-blooded black people lived a damn sight worse than some of the poorest white people I saw. I knew there was a difference but it made no difference to me. My folks seemed to get along with the white people in the area. Maybe it was a case of, "You got your place and I got mine." Probably we never crossed the line to cause the angers and hurts and lynchings that took place all over the South. Another funny thing. I never heard about lynchings, and nobody white ever called me a nigger until my family moved to Detroit.'

Louis played with white children, and while he was aware of differences, he accepted them as a matter of course. A quiet boy by nature, he was certainly less given to arguments than the others. He would recall on one occasion when a boy picked a fight with him in the school yard over something or other. The teacher had seen the fracas from the school window. She rushed and separated them, but for some reason, chose to reprimand Louis as an act of discipline. He never really understood why. 'Guess for no other reason than I was bigger,' he recalled in later years.

Louis would remember Patrick Brooks as the only father he ever really knew. 'He was a good man and worked hard and did the best he could,' said Louis. 'He always looked after my mother and all the children. He was always fair and treated us all as equally as he could. There were no favourites. He would just as soon lay a hand on his own young son, Pat Junior, as he would on Joe Louis Barrow. His kids and my brothers and sisters fit in like one big family, although we were too much for his little house or the one momma had. So we moved to a larger house in Camp Hill, deeper into the Buckalew mountains.

'My stepbrother, Pat Brooks Jr, and I were the same age and we got on well. Of course we did have disagreements sometimes. I remember one day we had a fight. He took up a brick and hit me on the head, and I still have that scar. Another time I'd fight if we had a disagreement about marbles. If somebody bothered my sisters, I'd fight too. But generally, we all got on well.'

Some of Patrick Brooks' relatives often came from Detroit to visit the family and talked of life in the big city. On more than one occasion, they talked about the family moving to Detroit for a better life. It was not idle talk but talk of reality. It was now 1926. It was a fact that tens of thousands of African-Americans were departing the South. Most boarded railway cars and watched as the cotton fields, tobacco farms and rich plantations of home gave way to land planted with corn and wheat.

In the Midwest, they stopped at stations without the familiar 'White' and 'Coloured' signs. Most continued to ride the train until it reached one of the booming Midwestern cities such as Detroit, Chicago, Gary or Cleveland, or one of the northern cities with established black communities. No longer was the landscape planted with crops. Instead of corn and wheat, they saw factories, some larger than towns, breathing fire and belching smoke. In the words of Randy Roberts, prolific author and Professor of History at Purdue University, Indiana, 'They had arrived in a place that looked like hell but promised heavenly opportunities.'

One day, Brooks was visited by relatives who told him that the Ford Motor Company in Detroit was paying good money to factory hands and it was a good place to work. Henry Ford was the son of an Irishman who had emigrated to the US from County Cork, via Somerset in England, and set up the company in 1901. He was considered a good and fair employer. Some 11,000 African-Americans were working in Detroit's auto plants. Ten years earlier, there had been none. World War One had brought about a change in attitude.

With many white workers called into military service, industrialists had no choice but to employ black people. Ford, tinkering with social problems as much as he did with mechanical ones, allowed them into all job classifications and paid them the same salary as whites. The paternalistic billionaire was regularly seen meeting with Baptist teachers and national race leaders such as Booker T. Washington. In the eyes of many African-Americans, he was their greatest white advocate since Abraham Lincoln.

A smile crossed Brooks' face at the thought of economic salvation in the North. He was also persuaded to move after a brush with the Ku Klux Klan. Arrangements were made for Peter Reese, a brother of Louis' mother, to look after the family until Joe's stepfather and Momma Louis had saved up enough money to bring them up to Detroit. They lived with a relative in Macomb Street on the city's East Side and Brooks soon got employment at the Ford factory.

Louis would say that he missed his mother and stepfather very much and couldn't wait to see them again, even though her brother was doing a very good job of taking care of the family. 'It seemed like a hundred years before I joined them, even though it was only a few months before they sent for us,' he said.

The big day arrived when they boarded the train for the 800-mile journey to Detroit. In their newly adopted city, they lived in a tenement house at 2700 Catherine Street, now Madison Street, in the poor Black Bottom area of the city. It was called Black Bottom not because of its black population but originally after the rich, black soil of its farming days. Another future great, Sugar Ray Robinson, who was also a resident of Black Bottom in his early days, said it was so called because it really was the bottom and that 'you couldn't sink any lower'.

Louis remembered, 'The place we lived in was crowded but you can't imagine the impact the city had on me. I never saw so many people in one place, or so many cars at one time. There were other things that I had never heard of – parks, libraries, brick schoolhouses, movie theatres. We had something too in Detroit that we didn't have in Alabama, an inside toilet. Another thing, there were electric lights.

'I had heard about electricity but I had never seen it at home. Seemed like everybody I knew had kerosene lamps that smoked and smelled all over the house. I used to think to myself, "What did we need electricity for when practically everybody was going to sleep by sundown?" But you can't imagine the impact the city had on me.'

Being the country boy he was, Louis was overwhelmed by the size of the city. He attended Duffield School where, he was dismayed to discover, his lack of good schooling in Alabama had put him at a considerable disadvantage. Older than the other children and big for his age, Joseph felt his size was accentuated when the school authorities, in consideration of the rural training he'd had, put him a year behind other children of his age. He was troubled and confused to be faced suddenly with facts he should have learned but had never even heard about. Lessons seemed a hopeless jumble.

Joe's pronounced Southern accent and the strange jargon which he had learned to use in the Buckalew region complicated matters further. It was not very easy to make himself understood. He was also embarrassed by a bad stammer he had developed in Alabama. One day, a classmate was asked by her father, 'What does Joe Barrow do in school?' 'Pop,' she replied, 'he just looks out the window.' The whole school thing seemed to him to be a complete waste of time.

It seemed a great relief when he got a job after school at an ice company. Now aged 12 and carrying blocks of ice, often weighing as much as 50lb, up flights of stairs, he would later claim helped to develop his powerful shoulders and muscular arms. More importantly, he was bringing in a dollar a week, a helpful addition to the family budget. Still, things were looking decidedly bleak before an unexpected boom changed things around considerably.

By applying to the Detroit Welfare Board, they were able to secure $269, paid to them over a period of seven months. It hurt Lillie's pride to accept charity, even for the sake of feeding and clothing her brood. It would not be until 1935 that she reconciled accepting the board's gift. Then Joe Louis, who had become the most famous heavyweight since the great Jack Dempsey, wrote out a cheque for $269 and handed it over to the board in repayment and heartfelt thanks.

After Joe had completed seventh grade at Duffield School, one of his teachers, Miss Veda Schwader, thought he would fare better in a trade school. 'Your boy is going to make a living with his hands,' she told his parents, 'and he had better start now rather than later.' They took Veda's advice and had their son enrolled at Bronson Trade School, where he learned how to use the tools of a cabinetmaker. He made tables, chairs, little closets and shelves, and when he brought them home, they added to the meagre furnishings his mother had been able to collect. Joe liked the woodworking trade and felt he might be able to make a good living at it.

Soon, America would be in the grip of the Great Depression. On the morning of 24 October 1929, panic swept the New York Stock Exchange on Wall Street. The bottom fell out of the market in stocks and shares. Investors ordered their brokers to sell at any price, and during the day a total of 12,894,650 shares were sold. America had been experiencing a boom and now the bubble had burst. Some had vast fortunes wiped out and many smaller investors also faced ruin. There were several suicides and the effect was felt worldwide. Patrick Brooks lost his job at Ford.

An aimlessness born of despair swept over Louis and the family. He spent long hours running with the Purple Gang and regularly got into fights. Concerned, his mother felt he ought to take violin lessons to take his mind off fighting in the streets and mixing with the wrong company. Lillie always loved music and at some sacrifice she purchased a violin and enrolled him with a teacher on Woodward Avenue at 50 cents a class. To please her, he went to his music teacher with what was, to him, monotonous regularity. While Joe's fondness for it sprang mostly from the sense of rhythm that guided his every movement, drums might have suited him better.

When he grew into adulthood, Joe would develop a deep love for jazz and blues. But classical music was just not his thing. It never was, so the move into cultural matters did not take hold. When out of his mother's sight, he strummed the violin instead of using the bow. After having five or six lessons, he quit. 'You cannot imagine the kidding I got from the other guys,' he said in later years. 'Here I was, a big guy over six feet tall and carrying a little violin. They used to call me a sissy.'

When the teacher came by the family home and asked Lillie where her son was, the answer she got was, 'I understood he was having his lessons.' When Joe came home later and was quizzed by his mother, she was told he had used the money to pay for a locker, where he hid the violin, at the Brewster Recreation Center. The centre had a gym where amateur boxers gathered and trained. Louis had been reading about famous boxers, notably his idol Jack Dempsey, who had fought his way to be heavyweight champion of the world. He told his mother he wanted to be a boxer, not a musician.

Angry at first, and anxious to keep the peace, she consented. 'If that's what you really want, that's OK,' she said, giving her son a hug. Joe told her he had sparred with some of the regulars there and enjoyed it. What he did not tell her was that kids used to jeer him when they saw him carrying his violin case, and that on his way from his last violin lesson, he smashed the instrument over the head of one of them and it broke into little pieces.

Privately, Lillie felt that some day he would come home with his face cut and eyes blackened and that would be the end of it. Joe was now working as a lathe operator at the Briggs car factory. Lillie only hoped that, if he did not want to be a violin player and get into an orchestra, then he might settle down at the factory and forget this crazy boxing lark.

Among those who trained at the Brewster Center was a promising young amateur flyweight named Walker Smith Jr, who would become famous as Sugar Ray Robinson. They would remain close friends all their lives. 'Louis was known as Joe Barrow and a good boxer, the big hero of the neighbourhood,' Robinson said in later years. 'We kids used to tag along behind him. He lived a couple of blocks away from me. When it was time for him to go to the Brewster Center to train, I'd go over and stand in front of his home waiting for him.

'When he'd come out, I'd grab the little bag he carried, with his shoes and stuff, and carry it for him. He got to know me and called me Junior, but I don't think he ever knew my name. When my mom took us kids to live in New York a few years later, I still followed Joe's career in the newspapers and magazines. Later on, we would meet up on big fight nights and always kept in touch.'

Another young boxer who trained at the centre was Thurston McKinney, his former classmate at Duffield School. McKinney had become amateur lightweight champion of Michigan and was something of a celebrity in the neighbourhood. He had earlier seen Louis from time to time carrying his violin case.

'Are you going to be a musician or a boxer?' asked McKinney one day.

'I'm taking violin lessons but I'd prefer the gym.'

'Oh, come on Joe. Give up the violin and take up the gloves.'

'I'll think about it, Thurston.'

One afternoon, McKinney told Louis he had an important bout coming up and Joe agreed to spar with him in the gym. For the first few minutes of the session, McKinney jabbed and hooked and made Louis very uncomfortable. After all, Thurston was the state champion and very experienced. In the second round of their spar, McKinney landed a hard right to Joe's chin that staggered him. But it had the effect of making Louis angry, something that seldom happened to him. Instinctively, he struck back with his own right and was astonished to see McKinney stagger back and start to fall. Louis, his anger gone, stepped in right away and held his opponent up. Apologising to Thurston, who said, 'That's OK, Joe,' the light had dawned. 'I could have knocked him out,' Louis kept telling himself. 'He's the champion of all Michigan, and I could have knocked him out.' Around this time, he told McKinney he had given up the violin lessons.

When he signed amateur forms at the Brewster Center in the early months of 1932 at the age of 17, the barely literate Louis wrote his name so large that there was no room for his last name. Thus Joe Louis Barrow became simply Joe Louis for the remainder of his boxing career, amateur and professional. His trainers were Holman Williams and Atler Ellis. They were two of the top coaches in the city, particularly Williams, who was also an active boxer with a busy career ahead of him as a middleweight.

In a 16-year career, Williams would have 187 fights in three divisions, losing just 30, defeating big names like future world light-heavyweight champion Archie Moore and perennial contender Charlie Burley. Williams lost a disputed decision to Jake LaMotta three years before Jake won the world middleweight title.

'In the early years, Williams won the Detroit Golden Gloves title in 1932 and would develop into a great boxer but he never got the recognition he deserved because he wasn't a puncher,' said Eddie Futch, one of Louis' sparring partners whose experience at the Brewster Center resulted in a long, distinguished career tutoring such world champions as Joe Frazier, Alexis Arguello, Larry Holmes, Ken Norton, Riddick Bowe and Wayne McCullough.

'Williams was probably the greatest technician who ever lived,' he said. 'He had an excellent jab, deft footwork and taut defence but after his hands were broken, he resorted to skilful boxing. He had the finesse of Sugar Ray Robinson but no punch. I would rather watch Williams shadow box than watch most other fighters in action.

'As for Louis, like many others I saw great potential in him. He had the makings of a world champion in his amateur days but it would take time. I remember he was always persistent. If you had an apple, he'd beg and beg for a bite until you gave him a little bite. So in the gym, he always got me into the ring to spar with me. But I told myself, "if he wanted to work with me, I'd have to know where those fast punches were coming from".

'Remember, I was just a lightweight and he was a light-heavyweight, so he'd have maybe a 50 or 55lb weight advantage over me. I'd have to know the moves he wanted to make before he threw the punches because he never telegraphed anything. The left hook came out of nowhere. Bang. You just saw a light in your head. Like a camera flash going off.'

Williams and Ellis arranged for Louis to meet Johnny Miller. 'Miller was a good fighter and he would be a member of the US boxing team for the 1932 Olympics in Los Angeles later that year,' recalled Louis. 'He was experienced and tough, and certainly the best in the light-heavyweight division. Holman was not keen on the match. He said I was going in over my head and he didn't think I was ready, considering my very limited experience. But my mind was made up. I felt I could beat him and it would be a great start to my amateur career.

'It would be over three rounds. Miller was better than I expected and he knocked me down seven times before winning the decision. I made the mistake of trying to knock him out instead of boxing him. The defeat didn't discourage me. Williams and Holman both assured me that anybody who can get up after seven times must have something. I was determined to carry on.'

The loss came as a shock as most boxers starting off would win their first bout, but in this case Louis learned from the defeat and would soon win the Brewster club championship. In 1933, he became the Detroit-area Golden Gloves novice division champion but lost in the Chicago Golden Gloves Tournament of Champions.

Everybody in boxing knew the prestige attached to the Golden Gloves. The competition started in 1923 when Arch Ward, sports editor of the *Chicago Tribune*, came up with the idea of a city-wide amateur boxing tournament. He secured sponsorship from the newspaper in 1927 and it became an annual tournament between Chicago and New York.

In later years the idea was taken up by other cities, and a national tournament was held. The New York and Chicago tournaments, however, were viewed as the two elite Golden Gloves championships in the United States. Winning a Golden Gloves title was considered a stepping stone to the professional ranks. One of the most famous Golden Gloves champions who went on to great success in the paid ranks was Barney Ross, winner of world titles at lightweight, junior welterweight and welterweight.

In 1934, Louis won the Tournament of Champions and the Golden Gloves open division tournament, both in Chicago. A hand injury prevented him from competing in the prestigious

New York v Chicago Golden Gloves event in the Windy City. Later that year, he was successful in the US Amateur Athletic Union tournament, effectively the American championships, in St Louis, Missouri.

'For the first time in my life, I was being away from my family,' he said. 'It felt strange but I liked it. It was like being in a new family. You knew all the guys in the amateur circle. You would eat and sleep together and you became friends. Going to new cities and new places, both in the US and Canada, opened my eyes.

'I saw things I wanted that I had never really known about. I met important people and I felt I wanted to be important too. Doctors, lawyers, big-time gamblers would come up to me and talk to me and encourage me. It gave me great confidence, and that was something I never had before, certainly in my schooldays and growing up.

'By now, Holman Williams felt I was moving too fast for him, especially as Williams himself had his own career to attend to. After consultation with his co-coach Atler Ellis, Williams recommended a new trainer, George Slayton, who ran the Detroit Athletic Club. Slayton had a good team at the club and looked after all his members very well. He knew his boxing too and had the reputation of being strict but fair. His mantra was, 'Live a good, clean life, learn the rudiments of the sport, train hard and you are on to a good start.'

Under Slayton's guidance, Louis continued to improve so much that the trainer suggested he should turn professional and make some good money with his undoubted talent. Joe said he would think about it but felt there was still a lot of learning to be done.

In the summer of 1934, with Louis now into his second year as an amateur and in the midst of his early success with rare losses, he was defeated by a former Notre Dame football player named Max Marek. The pair fought for the first two rounds on even terms but Marek came on strong in the third by outboxing Louis and winning the decision. By then, Louis had switched to the Detroit Amateur Club, where George Moody was in charge. Moody was a respected coach and had a good team of boxers to look after.

One afternoon, a prominent 40-year-old Detroit businessman named John Roxborough, who had boxing connections, dropped into the gym. It was something he often did to look over any young boxers he might consider signing up, amateur or professional. On this occasion, it was a visit that changed the destination of Louis' life and altered the course of boxing history. To paraphrase the words of Humphrey Bogart's character in the movie *Casablanca*, it was the beginning of a beautiful friendship.

A wealthy lawyer and insurance man, Roxborough made his money in the numbers game, an illegal Italian lottery played mostly in poor and working-class neighbourhoods in the US but overlooked in the context of the times. He also ran a nightclub. A dapper dresser, Roxborough was described by Randy Roberts as 'a singular-looking man whose face was almost round and looked like a balloon on the verge of popping, or something out of the workshop of *The Wizard of Oz*.

'He was bald and plump and had a tiny, perfectly trimmed moustache. Poised and well spoken, he dressed immaculately as a Wall Street banker and smelled like a flower shop. This man had real class. Very light skinned, he didn't seem flashy but stylish and rich-looking. He wore gray, silk suits, the kind you don't buy off the rack. It made me look twice. His attitude was gentle, like a gentleman should be.'

Roxborough was also a forceful figure in the Young Negroes Progressive Association and the Urban League, and people in the African-American community regarded him as a completely worthwhile man whose work on behalf of his race was quietly done and usually effective. He also ran an estate agency and had many connections in boxing, the type of links a promising young boxer would need.

In the gym, Roxborough liked what he saw of Louis in a sparring session. They chatted when Louis got out of the ring. He was soft of voice and mood, and early on gained from Louis a measure of respect that never declined. 'I'll tell you what I can do for you,' he told the young boxer. 'You come to live with me in my house. You can eat and sleep right. You'll eat the right foods and I'll make sure you get some good clothes. What do you say?'

Louis went home and discussed the proposal with his mother and stepfather. There was full unemployment in the household, and the family was on home relief. What was there to lose by moving in with Roxborough? Lillie was a bit concerned when Joe told her about the man's involvement in the numbers racket but consented when her son told her he would be well taken care of. Joe moved out the next day.

Straight away, life bloomed for the young amateur from Alabama. Some of Roxborough's expensive clothes were altered to fit him. He ate with his new mentor, who also provided $5 a week pocket money.

Louis went into the ring draped in a splendid terrycloth robe and instead of wearing old bandages to protect his hands, he wrapped his fists in new bandages for each fight. His old tennis sneakers were replaced by leather boxing boots. 'Sometimes he would invite me to his home for dinner,' said Louis. 'It was a beautiful house and he had a good-looking and gracious wife. I loved it. I never saw black people living this way and I was envious and watched everything he did.'

Finally, on 12 June 1934, Louis had his last contest as an amateur. Fittingly, it was held in Detroit, in an inter-city tournament. His opponent, Joe Butler, lasted only one round.

Louis landed a solid right just above the cheekbone and the man from Cleveland, Ohio sank to the canvas to be counted out. It had lasted just 90 seconds.

The newspaper reports the next day were impressive and noted that Louis was turning professional in the very near future. An exciting new star had arrived on the boxing scene and there was every indication that he would do well. He left behind an impressive record, losing only four of his 54 contests, with 43 wins either by count-outs or stoppages and seven on points.

Even before considering Louis' entry into the professional ranks, Roxborough knew of the problems involving African-American boxers. Racial discrimination was a thorny issue in America. It was one thing being a black amateur, where there was no evidence of any discrimination whatsoever, but it was different in the pro ranks. Roxborough knew only too well there would be problems to be faced but he also felt they would be overcome in time.

'I've always done all right in business and I've done business with whites as well as blacks,' he explained. 'I find no prejudice. If Joe is handled well, I don't think the public will care who manages him.' He would mould his boxer 'into a veritable ambassador of goodwill,' as he put it.

Some of Roxborough's friends advised him to forget his plan to get involved in professional boxing and instead help his people in a more conventional manner. They pointed out that as vice-president of the Great Lakes Mutual Life Insurance Company, he had gained a good deal of respect for himself and his cause. His activities as chairman of the board of the Superior Life Insurance Society for obtaining employment for African-Americans had performed a similar function.

What was he doing looking after a boxer? Should he not concentrate on the type of things that had gained good results?

But Roxborough, in his quiet way, had already made his mind up. He would do it his way. Even when he became Louis' mentor, he always made sure he was seen as little as possible. When Joe won the heavyweight championship of the world, he refused to climb into the brightly lit ring with him and work in the corner.

Roxborough had a business associate in Chicago named Julian Black. He too was in real estate, as well as having strong associations in the numbers racket. He also ran a successful nightclub and had a stable of boxers. A chunky man with a slight limp and shiny black hair combed back, he had the reputation of being cold and calculating, unlike Roxborough. However, on his first meeting with Black, Joe recalled, 'He was always friendly enough to me, but I knew he was basically a tough guy. Maybe the kind of guy I needed in the fight business.'

Black and Roxborough did a deal. With Louis' approval, they would be co-managers and both would invest a total of $2,000 in the boxer. The next move would be to get not just a trainer, but a good trainer. This is where Jack Blackburn came into the picture. A former great lightweight who never got the breaks because of the colour of his skin, Blackburn would achieve greater fame as a trainer. He now coached boxers at George Trafton's gym on the city's South Side. So it was in Blackburn's direction that Roxborough and Black looked for help. Maybe, just maybe, he could train Louis if a deal could be arranged.

Born in Versailles, Kentucky in 1883 and the son of a minister, Blackburn moved with his family to Terre Haute, Indiana, where he began his boxing. Later relocating to Pittsburgh and Philadelphia, he continued his ring career. *Ring* magazine described him as 'a fast, fearless, snappy puncher, with a fine left jab and a powerful left hook'. Although he weighed only 135lb and could comfortably make the lightweight limit, he often fought much heavier men, including welterweights and middleweights.

Blackburn put up good showings against greats like world lightweight champion Joe Gans and perennial contender Sam Langford, who fought from lightweight to light-heavyweight. Blackburn also gave world 175lb champion Philadelphia Jack O'Brien all he could handle in a no-decision bout. But he was continually sidetracked because of the contemptible colour bar.

In January 1909, Blackburn's career was derailed when he went on a shooting spree in Philadelphia. In the midst of an argument, he killed three people, including his wife. He was convicted of manslaughter and sentenced to 10 to 15 years in prison. Blackburn gave boxing lessons to the warden and his children, and was released for good behaviour after four years and eight months.

Returning to the ring, and still with no sign of a world title fight, he finally retired in 1923. His official record shows 38 wins, three losses, 12 draws and 50 no-decision contests, but he always claimed to have fought 385 times. Blackburn then became a trainer and guided Sammy Mandell to the world lightweight title in 1926 and Bud Taylor to the world bantamweight championship the following year. He also worked for a time with future world heavyweight champion Jersey Joe Walcott.

Roxborough travelled to Chicago in June 1934 and met up with Black before heading for Trafton's gym, where they met Blackburn, by then a grizzly, world-weary trainer. Outlining their plans for Louis, Roxborough told Blackburn, 'Jack, we would like you to train our boxer because I believe he has great potential and can be a world champion. You are one of the best and most experienced in the business.'

Blackburn, who was 51 at the time and showing the effects of arthritis and heavy drinking, was silent for a few moments.

Finally, he agreed to have a look at Louis, but insisted that if he were to train their boxer he would be on a regular salary every week. 'None of this percentage of the gate for me,' he said. 'A salary straight up.'

Arrangements were made the next day for Louis to have a sparring session in the gym with a local light-heavyweight. When Joe climbed out of the ring and exchanged greetings with Blackburn, the trainer said to him in blunt terms, 'So you think you'll get somewhere in this fight game. Well, let me tell you something right off. It's next to impossible for a black heavyweight to get anywhere, never mind a world title fight. He's got to be very good outside the ring and very bad inside the ring. Mr Roxborough here, who has known you for some time, tells me he is convinced that you can be depended on to behave yourself at all times, but inside that ring, you've got to be a killer but also you've got to be fair.

'Otherwise, I'm afraid I'm getting too old to be wasting my time on you. You see, too many people remember all the trouble there was when Jack Johnson was champion. Johnson is the only black man to have held the world heavyweight title, and he was a braggart. I doubt if the public is really ready for another Jack Johnson.'

A brilliant defensive boxer with a knockout punch in both hands, Johnson was champion for seven years, from 1908 to 1915. He was also a gaudy, bold fighter who lived just as he wanted, and enraged the defenders of white supremacy with his blatant refusal to accept anything less than equality. *The Boxing Register*, official record book of the International Boxing Hall of Fame, said of Johnson, 'He was beloved by blacks and some whites, but thoroughly hated and eventually conquered by those who saw him as a threat to America's divided society.'

Denied a title fight for many years, when he finally got the chance against Tommy Burns in 1908, Johnson made the Canadian pay dearly for every moment of frustration and discrimination he had endured over the years. He tormented and angered Burns, taunting him with phrases like, 'Is that the best you can do, Tommy?' and 'Hit me here, white boy.' The one-sided battle was stopped by the police in the 14th round as his handlers escorted the champion, now the ex-champion, to his corner.

Jack London, then boxing writer for the *New York Herald*, sent back a report that was graphic and reeked of racialism. 'The fight!' said London. 'This was no fight. No Armenian massacre could compare to the hopeless slaughter that took place here in Sydney. It was like a pygmy and a colossus, like a grown man cuffing a naughty child.' London concluded his report with, 'One thing now remains. James J Jeffries must emerge from retirement on his farm and remove the golden smile from Jack Johnson's face. It's up to you, Jeff.'

Other writers and politicians soon took up the call. Jeffries, who had retired undefeated six years earlier, finally agreed to put on the gloves again and face Johnson. On Independence Day, 1910, Jeffries climbed into the ring in Reno, Nevada and was subjected to a merciless beating before being stopped in the 15th round. The one-sided battle set off race riots, lynchings and gang fights across the United States. On 4 July alone, the day of the fight, there were reports of 19 deaths, hundreds injured and over 5,000 arrested. A specially commissioned film of the fight was banned by Congress.

As calls for a 'white hope' to dethrone Johnson continued, Jack's penchant for white wives and assorted girlfriends got him into trouble with the Establishment, which was looking for any excuse to bring him down. He befriended prostitutes and was prosecuted for 'transporting a woman across state lines for immoral purposes'. Avoiding a jail term, he fled to Europe and finished up in Havana, Cuba, where he lost his title under controversial circumstances to big Jess Willard on a knockout in 26 rounds on 5 April 1915. He claimed he sold his title after working out a deal with the US government that in defeat, the conviction would be quashed. Yet he served eight months in a Kansas prison. If a deal had been done, it was reneged upon.

Trevor Wignall of the *Daily Express* reflected how the liberals of the era viewed Johnson, 'Jack Johnson had many defects. He was a swaggerer by nature but this is not altogether surprising when it is recalled that for many years he was an absolute idol. If he had not been so insanely pestered by women, and if he had not been so ridiculously flattered by men, he would probably have been a better fellow.

'On one visit to see Johnson, I was compelled to force my way into the building past crowds of women. Johnson was conscious of the colour of his skin, and was firmly convinced he had a mission in life. He believed it was his duty to "lift the black race," that they would be superior to the whites. He did considerable harm to boxing but the men to whom he rendered the greatest disservice were boxers of his own hue.'

Even if Johnson had behaved in the manner that white America believed correct, the history of other sports suggests that the doors would still have been closed off to non-whites. The author Gerald Astor noted that before the turn of the 20th century, blacks had already been barred from major league baseball. US college football teams had few black players in the early 1900s.

Golf and tennis were never friendly to black players in the early days. Both games developed in private clubs that usually restricted membership to whites by cost and by choice, even up to the 1970s. Horse racing in America started almost exclusively with black jockeys. In the first Kentucky Derby of 1875, which attracted 15 entries, 14 of the riders were black. Colour bars began to appear in the next 25 years. By 1911, blacks had been excluded from the Kentucky event.

In basketball, few colleges used black players and professional basketball kept its colour line until 1949. In track and field, George Poage became the first non-white participant to represent the US in the Olympics when he competed in the 400 metres in St Louis in 1904. Several other black competitors took part in the London Games in 1908 but non-whites seemed to vanish during the 1920s before reappearing for good in 1932, preceding the triumphs of Jesse Owens in the Berlin Olympics of 1936.

In the immediate fall-out from the Johnson–Jeffries fight, its promoter Tex Rickard refused to stage another black v white world heavyweight title contest, resulting in the perennial No. 1 contender Harry Wills, the 'Black Panther', being denied a title shot.

With all this in mind, Black, Roxborough and Blackburn knew only too well that it was going to be very difficult to break down racial barriers and to have another black heavyweight in their midst. 'Mr Roxborough explained that white managers and promoters would have no real interest in seeing a black boxer work his way up to title contention,' Louis recalled. 'He told me about the fate of most black fighters, ones with white managers who were wound up, burned out and broke before they reached their prime.

'He said the white managers were only interested in the money they could make from them. They didn't take the proper time to see that their boxers had proper training, that they lived well or ate well or had some pocket money. Mr Roxborough was talking about Black Power before it became popular and accepted.'

Roxborough, Black and Blackburn made sure that Louis' image was carefully crafted. Remembering Jack Johnson's misadventures inside and outside the ring two decades earlier, they were keen for their charge not to alienate the public or make the mistakes Johnson made. They drew up seven commandments for Louis:

- He was never to have his photograph taken with a white woman.
- He was never to go to a nightclub alone.
- There would never be any soft fights.
- There would never be any fixed fights.
- He was never to gloat over an opponent.
- He would keep a 'dead pan' face in front of the cameras.
- He would always live and fight clean.

Blackburn revamped Louis' rather mobile, defence-orientated philosophy, a legacy of Holman Williams' instruction. 'You won't get anywhere nowadays trying to outpoint fellows,' Blackburn told Louis. 'It's mighty hard for a black man to win decisions. You will find the dice is loaded against you. Take it from me, I know. It happened to me many times. You have to knock them out, and keep knocking them out, to get anywhere. Let that right fist there be your referee and you will start to go places.'

Blackburn also worked on Joe's left jab, which had been a hallmark of all the boxers Blackburn trained. Louis had demonstrated a powerful left hook but with Blackburn's help, he developed a piston-like left lead with which to create openings in his opponent's defence. The trainer spent hours sparring with his boxer, showing him how to block punches without ducking, and stressing balance at all times. He preached that a boxer, properly balanced, could pick off a punch and fire off two, three or four of his own in return. Louis would in time develop into a powerful counter-puncher. The respect in which

Louis held Blackburn became mutual and both came to call the other 'Chappie'.

'When I began with "Chappie" Blackburn, he saw things I did not notice myself,' Joe remembered. 'He saw that I couldn't follow a left hook with a right without picking up on one foot. He said that was no good, and that a boxer had to keep both feet planted on the canvas to get proper balance and to get power to punch, or to take a punch. I used to be clumsy-footed when I was a kid in Alabama. He soon had me throwing a series of punches. Whatever he told me to do, I did it. He was the best teacher anybody ever had, and I'm convinced of that.'

As with all trainers and managers, Roxborough, Black and Blackburn planned to select Joe's opponents carefully. The idea was to build up the boxer's confidence and record by matching him with progressively tougher opponents. 'We felt we had a great prospect in Joe and we did not wish to take any unnecessary risks by overmatching him,' recalled Black. 'We'd seen too many prospects, outstanding prospects, rushed into fights for which they were not ready. We did not want to make that mistake with Louis. John and I had more confidence in Joe than Blackburn had, even though Jack felt he could make the grade, but caution was still the keyword.'

Late in June, Louis was informed by his co-managers that he would have his first professional fight in early July against an opponent yet to be selected. 'You know,' Blackburn said to Louis as the team took a breather one afternoon at Trafton's gym in Chicago, 'I've told you before that it's going to be tough because of the colour of your skin.

'There hasn't been a black heavyweight champion since Jack Johnson way back and I don't think the public really want another one, certainly not one like Johnson. People haven't forgotten the way he belittled white opponents and the way he carried on with his private life, acting like he owned the world.

If you do the right things, and fight the right way, you can make people forget Jack Johnson ever existed.'

When Louis became world champion, Johnson belittled him at every opportunity, calling him 'an amateur who does everything wrong'. But when they met socially while Louis was still an amateur, he had been full of praise for Joe, while Louis felt he himself was in the presence of greatness. Characteristically, he would always refuse to pass judgement on Johnson. 'Every man has a right to his own mistakes,' said Louis of that initial introduction. 'There is no man alive who did not make a mistake.' Years later, Louis again defended the former champion. 'When I won the world title, half the letters I got had some word about Jack Johnson,' he said. 'A lot was from old black people in the South. They thought he disgraced his race. I just figured he did what he wanted to do, and what he did had no effect on me.'

Johnson was a severe critic of Louis up to the end, and was destined to die in the same hell-bent fashion he had lived. Driving his sports car too fast on the afternoon of 10 June 1946 near Raleigh, North Carolina, he skidded off the road, slammed into a telegraph pole and overturned. He received multiple injuries that proved to be fatal. Ironically, Johnson had been on the way to New York to watch Louis defend his title in a return bout with Billy Conn at the Yankee Stadium.

Round 2

When Joe met Mike

On the warm evening of Independence Day, 4 July 1934, Louis climbed into the ring at Bacon's Arena, Chicago for his first professional fight. His opponent was Jack Kracken, a local favourite with a good record, 28-7-3. A former student at the University of Illinois, he was rated the best heavyweight in the Windy City. Because of Joe's reputation as an amateur, the fight was a main event and scheduled for ten rounds. The 1,133 capacity attendance at the arena, which was formerly a dance hall, expected to see a good fight as it had received plenty of advance publicity in the Chicago newspapers.

On the morning of the contest, Blackburn urged Louis to keep his guard up and jab, jab, jab in the opening minute. 'Feel him out, "Chappie,"' he instructed. 'But when you see an opening, shoot across that right hand. Remember, the fans want knockouts, not decisions. A heavyweight from the Jack Johnson era called Sam Langford, the "Boston Tar Baby", always said he carried his own referee into the ring. His referee was his big right.'

On fight night, Louis was ready to make a successful debut in the paid ranks. At 181lb and now a fully fledged heavyweight, he had a six-pound advantage over Kracken. 'In the dressing room, I told my team I was worried about going the full ten rounds,' Louis remembered. 'I was used to fighting three rounds as an amateur. Here I was now in a six-rounder and I wasn't sure I could make it. "Chappie" told me not to worry about it.

'He said if I can go three rounds, I can go six, and if I can go six, I can go ten. The talk was fine until I got into the ring. Kracken seemed big and strong. He looked confident, too. Pacing around, he looked like he hadn't a bother in the world and here he was going into a main event. I was definitely worried. "Chappie" could see I was nervous but he kept talking. "Remember everything I told you," he said. "When you see that opening, let him have it. One clean shot to the chin or the body is worth a thousand other punches." That bit of advice from him cheered me up a bit.'

With Blackburn's advice in mind, Louis jabbed the Chicago fighter while looking for that big opening, before going for the body. One hard shot to the midriff made Kracken double up and caused him to drop his arms momentarily and cover his stomach. It gave Louis the chance he was waiting for. Firing a hard left hook to the jaw, Louis sent Kracken down for a nine count. Louis closed in and shot over a powerful right that sent the Chicagoan through the ropes and into the lap of Joe Triner, chairman of the Illinois State Athletic Commission.

By the time Kracken had climbed back into the ring, 14 seconds had elapsed. It was all over. The official time of the finish was 90 seconds of round one, one of the quickest main event bouts in the six-year history of the arena. Louis received a $50 cheque for his brief encounter – the equivalent of two weeks' pay handling auto parts and valued at $1,098 in today's currency. Roxborough and Black allowed Joe to keep the entire purse. He sent most of it home to his mother.

Blackburn was not completely satisfied with Louis' win, as fast as it was, though Roxborough and Black felt he looked fine. The trainer felt he was a bit sluggish and asked him what he had eaten before the fight or the previous night. When he said he'd had a dozen bananas that morning before heading for the weigh-in, Blackburn was aghast. 'Joe, cut down on the bananas,' he admonished, with his two co-managers nodding in agreement. 'They put on extra weight and make you sluggish. One or two is fine but a dozen? Wow!'

With fans demanding another Louis fight, Roxborough and Black had him back at Bacon's Arena for his second bout five days later. It would be another scheduled six-rounder, this time against Willie Davies. His purse was $72. As had happened against Kracken, Louis felt out his opponent in the opening round, which had little action. The pace quickened in the second when Davis opened up with hooks from both hands.

Towards the end of the session, Joe staggered his rival with sharp left hooks to the body. In the third, Davis was taking heavy punishment before the fight was stopped, with Louis having his right hand raised as the winner. Blackburn was happier this time, but told his charge, 'Good show, "Chappie", but keep that left hand a bit higher.'

It was back to Chicago for fight number three, this time at the Marigold Gardens outdoor arena against the cagey Larry Udell on 30 July. It did not last long. A right to the chin in the second round of a scheduled eight-rounder sent Udell down for the full count. Joe left the venue with a cheque for $101 in his possession. His next outing four weeks later was another eight-rounder, this time against unbeaten Jack Kranz and again at the Marigold Gardens. Unexpectedly, this one went the scheduled distance.

Kranz was tough and resourceful but Louis landed enough punches to earn a unanimous decision. 'Don't worry that he went the full route,' said Blackburn. 'Fights like this give you experience, and that's just what you need now. Quick wins look good on paper but you don't learn from them. You'll have more of them but this was a good one. It'll pay off.'

Joe's pure money began to increase. He received $125 for taking on Kranz and $150 for his next opponent, Buck Everett. This one, on 27 August 1934, had Joe back at the Marigold for the third time in succession and again over eight rounds. It ended in the second round when he caught his man with a solid right hand to the body and Everett sank to the canvas to be counted out. His co-managers were still allowing Joe to keep his entire purse. The big money would come later.

Louis sent most of it home, and Patrick Brooks could hardly believe his eyes when the cheques came through the post – now totalling almost $500. In just a few short weeks, he had become a rabid fight fan. Brooks would chat to neighbours and the conversation would usually come around to his stepson, who was gaining a reputation for himself in the boxing ring. 'My boy will reach the heights,' he would proudly say. 'Just wait and see.'

Louis' co-managers now decided to show their boxer in his adopted home town of Detroit. The date was 11 September. Joe had fought there several times as an amateur but this time he was returning as a pro, and unbeaten in five fights at that. The venue was the Naval Armoury and Joe's opponent in a scheduled ten-rounder, his first over that distance, would be Al Delaney. A promising 18-year-old Canadian based in Buffalo, New York, Delaney was an aggressive fighter with a strong punch, particularly with his right hand.

Delaney was born Alex Borchuk but changed his name to Al Delaney on the advice of his manager, who felt that Delaney had more of an 'American' ring to it. He had won 23 fights with just one defeat, against Louis' meagre 5-0 record. Joe's co-managers were at first reluctant to put their promising heavyweight in against such an experienced foe, but Blackburn felt that this was the only way Louis would learn.

'He can't be fighting pushovers, although that is not to say his other opponents were patsies,' said the wise old trainer. 'Look, "Chappie" went in against Jack Kranz, who was unbeaten in 14 fights, and Larry Udell had lost only eight of his 45 fights. "Chappie" beat both of them, Udell in two rounds and Kranz on a unanimous decision. This guy Delaney is pretty good but I still think our boy will beat him.'

The match was put together by the *Detroit Times*, owned by William Randolph Hearst, the wealthy businessman and politician who established the nation's largest newspaper chain and media company. Like Hearst's other newspapers, the *Times* emphasised sensationalism and human interest stories but was very much anti-black, except for crime stories.

'We didn't cover much news about the black community,' remembered Edgar Hayes, who was a sportswriter on the newspaper. 'Blacks were kind of invisible as far as newspapers were concerned. We had one editor who came out of Knoxsville in Tennessee, I believe, or somewhere down South. Anyway, he was bitterly opposed to giving coverage to any blacks. Of course, it was wrong but that's the way things were in those days.

'The rise of Joe Louis was something else. It was kind of hard to ignore him.'

Shortly after the fight was announced, Roxborough, as Louis' chief negotiator, was called before Bingo Brown, chairman of the Michigan State Athletic Commission, for what they referred to as an 'important meeting'. It seemed that Brown, Eddie Edgar, sports editor of the *Detroit Free Press*, and several managers were being pressurised to have Louis sign with a white manager instead of Roxborough. Brown said it would be in everybody's interest. When Roxborough refused, Brown said the commission would allow the Delaney fight to go through as contracts had been signed and everything had been arranged and finalised. But it was a one-off and Louis could never fight in Detroit again.

When Roxborough got up to leave the meeting, Brown relented in part, saying that Louis could box again in the state of Michigan, but only against black boxers. This would mean that Joe would have a limited number of opponents, and almost certainly be getting small purses as a result. 'Then Joe won't fight in this state again, ever,' Roxborough insisted. 'But remember, when the fans start yelling that they want to see their hometown boy in action, I'll start telling them what exactly happened.' As it turned out, Louis boxed in the Motor City twice more in 1934 by public demand. Fans could not see enough of their hometown hero.

For his part, Louis was doing everything right in his quest to overcome the prejudice against the colour of his skin. He was adhering to the Seven Commandments that Blackburn had laid out. He was winning his fights well and showing sportsmanship and humility. 'The way I think about it now, I get even madder,' he said in later years. 'Those white people just couldn't stand to see a black man on the rise, and in the case of the Delaney fight back then, I was mighty glad Mr Roxborough took the stand he did, and forced them to back down. Besides all that, other managers wanted a piece of your contract. It wasn't easy all round.'

A large number of friends and family members turned out to see the Delaney fight. It was their first look at Joe. One person missing was his mother. Lillie said she did not want to go in case Joe got hurt. 'No danger, momma, but stay home if you feel better,' Louis said as he kissed her on the cheek on the way out. Delaney turned out to be a tough opponent and gave Louis some uncomfortable moments, continually coming forward with both hands. Countering one of Joe's jabs in the third round, the Canadian crossed over a solid right hand to the head that rocked Louis to his bootlaces, and broke a back tooth in the process. This would be a punch that Louis was always open to, and would be fully exploited by Germany's Max Schmeling later on. Going out for the fourth round, Blackburn said, 'This is it, "Chappie". Go get him in this round.'

Waiting for the right opening, Louis had his man on the boards three times before the towel came fluttering in from Delaney's corner with just 30 seconds remaining in the round. 'That night I was the toast of Detroit, and I think I earned it,' Louis would remember. His purse was $160, the best pay-night to date. Roxborough and Black suggested Joe should stay in Detroit for a few days, and he treated his family and friends to some bowling games and bought clothes.

Next stop for the Louis rollercoaster was Chicago, where five of his six fights had taken place. This time it was a different venue, the Arcadia Gardens. The date was 26 September and the man in the opposite corner would be Adolph Waiter, winner of all but two of his 18 fights, with one draw. At 22 years of age, he was born in Green Bay, Wisconsin and based in Chicago, where he had a big following.

Waiter was expected to provide strong opposition for Louis. During a training session, Blackburn picked up a red brick as if to throw it at Joe, who instinctively ducked. 'Chappie' laughed, 'See what I'm trying to teach you? Pretend you have a brick in your hand. Naturally, the guy is going to duck, then you hit him with the other hand. It makes sense.'

Waiter turned out to be a tough opponent, as expected. He kept the pressure on Louis with strong two-handed attacks and became the first to bloody his nose when landing a wide left hook in the third round. But Louis did enough to win the decision with his sharper boxing. Waiter acknowledged the result by going over to Joe's corner and shaking his hand. 'Good luck for the future,' he said. 'You're going places.' Louis' purse was $300.

The Arcadia Garden promoters wanted Louis back, and soon. Gate receipts were healthy. Four weeks later he ducked between the ropes to face Art Sykes, a strong New Yorker who fancied his chances against Joe and expressed his views to sportswriters. The fight started cautiously, with both men looking for openings, but by the third round Louis was beginning to assert his superiority with his better boxing and sharper hitting. However, Sykes was always coming forward, seeking the big chance to end it all as they traded blows toe to toe.

In the eighth round of the scheduled ten-rounder, Louis caught Sykes with a cracking right flush on the jaw that sent him down on his back to be counted out. He was unconscious for over 30 minutes as two doctors tried to revive him and was rushed to hospital. Louis would say that if Sykes failed to show signs of life, he would quit boxing there and then. 'I hit him a hundred times but couldn't keep him down,' he recalled. 'I didn't want to hit him any more. When he went to the floor in the eighth round and took the count, I was glad it was all over. I called the hospital regularly to find out how he was doing and I was glad when I was told he had recovered. It was scary.'

After the fight, when Louis met Damon Runyon, who had rooted for Sykes as a fellow-New Yorker, the famous writer said, 'You almost killed my boy.' Sykes retired from boxing soon after the Louis defeat. Roxborough had asked for a purse of $450, and got it. Louis was really in the big money now – and there were much bigger purses to come.

'I was boxing so often and training so much, I didn't get a chance to spend my money,' he said. 'Every time I could, I'd buy some really nice clothes. Thanks to my managers, I knew how to dress well. All I had to do was copy them. I sent my family regular cheques and they looked fine too in new clothes. The good things were that there was no more welfare and no more worrying about simple things like food. Even my sister, Emmarell, was bursting with pride. Mr Roxborough and Mr Black were proud of me and they encouraged me to buy my first car, a black Buick with whitewall tires. I would ride in that car for hours, even going round and round the block.'

Seven days later, Louis in Detroit for a fight at the Arena Gardens. It turned out to be a win in two rounds over Jack O'Dowd, a local boxer with a 25-8-2 tally. A right to the chin was the finishing punch. Joe was now unbeaten in nine fights, with only two going the scheduled distance. His co-managers now felt that the level of opposition needed to be increased if their prospect was to reap the full rewards of his fledging career. They also needed to showcase Louis in New York, the centre of the boxing world – and sooner rather than later.

Stanley Poreda was the first target. A protege of the great Joe Jeanette, a perennial contender around the turn of the 20th century, Poreda, 26, was from New Jersey of Polish extraction and at one time the number one contender for the world heavyweight title. He boasted a 29-8-1 record and had wins over future heavyweight champion Primo Carnera and ex-light-heavyweight king Tommy Loughran, as well as other leading contenders. An impressive victory over Poreda would enhance Louis' career and image immeasurably, and perhaps bring him to the attention of the influential figures in Madison Square Garden, boxing's most iconic arena.

'I handled Poreda at the time,' recalled Musky Jackson, the New York manager who had a stable of boxers. 'I handled nobody but heavyweights, and I also had Don "Red" Barry. I had heard about this promising fighter named Joe Louis who was knocking everybody out. Scotty Monteith, a Detroit matchmaker, called me one day and said he could set up a fight between Louis and Barry in a six-rounder.

'Barry wasn't interested so I turned him down. I asked Benny Ray, a Chicago promoter, how much he could get me for a Louis fight against Poreda. He offered a £1,000 guarantee, a week's expenses, the hotel bill plus two round tickets. I agreed and Poreda agreed but the Illinois State Athletic Commission said they would have to see Poreda work out first, to show that he was in shape.

'I agreed only to have him limber up. We're in the same gym with Louis and he's knocking his sparring partners all over the place. Julian Black, one of Louis' managers, was there too. I put up a punch bag with a swivel and asked Poreda to hit it. I knew what was going to happen. The bag flies off and I yell, "That's enough. You'll break the bag. But what a puncher!" Somehow, the commission officials fell for it and sanctioned the fight.'

On fight night, a big crowd turned out and expected action. They got very little. In the corner before the first bell, Blackburn told Louis to go for a quick win. 'Surprise him,' instructed the trainer. 'Move around and jab him. He'll probably expect you to continue on like that but then you move in and finish him.' Joe did just that.

Musky Jackson remembered it like this: 'I can tell you that Louis was all over my man. The first punch, a left hook, put Poreda down for nine. When he struggled to his feet, another punch, this time a right, dropped him for the second time, again for nine. The third blow, a left hook, knocked him clean out of the ring. The referee kept on counting but my guy had no chance. It was a clean knockout. When I got back to New York, I told everybody what a fighter Louis was but nobody paid any attention. Nobody wanted to know. He was a black fighter, and black fighters were a dime a dozen.'

In any event, New York could wait. One day they would come yelling for Louis – at any price. Next stop for Joe, now unbeaten in ten professional fights, eight of which had taken place in Chicago, where he was a big attraction, was the city's Coliseum on 30 November. In the opposite corner would be Charley Massera, an experienced Pittsburgher who had been around the block. His record included a win over Maxie Rosenbloom and a draw against Bob Olin, two former world light-heavyweight champions. He had also held heavyweight contender King Levinsky to a split decision. At the end of 1933, Massera had been ranked the number eight contender by *Ring* magazine. He looked a good test for Joe.

'The first time I ever broke training was in Chicago before the Massera fight,' Louis admitted in his 1978 autobiography. 'One of the ladies in the building I was staying in had a daughter who was much older than I was. About ten days before the fight, she talked me into going to bed with her. The next morning when I got up to do roadwork, I felt [so] guilty that instead of running five miles, I ran ten. I just ran, ran, ran. Instead of boxing three rounds, I'd box six. "Chappie" Blackburn said to me, "What the hell is wrong with you?" I told him I felt good. I didn't tell him what I'd done. It worried the hell out of me. Here I was getting ready for a big fight, and already I was fooling around.'

Louis' misdemeanour did not seem to have any effect on his performance in the ring. After two exciting rounds, with both boxers getting through with solid blows, Joe found an opening in the third round and connected with a heavy left hook followed by a right uppercut that sent Massera down for the count. Nineteen seconds remained in the round. Massera's trainer, the legendary Ray Arcel, went on record as saying that Louis was a genuine prospect for the highest honours in boxing. The fight earned Joe his first four-figure purse, $2,000.

For his final fight of 1934, Louis made his first appearance at the famous Chicago Stadium, a venue he would become very familiar with in the ensuing years. On 14 December, he climbed into the brightly lit ring to face Lee Ramage from San Diego, California in a scheduled eight-rounder. Ramage's record was impressive: 40 wins and five draws in 53 fights against Louis' 11-0 tally. At 24 years of age, he was two years older than Joe.

The Louis management team came under heavy criticism from the press for putting their promising charge in with a fighter of Ramage's reputation. Lee had recently held the reigning world light-heavyweight champion Maxie Rosenbloom to a draw, and anyone who could do that had to be good. Ramage had boxed in much better company and entered the ring a heavy favourite before a crowd that included movie stars Mae West, Clark Gable and Bing Crosby.

For the first three rounds, Louis took a hammering from the fast-moving, slippery Californian, who was in and out the whole time, catching his opponent with looping rights. It looked as though Louis had been overmatched. Ramage also had a fast, snappy left jab, as well as a dangerous right uppercut that he used effectively as Joe came in. For five rounds, Ramage had a commanding lead and Louis seemed frustrated in his efforts to nail him with any solid punches. Blackburn had advised him to go for the body and slow his man down, but Ramage was constantly on the move.

Before the start of the sixth round, the trainer insisted Louis keep aiming for the body. 'You'll tire him out eventually, "Chappie", so keep it up,' instructed Blackburn. Louis would remember, 'Ramage was easily the best boxer I had faced up to that time. I could hardly land a solid blow to his mid-section because he was so slippery. In the eighth, I noticed that his hands were starting to drop a little, so the plan to weaken him seemed to be finally working. "Chappie" had always told me to watch another fighter's arms.

'He had said, "When a fighter is fresh, he keeps his arms at regular length. When he's tired and wants to make believe he's fresh, he lifts them too high and that's the giveaway." I eventually got Ramage in the eighth and knocked him down three times before his corner threw in the towel. I was mighty relieved that I finally nailed him.' One ringside reporter wrote, 'Lee looked all in during the eighth. Following a barrage of blows, it was all over with just nine seconds remaining in the round.'

Around this time, Louis had met Marva Trotter, who would become his steady girlfriend. They were introduced by a mutual friend, Gerard Hughes, a rabid sports fan, after the Ramage fight. 'Joe,' said Hughes, 'I finally persuaded this girl to come along and meet you. Her name is Marva Trotter.' Turning to the girl, Hughes said: 'Marva, meet Joe Louis, the next world heavyweight boxing champion.'

Marva was a stunningly attractive girl of 19 and worked as a secretary at the *Chicago Defender*, a black newspaper. Louis would not easily forget her. He took her to the movies quite often, and together they enjoyed what was on offer, whether it was a drama *Treasure Island*, a comedy *The Thin Man*, a western *The Man from Utah*, a romance *Wonder Bar* or an actioner *The Lost Patrol*. The colour of their skin was similar but one thing bothered Joe.

The Trotters were from Chicago's high society. Marva had graduated from Inglewood High School and then from the Gregg Business School. Her grammar was perfect, her manners above criticism. She even had a brother who was a minister. She had known advantages that were denied to Joe and her every word and action showed it clearly.

Julian Black approved of the relationship and encouraged it. So did John Roxborough. They both had good reasons to agree with the match. Marva Trotter was smart and ambitious, and came from a good family. More important, both were of the same colour. Louis would later recall, 'There was no Jack Johnson problem there.' They had talked of marriage but that would not happen until Louis had achieved his ambition of moving into the big league, and more importantly the big money, in New York. Until then, they would not tie the knot or move in together.

The day after the Ramage fight, Louis went home to Detroit to spend Christmas with his mother, stepfather, brother and sisters. But Joe could not afford to take a long holiday. Roxborough and Black had arranged a ten-rounder at the nearby Olympia Arena against Patsy Perroni for 4 January 1935. Wily and tough with a strong chin, the native New Yorker was ranked the number seven contender for Max Baer's world heavyweight title. A professional for seven years, Perroni had a 50-13-7 record and had mixed punches with some of the best men of his era, and beaten many of them, even though he was only 22 years of age. The general feeling among boxing writers was that Perroni could be the one to really test the man from Alabama.

It turned out to be the toughest fight of Louis' fledging career. Perroni was agile and skilled, and made Joe do all the work. Louis had him down three times, twice with left hooks to the chin and once with a body shot, but could not keep him down. Once again, Perroni exposed Joe's openness to a right cross or right hook, although he managed to stay on his feet. It was a fault he was never able to eradicate fully.

The fans were disappointed, although Louis was happy. He got $4,227, his biggest purse to date. Not all of it went to him, as his co-managers were now taking their cut. But they had moved their prospect well and he was very pleased with the financial arrangements. He now had money beyond his wildest dreams.

Perroni sought a return fight, even when Louis won the world title, but Roxborough and Black turned him down. The

New Yorker remained a contender for several years and would go through the rest of his career calling himself 'the man Joe Louis refused to fight a second time'. It did not seem likely that he would defeat Louis in a rematch. Joe's subsequent career showed that he usually beat opponents more quickly second time around. But with a golden prospect on their hands, Louis' managers did not seem overly enthusiastic to take any unnecessary risks.

Instead, they matched Joe with Hans Birkie, an interior decorator when he was not throwing punches, at the Duquesne Gardens, Pittsburgh, scheduled for 11 January. Born in Germany and based in San Diego, California, Birkie had lost 28 of his 67 fights with eight draws. It was not expected that he would cause Louis any trouble, and that is how it turned out. Joe coasted through nine rounds before catching the German with a powerful right to the chin that put him down. As Birkie struggled to regain his feet, the fight was stopped at 1:47 of the tenth round.

'After each victory, while his hand was being raised by the ring announcer, Louis remained expressionless,' said Barney Nagler, who wrote on boxing for the *New York Morning Telegraph*. 'Not that he found boxing a melancholy task. His facial immobility indicated neither balefulness nor unconcern. He was simply impassive, although sportswriters read menace into his impassivity. His muscles, deeply buried beneath smooth brown skin, gave every promise of harnessed power.

'Only his buttocks and thighs appeared heavy, but the movements of his hands were so quick they disguised the relative slowness of his feet,' continued Nagler. 'He was still growing, approaching 190lb and not yet 21, but already people were beginning to think of him inevitably as a future heavyweight champion. He was less than a virtuoso, of course, but he was learning to taunt an opponent with a hammer-like jab that eventually struck the core of his subject. His left hook was his most potent weapon but he did not depend on it alone to flay his opponents.'

By this time Louis had won all his 14 fights, just three going the scheduled distance. Roxborough and Black were now casting their eyes towards New York, then the undisputed capital of the boxing world and where the big money lay, but Blackburn was cautious. 'Yeah, maybe "Chappie" is ready for New York, but is New York ready for him?' he told the management team. 'I don't think so. Not just yet. It's not too far off when there will be demand for an appearance there.'

Roxborough was still anxious for their prospect to box in New York and decided to test the waters. Louis was now the number nine contender for Max Baer's world heavyweight title. Roxborough put in a call to James J. Johnston, the entrepreneur who ran boxing at Madison Square Garden, asking if he could use Louis on one of his shows.

'He's a future world heavyweight champion,' said Roxborough. 'We think he's ready for the big time, and he'd go down well at the Garden. We're sure of that.'

'That's fine,' said Johnston, who had heard of Louis' progress. 'The only problem is that he's black, and we don't use black heavyweights. If we do use them, they must be prepared to lose if we want them to.'

'No deal,' answered Roxborough, and hung up.

Blackburn, who had always believed Joe's colour would be a problem, was beside Roxborough when he made the call. 'What did I tell you?' he said, remembering the Jack Johnson era and the tremendous antagonism it caused. 'We're going to have big, big stumbling blocks ahead.'

Johnston was the major boxing promoter in New York, controlling as he did the most famous boxing arena in the world, the Garden. Rarely seen without his bowler hat, Johnston called the shots if a boxer wanted to show his paces there. Born in Liverpool in 1875, he immigrated with his family to the US at the age of 12, settling in New York City's tough Hell's Kitchen district, where he had to fight to survive against neighbourhood gangs. He worked alongside his father in an iron foundry by day and boxed at night as a bantamweight – first as an amateur and later as a professional. In 1912, at the age of 37, he gave up active boxing but remained in the sport as a manager.

In a busy and colourful life, Johnston introduced a number of great British boxers to American audiences, notably Ted 'Kid' Lewis, Jim Driscoll and Owen Moran. Lewis, from London's East End, won the world welterweight title while Driscoll, from Cardiff, and Moran, from Birmingham, both laid claims to world championships, Driscoll at featherweight and Moran at bantamweight.

A talkative individual, Johnston was aggressive, pugnacious and ready to fight at the slightest provocation. He often leased Madison Square Garden to promote his own shows and it was often said that he got more publicity than his boxers because of his reputation. When he was promoting boxing at St Nicholas Arena in New York in the years before the First World War, he was fond of stunts such as midget boxing, which involved bringing in a suffragette speaker guaranteed to draw hecklers, introducing a white man with his face painted yellow, another masquerading as a Chinese champion and one posing as a gypsy. While these tactics might seem tawdry today, they won Johnston great acclaim in boxing circles at the time.

Johnston was regularly accused, too, of influencing referees to 'support' his own boxers, resulting in complaints of favouritism from other managers. He was dubbed 'Boxing's Boy Bandit' by famed sportswriter and novelist Damon Runyon. But he had a shrewd business sense. Besides handling the fistic affairs of Lewis, Driscoll and Moran, Johnston guided three other boxers to world titles, light-heavyweight Mike McTigue, middleweight Harry Greb and featherweight Johnny Dundee.

In 1933, Johnston became the official promoter/manager at Madison Square Garden following the death of Tex Rickard. He promoted three world heavyweight championship fights there over the next four years – and each time the title changed hands. Primo Carnera knocked out Jack Sharkey in six rounds in June 1933 and a year later, almost to the day, Max Baer finished off Carnera in the 11th. In June 1935, James J. Braddock outpointed Baer, a 15/1 favourite, over 15 rounds in one of boxing history's biggest upsets.

Madison Square Garden was still the prime target for the Louis management despite Johnston's conditions. But time was on their side and the promoter could wait a while longer. Blackburn was right. The trainer had said the demand for a Louis appearance in the big city would come, and come big. The cry would be, 'We want Joe Louis.'

Meanwhile, the Louis juggernaut stormed on. Louis was paired in a scheduled ten-round rematch with Lee Ramage at Wrigley Field, Los Angeles on 21 February 1935. It would be Joe's first ring venture out west and he was looking forward to climbing into the ring at the big outdoor venue. Louis had admitted after the first bout that Ramage had given him his toughest fight before he finally caught up with the Californian in the eighth. This time he aimed to bring him down in faster time, and before Ramage's own supporters at that.

It was all over in two rounds. Ramage made his usual fast start, jabbing and hooking the advancing Louis, and avoiding the counter-shots. In the second round, Ramage caught a hard Louis shot straight on the chin and wobbled a little but quickly recovered as he used the ring well. Louis went after him like a tiger sensing his prey but Ramage moved well and landed several hooks to Joe's body and head. With both men exchanging blows near the ropes, Louis connected with a whipping right cross that sent Ramage to the canvas on his back.

Taking full advantage of the nine count, Ramage arose only to run into another heavy right cross that sent him down on to his back again before the bout was stopped. The time was 2:11 of the second round and Louis had stretched his record to 15 consecutive victories. When Ramage was asked in the dressing room to describe the blows that put him down, he said, 'I honestly couldn't. I never saw them coming.'

The rematch, for which Louis collected $3,000, was notable for a significant reason. At ringside was Scotty Monteith, a boxing man from Detroit who combined his role of promoter and manager with that of matchmaker. He had previously offered Musky Jackson, a New York manager, a Louis fight against Don 'Red' Barry, only for Barry to turn it down. Monteith is generally credited with giving Louis his most famous nickname.

'The kid can't miss,' Monteith told a reporter in front of him. 'He's going to be champion of the world. Come to think of it, that boy is a real bomber, a brown bomber.' The claim is disputed, however, as some sportswriters were already referring to Louis as the 'Brown Bomber', including Charles Ward of the *Detroit Free Press,* who has also been credited with officially coining the nickname. Ward said the staff of his newspaper had a habit of sitting around their typewriters and tossing around names for various sports stars, and that the 'Brown Bomber' was one of them.

Musky Jackson came back into the picture in the spring of 1935 when he was approached by the Louis team for a bout with Don 'Red' Barry. When Barry had been offered a Louis fight the previous year, he had turned it down. This time he agreed, undoubtedly swayed by a $3,000 guarantee. The bout was arranged for the Dreamland Auditorium, San Francisco on 8 March 1935.

Barry, from Washington DC, was a run-of-the-mill heavyweight with a 52-20-13 record and was not expected to give the unbeaten Detroiter much trouble. 'The fight was funny,' said Louis in his autobiography. 'I had met this San Francisco sportswriter, Harry Smith. When he interviewed me, I told him I'd stop Barry in the third round. Smith printed this up as his own prediction. I really liked the guy and I didn't want to disappoint him by knocking Barry out in the first round, as I could have done. "Chappie" didn't know what was going on and he gave me hell, saying I should finish Barry off there and then.

'When I went back to my corner at the bell ending the second round, I explained what went on with Smith. "Chappie" gave me that funny grin and said, "OK, it's round three coming up and don't mess it all up now." At the bell I went out and after sparring around a bit, I hammered Barry and the referee intervened after a minute and a half.'

As it happened, Barry never won or even drew another fight, losing all of his next 20 bouts before announcing his retirement. 'I guess Louis kinda put the hex on me,' he said in later years. 'Even at that stage, the time of the Louis fight, I figured Joe was heading for big things. I reckoned he couldn't miss being heavyweight champion of the world. Any of his opponents around then would have said the same.'

It was back to Louis' hometown for his next fight. Roxborough and Black accepted a ten-rounder at the Olympia, Detroit on 29 March. The opponent would be Natie Brown who, like Barry, was based in Washington DC, although born in Pittsburgh. He turned out to be a tough and slippery rival. Billed as the 'New Deal', he had won 30, lost 18 and drawn seven in a career that had started in 1928 and would subsequently run for 21 years. He finally hung up his worn gloves in 1949, a year after Louis had defended his world heavyweight title for a record 25th time.

By now, Mike Jacobs had entered the scene. Jacobs promoted fights at the New York Hippodrome and had heard good reports from his contacts of 'an exciting, young unbeaten heavyweight named Joe Louis'. He decided to have a look at him and invited New York's leading boxing writers, sports editors and news agency reporters on a junket to Detroit for the fight, putting them up in a luxury hotel with all expenses paid.

As it happened, it was not Louis' best performance. Brown took Joe's best shots and always fought back with sustained attacks, often catching the Detroiter with looping right hands. But Louis was always in command against what boxing people call a spoiler, someone who makes an opponent look bad. Louis had Brown on the canvas in the opening round with a hard, sharp left hook but on rising, Brown went straight back on the attack, determined not to be caught again.

To avoid punishment, Brown often ducked and stalled, and several times draped himself over the ropes, even turning his back to the ring. Louis would have been within the rules had he hit Brown on such occasions but declined. Joe would step back until the Washington DC fighter resumed a fighting stance. A unanimous decision went to Louis. Brown knew he would not win but had succeeded in his objective – to finish on his feet and make the Detroiter look foolish.

'As you boys saw, Natie was a clumsy opponent with an awkward style,' Louis told reporters in the dressing room. 'I could hardly get through his guard. He was trying to show me up, and in many ways he did. I'm glad I won, sure I am, but I didn't feel happy out there. I can do better than that but Natie wouldn't let me.'

Louis and his team put his disappointing performance down to their boxer's state of mind. They felt he was overanxious and somewhat nervous because of the presence at ringside of Jacobs and the cream of the New York press corps. More importantly, however, Jacobs was impressed by Louis' power, his ability to take a good punch and his overall boxing skills. 'He can't knock everybody out,' he remarked to his ringside companion Nat Fleischer, founder and editor of *Ring* magazine.

At a victory celebration, Louis personally apologised to Jacobs for what he felt was an unimpressive performance but the promoter brushed it aside. He knew the young heavyweight had impressed the New York scribes and that was all that mattered. One of those writers was Harry Markson, who in later years would work for Jacobs and ultimately was employed as director of boxing at Madison Square Garden. 'Even though Louis did not knock out Brown, he was an exciting heavyweight, very impressive,' recalled Markson. 'You could see this kid had it in the way you could the first time you'd seen Sugar Ray Robinson or Willie Pep.'

As Louis remembered the occasion, 'Jacobs reminded me that not all my opponents would go down for the count, or be stopped by the referee. I was satisfied with that, especially coming from such an influential boxing man. He said I would go to the top and that I would break the colour bar that existed. In any event, he said there was a kind of silent agreement between promoters that there would never be another black heavyweight like Jack Johnson doing the bad things that he did. Those days were over. He said there would soon be a change in attitudes with black heavyweights, good black heavyweights. I took comfort from that.

'Jacobs told me that Jack Dempsey, heavyweight champion in the 1920s, had run all over the country to avoid fighting the top contender Harry Wills. Mike said he could break down that barrier and get me a shot at the heavyweight title, and that he'd make a lot of money for me. When my managers asked me how I felt about the whole thing, I said it was fine with me, and that's how it was.'

With the party in full swing, Jacobs, Roxborough, Black and Blackburn retired to another room to get away from the noise of the festivities. That happened to be the bathroom, of all places. Jacobs handed Roxborough a contract offering to promote all Louis' fights for the next three years under Mike's own banner, the 20th Century Sporting Club, with renewable options.

It meant that if all parties were in full agreement with the arrangement at the end of three years, the contract could be extended. If not, there would be no love lost. In Jacobs' own words – and this was the clincher that hooked the Louis team – Mike would have Joe box in New York by the end of the year. 'I am having talks with the people who run Yankee Stadium in the Bronx and they may have a free date in September,' he said. It seemed an offer too good to reject, and papers were signed by all principals. They all shook hands and returned to the party.

Jacobs would withhold news of the contract for two days before announcing it. He did not want it to clash with reports of the fight the next day. Louis, Roxborough, Black and Blackburn later went to the downtown Frog Club, a late-night spot frequented by black people, for drinks, although Louis did not touch alcohol.

Press reaction to Louis' victory was positive, even though Joe thought he could have done better by either stopping or knocking out Brown. Typical of the reports was Casey Adams' story in the *New York Herald Tribune*. 'Louis can punch with terrific power and can move with lightning speed,' wrote Adams. 'He can force a foe out of position, and his timing on the defence is so perfect that blows usually miss him and never land squarely. He is as cold as ice and when he moves, he does so as would a tiger or a lion.'

Two days later, Jacobs kept his promise and released news of his contract signing. A new era in boxing was about to start. Jacobs was the man who would play a greater part in Louis' career than anybody else. Known as 'Uncle Mike', he would, in turn, pull the sport out of the doldrums into which it had sunk in the early 1930s due to a series of controversial heavyweight title fights involving lacklustre champions and the influence of mobsters. Jacobs was on the cusp of changing all that and becoming the saviour of the noble art.

Fans had become somewhat tired of the recent heavyweight champions and their fights. The 1920s had been a golden age for the division, with the great Jack Dempsey, the 'Manassa Mauler', ruling the heavyweight class. Since then, there had not been a truly exciting fighter on the scene. Dempsey's successor, Gene Tunney, had retired too soon for his true worth to be assessed, and the champions that followed, namely Max Schmeling, Jack Sharkey, Primo Carnera, Max Baer and James J. Braddock, had failed to capture fans' or critics' full attention.

Boxing needed a bright, fresh face – a dynamic fighter who could put new life into boxing's premier division, the heavyweight class. The unbeaten Joe Louis seemed to fit that description. Jacobs would soon take the seventh son of a poor Alabama sharecropper to the pinnacle of his ring career, the heavyweight championship of the world.

Louis often said he owed his success to Jacobs. It was Mike who provided the boxer with the opportunity to get into the big money and effectively smash the colour bar that had prevented so many black heavyweights in the past from achieving their full potential. This is not to say that everybody liked Jacobs, although Louis could never say a bad word about him. On the other hand, Sugar Ray Robinson felt Mike was 'a true schemer'. Robinson would claim with justification that the promoter deliberately prevented him from boxing for the world welterweight title in the 1940s for years, even though he was the number one contender all along.

'Mike Jacobs eventually matched me with Tommy Bell in a title fight in December 1946, which I won, but I only got the opportunity because the press and public demanded it,' Robinson would tell this writer in later years. 'It was clear what Mike's intention was: "Keep Robinson out of a championship fight for as long as possible, as once he got the chance, he would win the title, mop up the rest of the contenders and quickly run out of contenders, and we'd be all out of a job."

'Jacobs wouldn't want that. There would be no more big welterweight title fights for him. It was more profitable for him to get other guys fighting for the title and drawing big gates. Even though we were always good friends, I always felt he was a bit of a schemer.'

Yet for all his crafty manoeuvrings, wheeling and dealing, and often divisive methods of doing business, Jacobs was a doer, and got things done, making him one of the greatest boxing promoters of all time. During the 12 years he dominated the sport, he staged 61 world championship fights and arranged 1,500 shows. On Louis' fights alone, he grossed $10 million. He was a worthy successor to the great promoter of the 1920s, Tex Rickard, who turned a one-time hobo in Jack Dempsey into a world heavyweight champion and introduced a new era in boxing. Jacobs would do much the same with Joe Louis.

Round 3

Roy gets the Lazer treatment

One of 12 children, Mike Jacobs was born in New York City on 17 March 1880 to poor Jewish immigrants from Eastern Europe. While both were in their early 30s, Isaac and Rachel Jacobs moved first to Ireland in an effort to make a better life for themselves, and settled in Dublin. A few short years after their arrival, the country found itself in the grip of mass starvation and disease as a result of the failure of the potato crop, known in Ireland as the Great Hunger. Being an agricultural country that depended on the potato, over a million people died and up to a million emigrated, mainly to Australia, Canada and America, causing the population to slump by over 25 per cent.

Isaac and Rachel took the boat to America and having already lived among Irish people, settled in a two-roomed apartment in an Irish community on New York's tough West Side. As a boy, Mike used to call himself an 'honorary Irishman', seeing that he was born on St Patrick's Day, the national festival. In his teenage years he worked at any jobs he could find, often digging with railroad construction gangs.

His most notable job around that time was selling newspapers, sweets and over-salted peanuts on Coney Island excursion boats docked at the Battery. To quench the thirst of customers, he would sell them bottles of lemonade he had bought in bulk on the cheap. Mike also had his own remedy for seasickness, which turned out to be nothing more than tea mixed with lemon.

In addition to his salesmanship, and possessing a keen business sense inherited from his parents, Jacobs noticed that tickets purchased for the boats docked at the harbour were often confusing to prospective passengers. He began what was known as scalping tickets, or buying them in bulk and selling them at a profit. He started off in a small way, gradually increasing his sales, and eventually ran his own ferryboat. Soon, he would branch out into buying and selling tickets for Broadway shows, opera nights and sporting events. He even started promoting events himself such as charity balls, bicycle races and circuses.

Through his connections at theatres, he signed the tenor Enrico Caruso to a series of one-night performances at the Metropolitan Opera House that guaranteed the Italian impresario $1,000 a show. Mike cleared $80,000 on that particular venture. Later on, he arranged theatrical tours nationwide for the actors Ethel and Lionel Barrymore, as well as the suffragette Emmeline Parkhurst, netting more tidy profits for 'Uncle Mike'.

Always on the lookout for ways to make money, Jacobs heard there was a big fight coming up in the mining town of Goldfield, Nevada on 3 September 1906, Labour Day. It was a world lightweight title fight between Joe Gans, the champion billed as the 'Old Master', and Battling Nelson, an uncompromising battler known as the 'Durable Dane'.

The event was getting mass publicity in the newspapers and many leading boxing writers and sportswriters would be attending, including the reporter and short story writer Jack London. The fight was being promoted by a flamboyant 35-year-old former gold prospector named Tex Rickard, who ran a gambling saloon in the town. Rickard had made and lost small fortunes in bars and theatres in Alaskan mining towns. He was a gambler pure and simple.

Jacobs felt he might try and get in on the promotion in some fashion and duly made his way to Goldfield. It was Rickard's first boxing promotion and Jacobs persuaded the promoter to employ him as an assistant ticket seller at the gate on the day. To gain publicity for the fight, Rickard dreamed up the idea of placing the entire purse for the two boxers, a total of $33,000, in $20 gold pieces in a bank in town, a clever publicity stunt that produced photographs in newspapers across the country. Gans had been told by his foster mother a day before the fight, 'Son, the eyes of the world will be on you tomorrow. Bring home the bacon.' The phrase caught on and is now part of everyday speech.

The fight got under way in blazing sun before 8,000 sweltering fans. Gans was much too clever for the rugged but unskilled challenger, but in the 42nd round Nelson landed a low blow and was disqualified as Gans sat on the canvas in obvious pain. Gans may have retained his title but he lost out financially, as Nelson's people had demanded $22,000 as their end of the purse, leaving just $11,000 for the champion.

After all expenses, Rickard came out with a good profit as the bout attracted $69,715, the largest ever for a boxing match up to then. Tex was no real boxing expert but he saw the potential of the sport in a financial sense. He would go on to stage other big fights, notably outbidding several leading promoters to stage the Jack Johnson–James J. Jeffries world heavyweight title fight in Reno, Nevada on 4 July 1910.

When the promoters got together in a hotel in Hoboken, New Jersey to make their bids, Rickard emptied out two bags containing $101,000 on the table. 'That's my offer,' he said to Johnson and Jeffries, who were present. 'Take it or leave it.' It turned out to be the top bid. Rickard also guaranteed Johnson and Jeffries two-thirds of the movie rights. In addition, they would receive $10,000 'just for signing up', said Tex. The offer was readily agreed. Jacobs would say in later years that it was one of the best deals he ever pulled.

Rickard kept in close contact with Jacobs, particularly when Tex shifted his operations to New York following the Walker Law, which legalised boxing in the state. With Jacobs' help, he made successful overtures to the upper strata of society, and became skilled in dealing with prominent politicians to facilitate the promotion of his fights.

Rickard really came into his own in the Roaring 20s, when he linked up with the world heavyweight champion Jack Dempsey and brought the sport into the million-dollar bracket. He had promoted Dempsey's title fight with Jess Willard in Toledo, Ohio in July 1919, when Jack slaughtered the big Kansas cowboy in three merciless rounds. Jacobs helped with ticket sales. In Dempsey's defence of the title against the Frenchman Georges Carpentier, a former war pilot, at a makeshift arena in Jersey City on 2 July 1921, over 80,000 fans paid a record $1,789,238 to see Dempsey win by a fourth-round knockout and create boxing's first million-dollar gate.

As Rickard's assistant in ticket sales, Jacobs earned a tidy $250,000 by disposing of more than 5,000 tickets at an average profit of $50 a seat. The only individuals to walk away with any regrets were Dempsey and his manager Jack 'Doc' Kearns, who opted for a flat guarantee. A percentage of the gate would have netted them several hundred thousand dollars extra. 'You win, you lose,' mused Kearns as he left the arena with Dempsey. 'But we came out of it all right, and Jack still has the championship.'

By 1924, Rickard was matchmaker at the new Madison Square Garden at Eighth Avenue and 42nd Street, where he arranged many important world title fights. Tex effectively controlled the boxing scene, and more importantly the heavyweight championship, the biggest money-spinner in the sport. As Rickard's right-hand man, Jacobs too was in a commanding position. Mike had an office in the Forrest Hotel a block away but often worked in a windowless storage room at the Garden, 'Where I can do my business in quiet surroundings, with no interruptions,' as he put it.

Jacobs continued to work with Rickard throughout Dempsey's career, advising the promoter on ticket sales to the best advantage. All Jack's fights were big draws, notably his sensational bout with the rugged Argentinian Luis Firpo at the Polo Grounds, New York in September 1923. It attracted over 82,000 spectators, who contributed to another million-dollar gate, with $1,888,603 taken in. Dempsey was knocked out of the ring in the opening round but came back in the second session to demolish Firpo in just 57 seconds.

'Rickard was the best promoter of all time,' Dempsey would remember in his autobiography. 'We never had a contract, ever. You didn't need one with Tex. A firm handshake would be sufficient. He was the greatest man of my life. They don't make them like Tex Rickard any more. I hadn't met a promoter before who gave a damn whether I lived or croaked.'

Following Rickard's death from pneumonia in 1929, Jacobs continued to invest in other promoters' shows but always yearned to put on his own, where he would be in complete control. The opportunity came when he did a deal with the owners of the New York Hippodrome in which he would promote boxing shows. A man who kept a very close watch on his finances, Jacobs always made sure he paid his boxers well and they had no complaints. 'Whatever they say about Jacobs, he's a straight shooter,' said one manager who regularly dealt with Mike.

It was not until 1933, when Jacobs linked up with prominent sportswriters Damon Runyon, Bill Farnsworth and Ed Frayne, who all worked for the William Randolph Hearst newspaper chain, that his career changed for the better. They asked Mike to stage Hearst's annual Milk Fund boxing show at the Bronx Coliseum. This was a charity event, with the bulk of the proceeds going to help underprivileged children in the city, which was still feeling the effects of the Great Depression.

Jacobs agreed but suggested they form a new company, the 20th Century Sporting Club, and they could put on this and other tournaments at the Hippodrome. The first show was held on 24 January 1924 and headlined by world junior welterweight champion Barney Ross outpointing Billy Petrolle in a non-title fight over ten rounds.

Mike had set his sights on Madison Square Garden, the prime indoor venue in the city, but it was controlled by James J. Johnston, the dapper Liverpool-born impresario, as covered in the previous chapter. When Jacobs formed the 20th Century Sporting Club in opposition to Johnston, Mike knew there were going to be big changes. He vowed to smash the monopoly operated by Johnston and the Garden – and he had the great undefeated heavyweight to achieve that aim, Joe Louis. In addition, Jacobs had the support of the powerful Hearst newspaper chain to give him blanket publicity and coverage. He would strike at the right moment.

Jacobs arranged with Roxborough and Black for Louis to box Roy Lazer in a scheduled ten-rounder at the Chicago Stadium on 12 April 1935. From Paterson, New Jersey, Lazer was considered one of the best Jewish boxers of the 1930s. With a 36-2-2 record and on a seven-fight winning streak, Lazer was expected to provide stiff opposition for Louis. He did, in the opening round at least, as he moved well around the ring, keeping away from his opponent's heavy shots and at the same time scoring with long lefts to the head.

Louis began to connect with sharp hooks to head and body in the second round, one left hand rocking Lazer to his bootlaces. It was all over in round three when a left-right combination dropped the Jersey fighter in a neutral corner. After he rose at the count of eight, Louis sent over the finisher, a big right, and Lazer went down again to be counted out at 2:28 of the round. The gate receipts amounted to a respectable $42,000. Roxborough would say later, 'We didn't realise how many fans would turn out, otherwise we would have asked for a percentage of the gate instead of a $12,000 guarantee.' The purse was double what Louis got for his previous fight against Natie Brown two weeks earlier.

Jacobs believed in keeping Joe busy. Mike admitted he had been having preliminary talks with the people who looked after the affairs of the big Italian, Primo Carnera, the former world heavyweight champion. It would be a real test for Louis, and Jacobs felt he could beat Carnera. Negotiations were proceeding well and he would soon bring Roxborough and Black into the discussions. Jacobs also had his organisation, the 20th Century Sporting Club, enquiring about the availability of the Yankee Stadium in New York for a big outdoor fight there in June.

'Forget about the "black heavyweight" issue,' he told Roxborough. 'New York are now crying out to see Joe, and there won't be any problems, mark my words. Let's leave Madison Square Garden for the moment. We'll shoot for a big open air show at the Yankee Stadium first.'

To all intents and purposes, Jacobs seemed to be running the Louis show rather than his co-managers. Roxborough and Black saw no difficulties there. Remembering the reluctance in the past about a Louis appearance in New York, and the shadow of Jack Johnson hanging over the situation like a black cloud, they encouraged Jacobs to go ahead. After all, without New York, the world's leading boxing capital, things could look bleak.

Jacobs recommended keeping Louis busy. He planned to put the name Joe Louis on everybody's lips, with four fights in quick succession leading up to the clash with Carnera, now provisionally set for 25 June. The first date was at the Memorial Hall in Dayton, Ohio on 22 April, ten days after the Lazer fight. The opponent would be Biff Bennett, based at an army camp at Fort Sheridan, Lake County, Illinois.

Loosely described as a journeyman at best with more losses than wins, Bennett had been victorious in only 12 of his 27 fights, with one draw. It was Louis' first appearance in the state, and he wanted to put on an impressive performance. Scheduled for six rounds, the fight was given prominent publicity by local newspapers. The fans, however, did not see much of Joe. It was all over in two rounds.

After sounding out his rival in a quiet first round, Louis landed a lightning right cross in the second session that sent Bennett down and out. The round had lasted just 57 seconds. When Biff recovered his senses in the corner, he exclaimed wide-eyed, 'What happened?' From then on, in Louis' own words, 'it was like a blur'. He said in his autobiography, 'I was storming the country with three more knockouts and there was hardly anyone who hadn't heard of me.'

As busy as he was, Louis managed to buy a house for his mother, a promise he had made in his early days in Alabama. 'I surprised her with it on Easter Sunday 1935,' he recalled. 'This was what the game was all about. I was making good money. The house was at 2100 McDougal Avenue in Detroit. It had two bedrooms downstairs and two upstairs. Momma couldn't believe it when I showed her the house and she broke down and sobbed. Tell you the truth, I did too. I paid $9,000 for the house, cash, no bills. That was one time when I saved up my money. I was prouder of this than anything I had ever done. Soon after, I bought momma a chicken ranch on the outskirts of Detroit.'

Louis was also thinking of his girlfriend, Marva. He wanted her to meet his family. Joe had never invited a lady to his mother's house, so he had to do something special for that. He asked Marva to meet him in Detroit to see a tennis match. They met as arranged – but Marva came along as usual with her sister. Louis' thoughts were something on the lines of, 'When am I going to see this girl alone?' When Marva did eventually meet his mother, they hit it off. 'We started off straight away like mother and daughter and that was nice,' Marva recalled.

Meanwhile, Jacobs had been working on the Carnera fight and announced that the bout was arranged for the Yankee Stadium on 25 June 1935. It would be Louis' 20th fight and the most important of his fledging career. Mike had kept his word to get Joe into New York. Moreover, he had capitalised on the failure of James J. Johnston and his associates at Madison Square Garden to sign up the local ballparks to prevent any other promoters, particularly Jacobs, from renting them. It was a major coup for 'Uncle Mike'.

Carnera had lost his world heavyweight title a year earlier when he was knocked out in 11 rounds by the hard-hitting Max Baer at the Long Island Bowl, New York. The big Italian had been on the canvas 12 times in the one-sided bout, and the only thing that could be said about Primo was that he was gameness personified. Coming into the Louis fight his record read 82-7-0, which looked good on paper but was much less in substance. The problem with Carnera was that many of his fights were fixed. There were allegations that even his title-winning bout with Jack Sharkey was crooked, with many ringside observers claiming they never saw the punch that put Sharkey down for the full count in the sixth round.

The jury is still out on that one, nearly 90 years on, but at his best, and when his fights were on the level, Carnera was a good, skilful boxer with a strong right hand. It would be Louis' most important fight to date. The first, and still the only Italian to win universal recognition as heavyweight champion of the world, another of his claims to fame is that he had had more nicknames than any other heavyweight champion, such as 'Man Mountain', 'Old Satchel Feet', the 'Gorgonzola Tower', 'Da Preem' and the 'Noblest Roman of Them All'. However, it was Damon Runyon of the *New York Journal American* who tagged him with the sobriquet that stuck, the 'Ambling Alp'.

The son of a poor stonecutter, Carnera was born in the little village of Sequals in north-east Italy on 26 October 1906, the eldest of six children. His parents were of normal size and none of his brothers were over 6ft. By the time Primo was 21, he was 6ft 6in and weighed 240lb. Growing up during World War One, his village was occupied by Austro-German forces, so there was very little food about. The youngster had to help out and search the fields for anything edible to supplement the family larder. Things improved after the war, but with hardly any education young Primo could barely read or write. He got a job as an apprentice to his uncle, who was a carpenter, but there was still not enough food to satisfy his big appetite, let alone the remainder of his family.

Carnera made up his mind at the age of 14 to leave home and try to make his way in the world, travelling around northern Italy and leading something of a hobo existence, picking up whatever work was available – labourer, bricklayer and occasionally stonecutter. Primo eventually made his way to France and arrived in Le Mans wearing one of his father's old suits, his feet encased in worn rope sandals and carrying all his worldly goods in a cardboard box. He stayed with an aunt and got a job in a circus, where his size and strength were useful in setting up and dismantling the big top.

Carnera eventually became part of the show, working in the circus ring as a strongman, weightlifter and sometimes boxer, even undergoing a nationality change by the circus proprietor, who billed him variously as 'Juan the Unbeatable Spaniard' and 'Terrible Giovanni, Champion of Spain'. Seemingly, his boss felt that being a 'Spaniard' was a bit more exotic than merely an Italian. Primo's speciality in the strongman act was a tug-of-war in which he outpulled a heavy motor vehicle heading in the opposite direction.

When the circus reached Bordeaux, he was spotted by a former French heavyweight boxing champion, Paul Journee, who suggested that Primo take up boxing seriously due to his strength and size. 'You could well go places,' suggested Journee. A contract was duly signed. Journee put Carnera up in his home and trained him for three months before turning him over to his own former mentor, the diminutive Leon See, who was France's most successful boxing manager and had a training camp outside Paris.

See was a former amateur bantamweight who boxed in England as a 17-year-old by virtue of his father having a home and business interests in Birmingham. At the time, *la boxe anglaise* was little known in France, where a form of kickboxing, or *la savate*, was more popular. Later on, See would do much to introduce the Queensberry style in France and subsequently formed the French Boxing Federation.

See said he would take 35 per cent of Carnera's earnings but promised he would move Primo ahead. What had the big fellow to lose? At least he would eat regularly. Carnera signed the contract. See arranged for some local boxers to coach his new charge in the rudiments of the sport and asked Jeff Dickson, an American promoter domiciled in France, to fix up some fights. Dickson soon matched the Italian with local fighter Leon Sebillo for a purse of 1,000 francs at the Salle Wagram in Paris on 12 September 1928. Carnera knocked his man out with a mighty right to the chin in the second round.

See would later admit that he handed Sebillo 500 francs out of his own pocket to throw the fight and that Leon agreed to leave his guard open so that Carnera could land a blow that would lay him out for the full count. The shrewd See clearly did not want to take any unnecessary risks with his new meal ticket.

This practice would set the trend in Carnera's career. See later revealed in a book he wrote that at least 28 of Primo's fights were fixed as the naive Italian 'knocked out' opponent after opponent – and all this before Primo got into the big time when American mobsters moved in and took over his management. In those early fights, Carnera did not know how much he was being paid. See simply oversaw each contract and conveniently never kept receipts.

For Primo's second fight, against Joe Thomas, See visited the Frenchman's dressing room and quietly slipped half of Carnera's purse of 3,000 francs into Thomas' hand and promised, 'That's in addition to your purse. All you have to do is go down in the third round.' Thomas duly obliged. And so it went, See coming to financial arrangements with Carnera's opponents, many times the money coming out of Primo's purses. The big Italian was still none the wiser. Those who were not paid to lie down or merely surrender were either faded veterans or no-hopers who would lose anyway.

Ironically, in his first real test, against Germany's Franz Dener in Leipzig in April 1929, Carnera was caught with a vicious right hook to the groin in the opening round. He went down groaning, but the referee, instead of immediately disqualifying Dener for a blatant foul, ordered Carnera to continue after a five-minute rest. When Primo, still in discomfort, refused to leave his corner after a further five-minute rest, the German was awarded the fight on a disqualification. In addition, Carnera's purse was held up by the boxing commission.

Carnera soon moved back into his winning streak with the help of See and willing opponents. Promoter Jeff Dickson decided to move Carnera into the London scene. He matched the Italian, following See's approval, with the talented American, Young Stribling, at the Royal Albert Hall on 18 November 1929. The arrangement was that Stribling would strike Carnera below the belt in the fourth round and be disqualified, leaving the way clear for a lucrative return fight in Paris, where Stribling had a big following.

The fight went according to plan, with the American landing a right uppercut well below the beltline in the fourth round 'with all the force of a dessert spoon dipping into a rice pudding', according to Carnera's biographer Frederic Mullally. Primo slithered down the ropes and hit the canvas, rolling over from side to side, whereupon the American was disqualified.

They met again three weeks later before a sell-out crowd, at the Velodrome d'Hiver arena in Paris, and again promoted by Dickson. The plan was that Stribling would win this fight, with the exact finish worked out later. Following the script, Carnera punched after the bell had ended the seventh round, even backhanding the referee to make certain he was disqualified. Sure enough, he was promptly thrown out. Plans for a third fight never materialised because See now had his sights set on the more lucrative American market and a world title fight.

To ensure that Carnera's interests were well looked after across the Atlantic, See was 'persuaded' to hand over his claim on Primo to a syndicate comprised of a New York manager/talent scout named Walter Friedman, known as 'Good Time Charlie', and two of his associates, Bill Duffy and Owney Madden, both well-known hoodlums but with the right connections. Madden was actually born in Leeds, England but moved to the United States as an 11-year-old, and in his teens would find himself at home in the impoverished Hell's

Kitchen neighbourhood on the West Side of New York, not too far from where Mike Jacobs got his start.

There were also two others in the syndicate, 'Big Frenchy' de Mange and Frank Churchill, two mobsters with an interest in the fight game, undoubtedly a financial interest. Both also had close and convenient friendships with referees, judges, officials and boxing commissioners. Christmas cards would be sent out to one and all every year without fail.

At first, See was reluctant to part with Carnera as he had developed a close, warm friendship with the gentle giant. But when it came out later in the newspapers that he had agreed, the supposition was that some additional incentive had been offered to the little Frenchman by the hoodlums, such as 'insurance against accidents detrimental to his health'. In any event, under American rules, Carnera had to have a licensed manager. In his case, he had several.

Duffy, a shady New Yorker known as 'Big Bill', owned several speakeasies and had served prison sentences for an assortment of crimes, including armed robbery. A bootlegger, nightclub owner and hotelier, he had interests in slot machines and lottery games. Madden, dubbed by the FBI as 'Public Enemy No 1,' he was known in the underworld as 'Owney the Killer'. He too had a long prison record, with several murders and a manslaughter to his name.

The syndicate, after some consideration, allowed See to act as Carnera's European manager and said he could also come on Carnera's planned American tour as an advisor. After all, they did not want Primo to feel lonely or isolated from the man who had been with him from the start. Dickson would stay behind as Carnera's European promoter. Both Dickson and See would be on a small percentage of Primo's American earnings.

Also on the Carnera payroll was Luigi Soresi, an Italian with banking interests in New York. Soresi would be the front man and look after Primo's financial affairs when his pals Duffy and Madden, who both had a major share in Carnera's purses, were 'otherwise engaged'. Is it any wonder that Primo himself usually received less than ten per cent of the money earned from his fights?

Carnera would be introduced to American fight fans by means of a cross-country tour featuring quick knockouts. 'Primo's opponents either came into the ring leaning on, or were more than normally sensitive to "strong drafts",' recalled the boxing historian and prolific author John McCallum. 'Primo only had to swish his great glove through the air and – crash! – down they would fall.' As was the case in Europe, Carnera was not aware that many of his opponents were taking dives, and when he was told, it caused much embarrassment. On one occasion, when a rival fell down from a light punch and was later fined by the boxing commission for not giving of his best, the soft-hearted Primo insisted on reimbursing him.

The tour got off to a quick start. On his US debut at Madison Square Garden on 24 January 1930, Carnera knocked out the Canadian, 'Big Boy' Peterson, in 70 seconds with a heavy right to the chin. What the spectators were not aware of was that Peterson had agreed to take the punch and go down for the count. Owney Madden was unavoidably absent from ringside. He was back behind bars in Sing Sing prison on a first-degree murder rap.

A week later at the Chicago Staduium, Carnera was down to meet Elzear Rioux, a French-Canadian lumberjack who weighed 210lb. The day before the fight, the International News Agency reported, 'Carpenters went to work early this morning to strengthen the ring to make sure the boards will support the two behemoths whose combined weight is nearly a quarter of a ton.'

The ring stood up better than Rioux. He slumped to the canvas for no particular reason after 47 seconds of the first round. When Carnera yelled at Rioux to 'get up', he did so only to be immediately put down again for the full count with a light right cross to the head. The Illinois State Athletic Commission confiscated the Canadian's purse and fined him $1,000 for 'playacting unbecoming for a fighter'. Primo was held blameless of any charges and exonerated, getting his $16,000 share of the gate receipts.

On 3 March in Philadelphia, rugged Roy 'Ace' Clark, all 6ft 9in of him, chose to ignore his corner's instructions and was giving Carnera all kinds of problems for five rounds. As he sat on his stool awaiting the bell for the sixth, a gruff voice shouted up at him, 'Look down here, Ace.' When he did so, his jaw dropped, because sitting at ringside was a mobster pal of Duffy's with a long, glistening knife on his lap. Clark got the message and took the full count after 30 seconds of the sixth round.

There was the occasional mishap. In Oakland on 14 April, a tough individual named Leon 'Bombo' Chevalier refused to be bribed and felt he could beat Carnera. He duly bombed Primo with heavy rights for a few rounds, splitting the big Italian's left eyebrow and bruising his self-confidence. The hoods who controlled Primo, however, were fully prepared for such an eventuality. Between the fifth and sixth round, one of Chevalier's handlers rubbed resin into their man's eyes.

The half-blinded Chevalier still managed to put Carnera on the canvas in the sixth round with a swinging right for a count of five. But on instructions from Primo's corner, Chevalier's chief second Bob Thomas threw in the towel, even though 'Bombo' was capable of continuing the fight. The arena erupted in protest, and Chevalier was attacked by several spectators after the sudden finish. Both boxers' purses were withheld by the Californian State Athletic Commission, which also suspended the state licence of Carnera as well as those of Primo's team, Duffy, Soresi, Friedman and See.

New York followed the lead of California and suspended all their licences as well as ordering a full investigation into all of Carnera's fights, but the syndicate controlling his interests simply moved elsewhere – Portland, Detroit, Philadelphia, Omaha, Cleveland, Atlantic City, Newark, Chicago and Boston.

One particular opponent, Riccardo Bertazzolo, a proud and gutsy Italian, refused to take a dive in Atlantic City on 30 August, despite being guaranteed a percentage of the gate receipts on top of his purse, which would have netted him $10,000 overall against Carnera's $6,000. Bertazzolo, however, was double-crossed by his own manager, Aldo Linz, who split Ricardo's eyebrow with a razor between the second and third rounds, covering up the wound with Vaseline. With the first blow that landed on the eyebrow in round three, blood spurted, prompting the referee to stop the fight and award the verdict to Carnera on a technical knockout.

Primo had three more fights, in Newark, Chicago and Boston, before planning a few months' break in Europe. Pat McCarthy took the easy way out in the second round in Newark, New Jersey on 8 September, going out to meet Carnera with the enthusiasm of a man facing a walk to the electric chair. Jack Gross did likewise in the fourth round in Chicago ten days later. Jim Maloney, a seasoned campaigner of Irish heritage but long past his best, refused to be bribed in Boston on 7 October and in one of the few genuine fights in Carnera's pre-championship career, Primo lost a points verdict, although most observers felt he should have won.

Carnera had planned to have no more fights in Europe before resuming his American campaign but See, as his European manager, arranged two contests before year's end – a points win over the rugged Spaniard, Paulino Uzcudun, in Barcelona and a second-round stoppage of the 203lb future British heavyweight champion Reggie Meen in London. There had been letters in the British press calling for cancellation of the fight on the grounds that it was a travesty to put any human being up against the giant Italian.

Trevor Wignall, boxing writer for the *Daily Express*, almost seemed to be on the side of the protesters when he wrote, 'When Carnera removed his gown, there were gasps of astonishment all around from where I was sitting. His phenomenal chest and arms were the things that produced the astonishment. The man is much more than a "normal abnormal", as he was once described to me by a doctor.

'Professional boxing has never known anyone like him. Most certainly he is a giant, but he is also a giant who is most marvellously equipped both mentally and physically. Any present-day fighter who is matched to meet him is going to look like an infant by comparison, and I cannot help but think that the day is rapidly approaching when it will be found impossible to get opponents for him, except perhaps in exhibitions.'

Carnera continued with his ring appearances but only with a series of exhibitions in Britain, Sweden, Denmark and Norway. The exhibitions seemed to bolster Carnera's morale as well as the bank accounts of See and promoter Dickson who, between them, could pocket 45 per cent of the money rolling in before deducting their and Primo's expenses. The fans turned out in droves to see 'the Man Mountain' in the flesh as he sparred with local heavyweights and performed his physical exercises. It was estimated that no boxer had put in so many public exhibitions over so short a period, eight or nine weeks.

Carnera was back in the US in the spring of 1931 on a concentrated campaign that his syndicate promised would lead to a world heavyweight championship fight with Germany's Max Schmeling. First stop was at Miami's Madison Square Garden arena on 13 March for a return with his earlier conqueror, Jim Maloney. In a sparring session a week before the fight, Carnera sustained a cracked rib from a hard-hitting sparring partner, Walter Cobb. Primo's people asked for a postponement but the local boxing commission rejected the plea as most of the tickets had already been sold and the Italian had to enter the ring with part of his chest in plaster and bandages.

Carnera was also going through an emotional battle with his girlfriend, Emilia. She wanted marriage while Primo preferred to wait until he had made further progress in his boxing career. What with the injured rib and the private stress, it was perhaps surprising that he even went the full ten rounds with Maloney, let alone got the decision – one that brought boos and whistles from the 20,000 crowd for at least 15 minutes. Maloney was mainly the aggressor while Carnera appeared not to be punching his full weight. The press corps was split but the Associated Press news agency called it 'a robbery' and gave Maloney five rounds, Carnera three and two even.

The fight did little to raise Primo's status as a contender for Max Schmeling's world heavyweight title. The American boxing public seemingly were in no great hurry to have two non-Americans fight for the sport's most prestigious prize, a title they felt was something of a national institution anyway. This did not stop the Carnera managerial team plugging away for the championship bout. They flooded the New York newspaper offices with press releases, stressing his 'impressive' record and even inflating Primo's size to 6ft 9in and 284lb, and his shoe size between 17 and 18. Some newspapers stretched his foot to a size 22. In truth, Carnera's shoe was a mere size 13.

By now, Primo was moving up among *Ring* magazine's top ten contenders, and continually adding to his list of victims. Following his disputed win over Maloney, he had six quick wins, two in the first round, three in the second and one in the third. On 5 October 1931, he made the cover of *Time*, with the big-selling news magazine running a complimentary feature story on the Italian, part biography, part evaluation of his career and prospects. It was very good publicity and helped in keeping Carnera in the public eye. The rival *Newsweek* was also featuring him and he graced its cover several times.

Demand was seemingly growing for Primo to get into the championship picture. Finally, an offer came in for a heavyweight elimination contest over 15 rounds against Boston's Jack Sharkey, the number one contender, at Ebbets Field, Brooklyn on 12 October. The winner would be matched with world champion Max Schmeling in a title fight. It was an offer too good to miss. The old nagging problem of two 'foreigners' boxing for a world title in the United States was apparently forgotten.

'What's wrong with an Italian fighting a German in an American ring anyhow?' said one New York paper. 'It's unusual, to say the least, and it would undoubtedly be a big attraction.' Sharkey was a good boxer at best but he was inconsistent, an in-and-outer. In 1930, he had been disqualified for striking Schmeling below the belt in a fight for the heavyweight title left vacant by the retirement of Gene Tunney two years earlier. He promised to be 'a good boy' against Carnera.

A capacity crowd of 30,000 turned out to see the Carnera–Sharkey encounter. Associated Press boxing writer Herbert W. Barker had written the day before, 'If this fight confirms Sharkey as leading contender, it will serve also to remove any lingering doubt as to Carnera's courage and stamina.' Joe Williams of the *New York World Telegram* had a totally different view – and refused to even cover the fight. A week before the bout, he wrote, 'Put on the hot seat, I would not trust either one of these as far as I can throw the Empire State Building with my left hand. Which is another way of saying that in this fight, you can make your own choice. I don't want any part of it.'

Carnera fought well in the first three rounds, prompting Barker to report, 'The big Italian amazed Sharkey and the crowd with his speed and skilful boxing.' But in the fourth, the course of the fight changed rapidly when Sharkey dropped Primo to the canvas. According to John Kieran, chief sportswriter on the *New York Times,* 'the ring platform quaked and quivered under the terrific impact. Doubtless, the seismograph at Fordham University registered the shock on the revolving drum.'

Scrambling to his knees, Primo began pulling himself up by the ropes as referee Ed 'Gunboat' Smith reached the count of six. Carnera's corner had been exhorting him to stay down until the count reached nine to clear his head. As he stood up, he suddenly lost his balance and went down again. As soon as Primo hit the boards, Sharkey yelled, 'Hey ref, he went down without being hit. Disqualify him.' Ignoring the plea, Smith waved them on. Sharkey continued to call for a disqualification in the fifth round and failing to change the referee's mind, he began to climb out of the ring. His manager pulled him back and barked, 'Get on with it, Jack, and beat this guy. It's an important fight, remember.'

Sharkey and Carnera resumed the fight but it was the Boston boxer who dominated from there on. His long left jabs and hooks to the head and body continually unsettled Primo, who seemingly could not figure out Sharkey's shifty style. In the 15th round, Sharkey almost toppled the Italian with hard left and right crosses. At the last bell, there was little disagreement with the result. Smith and the two judges all marked their cards the same, awarding Sharkey a unanimous decision.

Five weeks later Carnera was back in the ring, this time in a scheduled ten-rounder against the hometown contender King Levinsky at the Chicago Stadium. Levinsky started well, crowding the favoured Italian with clusters of punches from both gloves, causing the crowd to go into a frenzy as they sensed an upset. But from the third round it was all Carnera, who leaned on the local in the many clinches that marred the fight. A strong finish by Primo in the final round, when he landed jarring rights to the head, earned him the verdict of referee Eddie Purdy and two judges.

After the fight, Carnera was tired but ready to celebrate his victory when two policemen walked into his hotel room and arrested him and his official manager Leon See. The charge was in connection with a $3,754 judgement filed against them by Indiana promoter George Biener, who was seeking damages, alleging that Primo failed to show up for a fight the previous June in Fort Wayne. Taken to the local jail, Carnera and See were soon released pending further review but the case was later dropped, reportedly due to See coming to a secret financial arrangement with the promoter.

Primo, meanwhile, continued with his ring career, and saw out 1931 with a scheduled ten-rounder against the 6ft 9in Victorio Campolo on 27 November. An Italian by birth but living in Argentina, Campolo was a rising heavyweight star who had featured on the cover of *Ring* magazine. But his reputation had suffered when losing earlier in the year to the former world light-heavyweight champion Tommy Loughran and the capable Ernie Schaaf. He was now out to re-establish himself and improve his 17-5-1 record.

Carnera entered the ring at Madison Square Garden a 2/1 favourite to topple a man who was even taller than himself. It was a busy if short fight, with plenty of action while it lasted. The first round saw the two big men mixing it freely. 'Resin dust rose in clouds as the gigantic warriors tramped around the ring,' reported the *Chicago Tribune*. Campolo won the first round on most ringside cards with his sharper punches. With seconds left in round two, Carnera went to work, unleashing a volley of hard lefts and rights, each reaching their target.

One powerful right found Campolo's chin and sent the Argentine boxer crashing to the canvas for a count of nine from referee Ed 'Gunboat' Smith. On rising, Campolo was subjected to a barrage of heavy blows, with a sweeping left hook sending him sinking to the floor for the second time. He managed to struggle to his feet but failed to make it up and was counted out at 1:20 of round two. See then hurriedly climbed into the ring and raised Carnera's hand.

The year 1931 had ended on a successful note, with nine victories and one loss bringing Carnera's overall record to 50-4-0. The following year was even busier with 25 fights, including 23 wins, 17 by knockouts or stoppages. With demands from European promoters to have a look at the big fellow 'putting the scare into the Americans', as one writer put it, Carnera had a frenetic schedule. He squeezed in eight fights, with seven wins, in five months, opening his schedule in Paris in January 1932 with a stoppage against the French champion Moise Bouquillon in the second round.

Primo made his first London appearance in over a year on 23 March with a fourth-round knockout of the Australian George Cook at the Royal Albert Hall, and returned there by popular demand two weeks later with a points win over Don McCorkindale, dropping the South African three times.

In his final appearance on the tour, Carnera was matched with Larry Gains, a black Canadian who held the British Empire heavyweight championship, now Commonwealth, at the White City Stadium, London on 30 May. An extremely talented boxer with an impressive 72-12-4 record, Gains left his native land on a cattle boat and settled in England, gaining a reputation as a boxer with class.

Before a crowd of 70,000, a new record attendance for a boxing tournament in Britain, Gains avoided Carnera's heavy punches and boxed his way to a unanimous decision over ten rounds, taking eight rounds to two on most cards. It was a serious setback to Primo's world title hopes. As for Gains, he set off with his manager Harry Levene, later one of Britain's leading promoters, to the United States in search of a world title fight, only to become another victim of the notorious colour bar.

Back on American soil, Carnera soon returned to the winning side with the assistance of his mobster associates and ran up 17 consecutive victories all over the nation, from New York to Boston, from Louisville to Chicago, from Grand Rapids to Galveston, from St Louis to Dallas and other stops in between.

In Primo's first fight of 1933, disaster struck when his opponent, Ernie Schaaf, died of head injuries sustained in the contest. Schaaf, 24, from Elizabeth, New Jersey, was among the top contenders for Sharkey's world heavyweight title. A good, solid body puncher, he had easily outpointed two future world heavyweight champions in Max Baer and James J. Braddock, as well as future title challengers Young Stribling and Tony Galento. However, in a return fight with Baer on 31 August 1932, six months before the Carnera fight, Schaaf was knocked down by Max two seconds before the final bell, which saved him from an official knockout. Baer won on points.

It took several minutes for Schaaf to be revived. He complained of headaches thereafter, and it was believed that he suffered brain damage. Six months later, on 10 February, he went against Carnera before a capacity crowd of 20,000 in a scheduled 15-rounder.

The fight turned out to be a dull affair, with more clinching and holding than solid punching, and the fans started booing for more action. By the end of the 11th round, Carnera was ahead on points and Schaaf, by now, had slowed down to a laden-footed amble. He rallied briefly in the 12th but was floored in the 13th by a couple of right uppercuts followed by a left hook to the jaw, seemingly with no great power behind it.

As he was being counted out, many in the big crowd started yelling, 'fake, fake'. They could not believe that an apparently light punch could have knocked out Schaaf. Carried from the ring on a stretcher, he remained semi-comatose in the Polyclinic Hospital across the street with an inter-cranial haemorrhage and underwent three hours of surgery.

During this time Carnera, greatly agitated and unable to sleep properly, called the hospital almost hourly for news of his opponent's condition. Upon Schaaf's death five days after the fight, Primo was put under technical arrest on a charge of manslaughter and twice interrogated by the homicide squad while the post-mortem was being conducted.

The autopsy revealed that Schaaf had entered the ring with a blood clot on the brain, sustained in the Baer fight. His death had resulted from an accumulation of blows rather than the 13th round knockout, but it seemed that the crucial damage had been done by Baer almost six months earlier when he battered Schaaf during the tenth round of their return fight. Primo was exonerated on the charge.

Despite this finding, William Muldoon, the New York State Athletic Commission chairman, announced that Carnera would not only be banned from fighting Sharkey but he was too big to box any average heavyweight. In future, Carnera would be allowed to fight only in a 'dreadnought' class of fighters, defined as weighing 240lb or more and of a height not less than 6ft 2in. As the furore died down, Muldoon's plan was forgotten and normal service, such as it was, was restored to the heavyweight division. With repeated calls from the Carnera camp for a world title fight with Sharkey, aided by the press and public, the contest was set for the Long Island Bowl, Madison Square Garden's outdoor arena, in New York for 29 June 1933.

Expert opinion was divided as to the likely outcome right up to the night of the fight. A poll of 13 ringside boxing writers showed ten were predicting a Sharkey victory. Damon Runyon could not make up his mind. Writing in the *New York American*, he said, 'Carnera is not an instinctive fighter. He has no ferocity but has amazing speed for a big man. When upwards of 250lb is merely shoving a ham of a hand encased in leather against a human object, that object is bound to be damaging.' Writing in the same newspaper, Ed Frayne commented, 'It's a tough one to call as neither are great fighters but I will put my money on Carnera to win over the 15 rounds.'

The Italian was installed as 6/5 favourite. By tradition, Sharkey was first into the ring and given a resounding cheer, despite not being the most popular of champions. A model of inconsistency, he could look like a world beater one night and a journeyman the next. Sharkey's biggest liability was his moodiness in the ring. If he disagreed with the referee's call or felt an opponent's foul had been overlooked – even though he was not averse to hitting below the belt himself — he became distracted and made mistakes.

Carnera climbed through the ropes a few minutes later and extended his arm in the Italian salute as the Italo-Americans kept up a chant of 'Primo, Primo' right up to the opening bell, when referee Arthur Donovan barked the ritual, 'Shake hands now, and come out fighting.'

Carnera won the opening round by virtue of his fine left jab and greatly improved footwork, which was keeping him away from the Boston boxer's sharp lefts to the head and body. Sharkey took charge in the second round with his better boxing but he was finding it hard to handle the heavier challenger in the clinches, though he still won the round with his long-range work.

Sharkey had a good third round, too, but in the fourth Carnera's thumping blows to the body were having an effect on his ability to reach Primo's chin. His confidence was waning, too. Near the end of the fifth, with both boxers exchanging hard blows, Sharkey seemed to get a second wind after landing a crashing right to Carnera's head. Primo held on like a limpet and blocked the champion's follow-up punches.

In the sixth, Carnera seemed to be strengthening and hurt Sharkey with long left hooks to the body and head. One left uppercut caught the champion on the chin and sent him to his knees and halfway through the ropes. Sharkey got up quickly but the Italian would not be denied. With a grimace on his face, Carnera landed an inside right uppercut that caught Sharkey square on the jaw.

As Associated Press sports editor Alan Gould saw it, 'The punch felled Sharkey as though he had been a tree hit by the woodman's final blow.' Sharkey, face down on the canvas, never moved a muscle as Donovan counted to ten. On its front page the next day the *New York Times,* under James P. Dawson's byline, described the blow as 'a terrific right-hand uppercut to the chin which almost decapitated Sharkey and brought Carnera the title'.

John McCallum, in his book *The World Heavyweight Boxing Championship,* wrote, 'A strange hush fell over the audience. They sat in stunned silence, while Carnera danced happily around the ring. John Buckley, Sharkey's manager, playing his role to the hilt, leapt into the ring and demanded that Primo's gloves be examined. His inference, of course, was that no mere mortal could cause such havoc with just skin, bone and leather.'

Following a thorough examination of the gloves, no irregularities were found, yet the allegations of a fixed fight still remained, given Carnera's past history of crooked fights. Clips of the fight, shot from one angle, as was the custom of the time, shows the Italian landing a right uppercut and Sharkey slithering to the floor. Some asked, was the blow hard enough to knock out the world champion? Or was it a punch packed with real power?

Paul Gallico of the *New York Daily News* said, 'Nothing will convince me that it was an honest prizefight, contested on its merits.' On the other hand, *Ring* magazine's Nat Fleischer, considered the doyen of America's boxing writers, always felt it was a genuine knockout. 'The blow that felled Sharkey was one of the hardest I have ever witnessed,' he said.

Carnera never said too much about the fight and the controversial knockout, though he always maintained he put all he had into the punch that put Sharkey on the canvas for a full count. 'I had too much power for Sharkey,' he told an interviewer in later years.

Sharkey was much more forthcoming. 'I'll never live it down,' he said in 1982 when he was 80. 'People don't remember me for being the heavyweight champion of the world. They think of me as the champion who took a dive. I didn't, and I'll swear on my grave I didn't. I saw a vision of Ernie Schaaf, the guy who died after a Carnera fight, in front of me. The next thing Carnera hit me, and that's the end of the story, but I could never convince anybody. I couldn't even convince my manager or my wife. They wanted to know if I had bet my whole purse on Carnera.'

Primo held the title for only 12 months. After two successful defences, points wins over Spain's Paulino Uzcudun four months later and the ex-world light-heavyweight champion Tommy Loughran, who was 84lb lighter, in March 1934, Carnera signed to put his title up against leading contender Max Baer. In June 1934, he was knocked out by the power-punching Baer in 11 rounds at the Long Island Bowl after being floored 12 times.

Ring magazine's headline was, 'Heavyweight crown returns to US. Baer thrashes brave Carnera.' Gene Tunney, the former world heavyweight champion, commissioned to write a report for the Associated Press, said, 'The Italian cannot hit and he is bewildered as soon as his defence starts to break down. His confidence was shattered from early on and it was simply a question of how long it would last.'

Carnera had four more fights, winning three inside the distance, before an offer came in to meet the new sensation Joe Louis. It would be an opportunity for Carnera to re-establish himself in the eyes of the public and the press, but a difficult one at the same time. A powerful hitter and the younger man by eight years, Louis was on a roll with 19 consecutive victories, 15 without the aid of officials' scorecards.

Round 4

Conquering the 'Man Mountain'

Promoter Mike Jacobs called a press conference in the offices of the 20th Century Sporting Club to announce that Louis would meet Carnera at the Yankee Stadium, New York on 25 June 1935. Louis set up training camp at Pompton Lakes, an hour's drive from the city and away from all the hustle and bustle, on the large estate of Dr Joseph Bier, a wealthy dentist.

While Louis went through his paces with Blackburn, Jacobs hired press agents to work at the camps of both boxers, as well as another based in his Manhattan office sending out daily press releases to publicise the big fight, often exaggerating the abilities of both men. In order to cope with Carnera's size, the Louis entourage brought in three exceptionally tall sparring partners in Leonard Dixon, Roy 'Ace' Clark and Cecil Harris, 'a trio of giants', as Blackburn called them.

Pressmen found Louis shy and uncommunicative, and he managed only monosyllabic responses to the rush of reporters' questions. It was his nature. He was still a quiet black boy out of Alabama suddenly thrust into the world of media and publicity. Some newspapermen mistook his silence and somewhat wooden expression for hostility and stupidity, but that was not the case at all. Louis was that way throughout his life, even when his boxing career had ended. When this writer met him on a personal tour of Britain and Ireland in 1970, you had to literally draw the answers out of him.

Back in the 1930s, the Louis entourage went out of their way to project their boxer as a 'clean-living sportsman who does his work in the ring'. There was no way another Jack Johnson would be created. That era was long past. Reporters wrote many stories about how well behaved Louis was, mostly patronising.

Richards Vidmer said in the *New York Herald Tribune*, 'Joe Louis is as different a character from Jack Johnson as baseball's Lou Gehrig is from the gangster Al Capone. It seems to me that the "Brown Bomber" is just what the doctor ordered to restore life in the business of boxing. He is a God-fearing, Bible-reading, clean-living young man, to be admired, regardless of creed, race or colour. He is neither a show-off nor a dummy. Modest, quiet, unassuming in his manner, he goes about his business, doing the best job he can every time he climbs into a ring.'

At his camp at Oswasco Lake in Upper New York State, Carnera expressed full confidence in his ability to handle his younger opponent, and qualify for a return fight with his conqueror Max Baer for the world title. Max told newspapermen at an impromptu gathering after a round of golf in Sacramento, California that Primo would 'explode the meteoric rush' of Louis.

He said that while Joe might well knock Carnera down, recalling his own fight with the tenacious Italian nine months earlier, he predicted with his usual certainty that Primo would get right up and fight back. 'If Carnera is in the top physical condition he was for me, then he will wear Louis down,' he confidently forecast.

On 13 June, the entire boxing world was sensationally turned upside down when Baer was outboxed, outfought and outpointed by the unfancied James J. Braddock and lost his title. It was one of the sport's biggest surprises of all time as Baer had entered the ring at Long Island Bowl a solid 15-1 favourite to beat the challenger, who was on a comeback at the time. Now the focus was on a Braddock–Louis title fight, or even Braddock against Carnera, with Jacobs keeping a close watch on proceedings.

As the Louis–Carnera fight approached, some people started to have qualms about the contest. Among these was the newspaper magnate William Randolph Hearst, whose *New York American* played up the bout because Mrs Hearst's Milk Fund stood to receive a percentage of the gate receipts. Mr Hearst finally decided he wanted the fight called off. He pointed out that trouble was brewing between Italy and Ethiopia and was receiving a good deal of publicity in the press, including his own newspapers.

To match a black boxer with a white man in an important fight would have been daring at any time. But to pair one with an Italian when the world was super-conscious of the Italian–Ethiopian crisis struck him forcibly. Italian supremo Benito Mussolini was making no secret of his intention to invade and subjugate Abyssinia in defiance of the League of Nations while German chancellor Adolf Hitler was making a lot of noise about world dominance in the Fatherland. Jacobs paid no attention to Hearst.

A crowd of over 60,000 passed through the turnstiles on fight night for what was the largest crowd to attend a boxing match since the Dempsey era. The gathering included 1,500 police officers, both uniformed and in plain clothes, on foot and mounted on horseback. There were over 400 journalists from around the world, including Britain, the most to cover a boxing event in over a decade. Invited guests included the mayors of New York, Newark, Jersey City and Chicago, as well as Postmaster General James A. Farley and President Roosevelt's sons James and John. State business prevented the president himself, a fight fan, from being there and he sent his apologies to promoter Jacobs.

The boxing world was well represented too, with five world heavyweight champions in attendance. Each stood as they were announced from the ring – former champions Jack Johnson, Jack Dempsey, Gene Tunney, Max Baer and the reigning title-holder James J. Braddock. Two other world champions were also on hand, welterweight Barney Ross and lightweight Tony Canzoneri.

The gate receipts came to $340,000, with expenses trimming the net to $277,000. Newsreel films were theoretically banned for the fight but some mobsters managed to film the action with Jacobs' permission, and in later years the promoter admitted he received an additional $10,000 for the rights to these. It was not until 1940 that it was legal to show films of a fight through interstate commerce.

At the weigh-in earlier in the day, Louis had scaled 196lb and Carnera just over 260. When asked by reporters to give a forecast, Louis glanced at his team and, addressing the press gathering, said diplomatically, 'May the best man win.' When Carnera was prompted for a quote, he was quickly interrupted by Luigi Soresi, Primo's financial advisor.

'Primo will win,' Soresi bravely forecast. 'I am assuming, of course, that Joe Louis behaves himself and does not get fresh in the first two rounds. If he is a good boy, Primo will make the finish as painless for Joe as possible.' Carnera boosters had said at the camp that the short-punching Louis would not be able to reach Primo and that the bigger man would be able to wear down the Alabama man in the clinches.

It was just before 10pm when the principals left their dressing room for the ring and the announcement by MC Harry Baloch. 'Tonight we have gathered here to watch a contest of athletic skill,' he said in his long-winded fashion. 'We are Americans. That means that we have come from homes of many different faiths, and we represent a lot of different nationalities. In America, we admire an athlete who can win by virtue of his skill. Let me then ask you to join me in the sincere wish that regardless of race, colour or creed, the better man may emerge victorious.'

Blackburn advised Louis on the proper tactics to conquer the Italian. 'Listen to me, "Chappie", a tree like this you gotta chop down,' he said. 'Fancy work is no good. Go after him right away.' Blackburn had long believed in the old boxing maxim, 'Kill the body and the head must fall.' It was Carnera who landed the first blows, jabbing effectively and landing a quick left hook to the ribs as he moved around the ring. Louis, waiting for the right moment, countered with a hard right that landed squarely in Primo's face and opened a bad cut on his lip. The Italian now realised the massive task that lay ahead of him.

'What he was up against was perhaps the most efficient pugilistic machine ever transformed into human shape,' wrote the author and novelist Frederic Mullally. 'Joe Louis moved as if every part of his body enjoyed its individual intelligence while responding smoothly and elegantly in the super-intelligence screened by an otherwise totally expressionless face. He wasted no punches.

'His powerful body could weave and bob with the fluid grace of a lightweight. He was a master of the feint – that sudden threat from a fist, or a sway, or a look in the eye, sometimes three at once, that raised or lowered an opponent's guard and opened the way to a hook as joined to the feint as the pain is to the sound of the whiplash.'

Carnera lost that round by the length of Broadway but seemed to regain his composure somewhat in the second round when he connected with a good left hook to the body and followed through with a long left to Louis' jaw. The American countered with a cluster of punches that drove Primo back across the ring and against the ropes. There was a clinch after Louis came in, and referee Donovan quickly broke the pair. When they resumed, Louis seemed to invite a right from Primo, then slipped under it and caught his man with a smashing left hook to the face, re-opening the gash on Carnera's lip.

Primo came out fighting in rounds three and four. But apart from a glancing left hook to Louis' chin, his main concern seemed to be keeping the 'Brown Bomber' at bay and clinching whenever he could. Even in the many clinches, his advantage in weight failed to work. Carnera's surprise at this caused him to make his only remark during the fight. Louis later recalled, 'In the fifth, when I turned him around in a clinch, he said, "Oh, I should be doing that."'

After the fifth round, with reporters tapping away at their typewriters and ready to wrap up another Louis early victory, Carnera was told by his cornermen, 'If you have any chance of winning this fight, you have to make your move quickly.' Primo came up for the sixth round with that in mind, driving Louis to the ropes, but could not seem to get through Joe's defence as the Alabama fighter jabbed him off. Adding to Carnera's problems by now were horrible cuts on his face, and his left eye was badly swollen, making him look more like one of those grotesque stone gargoyle faces you might see carved on a building. But the Italian was game. Nobody could dispute that.

Carnera swung a right at Louis' head, more in desperation than anything else. It missed the target and Louis countered with a jarring right cross and jolting left hook that sent Primo to the floor, where he took a count of four. On rising to face his tormentor, he was met by a hail of blows from an opponent with imminent victory in his sights. Carnera was down again before staggering to his feet on rubbery legs at three. Louis came in for the finish but the referee got there first. Acting humanely, Donovan waved his arms wide and raised Louis' right arm as the winner.

What was developing into a massacre was now all over, with 28 seconds remaining in the sixth round. Not surprisingly, the black section of the crowd erupted in wild jubilation but many Italians booed their man's performance. Yet Primo did his best. He could do no more against a potentially great heavyweight. Carnera's own manager and second, Bill Duffy, earned no plaudits for bawling out his fighter and main meal ticket for 'a stupid performance'. More neutral observers praised Primo's courage. Louis' own brother, DeLeon Barrow, would say in later years, 'Carnera fought from bell to bell and got no credit for it.'

In the dressing room, Louis praised Carnera's brave performance but conceded he was confident of victory. 'I knew in the fifth round I would get him,' he said. Some 12 years later and close to retirement, he told an interviewer, 'The Carnera fight was my first in New York and this was the night I remember best in all my fighting. If you ever were a ragged kid and you come to something like that, you'd know. I don't thrill to things like other people. I only feel good, and I felt the best that night.'

In his autobiography in 1978, he elaborated, 'Carnera never hurt me once. I felt ready for any heavyweight in the world – the new world champion Braddock, ex-champion Baer, anybody. I had made it in New York, the boxing capital of the world. Now there was no question of my fighting ability, or my ability to draw a crowd. I had $60,000 to prove it, and that was after my managers, for the first time, took their share and ten per cent had gone to the Hearst Milk Fund.'

In defeat, Carnera offered no excuses. 'Louis certainly hit harder than Baer, that's for sure. He's a very good boy, a very good fighter and will go far, I'm sure. Some day, he may be champion. He punches harder than anybody I've ever met.' When H. Allen Smith, the humorist who was then feature writing for the *New York World Telegram*, asked him, 'Did he hit you hard?' the battered Primo stared at him. 'Jesus God, he does hit.' When Smith enquired, 'Do you want to fight him again?' Carnera's badly cut face took on a look of terror. 'Oh Jesus God, no,' he said.

The newspapers heaped praise on Louis the following day. James P. Dawson told his readers in the *New York Times* that he had seen one of the greatest fighters of modern times in action. 'He punches like Dempsey. He is a reminder of the one and only Sam Langford.' However, several of them depicted Louis as something animalistic or savage.

Grantland Rice, considered the doyen of American sportswriters of his time but blatantly racist by today's standards, referred to Louis in the *New York Herald Tribune* as a 'bushmaster' and said his movements were 'the speed of the jungle, the instinctive speed of the wild'. Rice used another animal image to describe Joe in the ring, commenting, 'Joe Louis was stalking Carnera, the mammoth, as the black panther of the jungle stalks its prey.'

Davie Walsh's report for the International News Agency began, 'Something sly and sinister and perhaps not quite human came out of the African jungle last night to strike down and utterly demolish the huge hulk that had been Primo Carnera, the giant.' Paul Gallico, sports editor of the *New York Daily News*, who would later abandon journalism and write hugely successful novels such as *The Snow Goose* and *The Poseidon Adventure*, saw the 'fat-faced safe-au-lait coloured, sloe-eyed' boxer as 'something utterly vicious and pitiless. Not once is there a glimmer of sympathy or feeling on Louis' face. He is a splendid, vicious male animal, completely destructive. He was made for fighting and nothing else.'

Shirley Povich of the *Washington Post* said, 'No killer with the ferocious scowl of Jack Dempsey or the fiendish leer of Max Baer is this Joe Louis, but a killer nevertheless. Like some machine, a methodical, mechanical destroyer, geared for destruction, did he attack the gargantuan specimen who opposed him with a 64lb weight advantage, and was cut down for the finish.' Povich's colleague on the *Post*, Bill McCormack, referred to 'a cruel, destructive fighting machine trade-marked Joe Louis'.

Whatever his ability, sportswriters generally saw Louis as the best young heavyweight since Dempsey. It was obvious he would be in the upper ranks of the heavyweight division for years to come and, if given the chance, almost certainly become world champion. He was breaking down the race barrier, or at least chipping away at it. In what was in effect an open letter to Louis, Bill Corum of the *New York Evening Journal* wrote under a headline 'Stick To Your Ma, Joe', 'You saw for yourself against Carnera that everybody means to play fair with you. They'll keep on being that way if you give 'em the chance.

'Don't get big headed. Don't think when you get a bad break – and you'll get some, the game calls for it – that you got it because of your race. That's the bunk in sports. The people who make race feeling are the people who keep harping on it. Those who do most to kill it are those who don't think about it one way or the other. Be that way, Joe. Be yourself. Behave yourself. Be an example to your race.'

Promoter Jacobs suggested the Louis team come out for a meal in a fashionable club, but Joe shook his head. 'Ma cooks the best meal in the United States,' he said. 'I'm going home now and tomorrow ma will cook me a big steak, one of those lovely steaks she does so well.' For the most part, Louis liked home cooking, especially when his mother prepared it. Just before the meal was on the table the following day, Joe said he wanted to first say a quick hello to some pals who lived nearby.

He smiled at her and as he was striding briskly towards the door, Lillie put her hands on her hips. 'Joe Louis Barrow,' she said as Joe stopped and turned around. 'My son is never going to be too busy to eat a meal his ma cooks for him. It's good food. You need it. Where did you get such high-falutin' ideas anyhow? Now come on, sit down and have my meal.' Louis thought for a second then went into the dining room and ate his steak and potatoes. 'That,' he told his mother when not a scrap of the meal remained on the plate, 'was the best steak I ever had.'

Louis meant it too. He wanted to repay his family, who had struggled in those early days back in Alabama to rear himself and the other siblings and to bring them up as good people. Joe did not wish to be regarded as a kind of 'Goody Two Shoes'. He merely felt he could show how much he appreciated them all. He did not stop at buying presents. He did a lot of little things every other day to convince them he was as proud of them as a family as they were of him as a son and brother.

A month before the Carnera fight, he had taken a short break from training to take his kid sister Vunies to California on a pleasure trip as a reward for having graduated from high school with high honours. Now he was helping her plan the course she would take at Howard University in Washington DC, where he promised to take her in the autumn.

Carnera never again reached the heights in his boxing career. In any event, his heavy loss to Baer was effectively the beginning of the end, and now this conclusive defeat against Louis. Primo continued to fight through 1936 and 1937 with little success. During the war years, he went back to his hometown of Sequals but returned to the US in 1949 and had success as a professional wrestler with a large following. He appeared in half a dozen major Hollywood movies, starring opposite the likes of Marlon Brando, Bob Hope, James Mason, Janet Leigh, Rod Steiger and Diana Dors.

During his time there, the story of his exploitation by gangsters and undesirable individuals who cheated him out of most of his ring earnings became public knowledge. Returning to Sequals in 1967, Primo died, largely of symptoms related to alcohol. Even then, when his obituary appeared in the *New York Times,* columnist Arthur Daley cruelly called him 'a hoax'. Carnera deserved a better send-off than that.

***

In the summer of 1935, Louis was the golden boy of boxing, the saviour of the sport, the new Dempsey. Nobody knew that better than Mike Jacobs. There was talk of another big outdoor fight in New York in the autumn against the former champion Max Baer, which Jacobs confidently predicted would draw a million-dollar gate. Meanwhile, the promoter suggested a ten-rounder with King Levinsky, who had been ranked fifth in the world the previous year. Levinsky had fought most of the leading heavyweights of his era, and had a reputation for being one of the toughest. He held wins over two former world champions in Jack Sharkey and Tommy Loughran.

Born Henry Krakow of Polish origin, Levinsky was a member of a family who sold fish from a pushcart in Chicago's old Jewish ghetto in Maxwell Street, hence his nickname 'Kingfish'. For part of his career, Levinsky was managed by his sister, Lena. Known as 'Leapin' Lena', she was a colourful character who swore like a sailor, and rooted loudly for her brother during his bouts.

In May 1932, *Time* magazine stated, 'If you defined the efficiency of a prize-fighter by his ability in the ring, Levinsky would not rate better than tenth among US heavyweights. Last year he had 15 fights, won only eight. If you defined efficiency as a fighter's ability to earn money at his trade, Levinsky might rank as the best fighter in the US.

'In the last 15 months, gates at his fights have amounted to $254,124.68. He may this year earn more than Dempsey, Schmeling, Sharkey, Carnera or Schaaf. Kingfish Levinsky's earning power is due partly to an engaging slapstick manner in the ring, an engaging entourage. It is due partly to the fact that most of Levinsky's fights have been in Chicago, where he came from.'

The fight was scheduled for Comiskey Park, Chicago on 7 August 1935, so Jacobs felt there would be a big turnout to cheer on the local boy and give him every support, even though Louis was a solid favourite. Uncle Mike was right, as a crowd of over 50,000 paid their way through the gates. At the weigh-in a few hours before the scheduled start of the fight, Jacobs noticed Levinsky looked very nervous. When the promoter approached him and asked if there were any problems, the Chicago boxer waved his hands dismissively. 'Nothing's the matter, Mr Jacobs. All's fine,' he replied.

Jacobs had an official trail Levinsky during the day to make sure nothing went wrong with his big promotion. On fight night Jacobs still feared the worst, so he had the Illinois State Athletic Commission start half an hour earlier than planned.

'That's too early,' said one of the officials. 'The crowd is still coming in.'

'Get Louis and Levinsky into the ring,' barked Jacobs. 'It's going to rain.'

The official looked up. The stars were shining brightly in a cloudless, moonlit sky.

When the fight was due to start, Jacobs decided to check that everything with Levinsky was all right. Entering his dressing room, there was no sign of the boxer, only his handlers and several friends. 'Where's the fighter?' he asked anxiously.

He was told that Levinsky had locked himself in the toilet. 'Open up, open up,' demanded Jacobs, banging on the toilet door. 'Go away, please,' responded Levinsky. Jacobs had to send for two workers to break down the door with an axe and take the boxer out.

When Levinsky eventually climbed into the ring, he had to be shoved out at the bell by his seconds for what was his 98th professional bout, of which he had won 68 and drawn five. The grim prospect of disaster was in the air. Moving on stiff legs, he was hit by a terrific right cross to the head. Responding, he tossed his own right but missed by at least 12 inches. Louis countered with a straight right and the Chicago fighter toppled to the canvas, his legs buckling under him.

Levinsky struggled to his feet at the count of three with a look of sheer terror on his face before Louis landed with a short left hook to the head that sent Levinsky back against the ropes, leaving him in a sitting position on the bottom strand. Regaining his feet at the count of four, he was hit by another sweeping left hook, this time taking another count of four. Levinsky was in there only by instinct at that stage. As Louis moved in to finish him off, referee Norm McGarrity got there first and yelled, 'That's all.' The affair – it could hardly be called a fight – was all over, two minutes and 21 seconds after it began.

Later, Louis, normally deadpan, allowed himself what *Newsweek* magazine described as 'his first sincere smile' to the cameras. The reason was that he had made a bet with his handlers that they would all go on the wagon for six months if he took care of Levinsky in one round. 'I don't remember how many times he was down but it was an easy fight,' he said. As for the loser, 'Kingfish' was far from downcast by his summary defeat. 'Yeah, Louis is a good fighter but I'd fight him again tomorrow,' he said. 'I guess I was just a little careless.'

Two years after the Louis fight, Levinsky visited London for a bout with the popular Irish heavyweight Jack Doyle. At the press luncheon, the three-weight British champion Len Harvey, who was then acting as matchmaker for Wembley, where the fight was to take place, stood up to propose a royal toast, a time-honoured tradition. 'Gentlemen, the King,' he intoned.

The assembled company rose decorously and drank with the familiar hushed murmur – all except Levinsky. He quickly got to his feet and, with an expansive wave of his hand, said, 'Thanks pals, that's big of ya.' As the gathering sat down, nobody knew how to explain without hurting Levinsky's feelings. But Harvey saved the day by announcing, 'And now, let us drink a toast to our guest of honour, King Levinsky.'

Doyle won the fight, the only one involving the 'Gorgeous Gael' that went the distance. Years later, in an interview with this writer, Doyle said that one of his supporters had made a bet with him. The fan, anxious to encourage Jack to box rather than fight and avoid a possible disqualification, as had happened in a previous title fight, promised to pay Jack £1 for every left he landed on Levinsky's somewhat battered features. The Irishman came out of that little arrangement with over £100.

With Louis' impressive record now standing at 21 fights without a blemish, plans were quickly put in place by Jacobs and the Louis team for the Baer fight. Mike announced it would be held at the Yankee Stadium on 24 September 1935. But first, Louis had another important engagement. He was getting married to his long-time girlfriend Marva Trotter on the morning of the fight. Always the businessman, Jacobs baulked at the idea, feeling that the nuptials would take Louis' mind off the contest, but Joe told him not to worry. 'I want to come home to a bride after the fight,' he told the promoter.

Max Baer had all the attributes to be a great boxer. Possessing one of the hardest right-hand punches in boxing history, he fought his way to the heavyweight championship of the world, the ultimate prize in the sport. Yet having reached the top with minimal effect, he let it all go with minimum resistance. He was a playboy, pure and simple. 'Baer's huge enjoyment was infectious,' said author and boxing writer John McCallum. 'Guys and dolls loved him. Handsome, carefree, incorrigible Max preferred a female "knockout" than a fight "knockout."'

One sure thing about Max was his unpredictability. Nat Fleischer, founder and editor of *Ring* magazine and in his day the most knowledgeable boxing expert in the world, wrote, 'Baer stalked the arena with the sweep and dignity of a master-tragedian one moment, and the rollicking abandon of a circus clown the next.'

Maximilian Adilbert Baer was born in Omaha, Nebraska on 11 February 1909, the second child of Jacob Baer, a German whose father was Jewish. Max's mother, Nora Bales Baer, was of Scottish-Irish descent. After Max was born, the Baers had two more daughters, Frances and Bernice, and a second son, Buddy. They would later adopt a third boy named August. The fact that Max and Buddy grew up to be heavyweight boxers would not have surprised those who knew their parents, for both Jacob and Nora were 6ft tall and weighed over 200lb. Jacob worked in a slaughterhouse and was regarded as one of the strongest men in a trade where no weakling could earn a living.

When Max was four, Jacob felt it was time for a change of scenery, particularly as he was made redundant in the slaughterhouse. The family moved to Denver, Colorado but things were not much better there and they moved again, to Durango, a smaller town in the state.

Five years later, with his growing family needing support, the wanderlust again took hold and they moved to California, first to Hayward, where Max remembered his father could not get any work, and then to Galt, where he worked at various jobs. It was in Galt where Max joined the local baseball team. Finally, the family settled in Livermore, which would later provide Max with yet another nickname, the 'Livermore Larruper', and where Jacob rented a ranch.

When Jacob found himself unable to handle the daily chores, young Max quit school and helped out on the ranch, where he filled out and built his great physical strength. By the time he was 19, he stood over 6ft tall and weighed 190lb of bone and solid muscle. He had not paid too much attention to boxing growing up, although he remembered his father taking him to a local tournament in Oakland when he was 16. 'I wasn't particularly interested as baseball was my favourite sport, but I do recall being in tears the following year when Jack Dempsey lost his world heavyweight title to Gene Tunney,' he said.

It was at a weekly dance that Baer got his real introduction to boxing. He was shy around girls and often used to stay outside the hall for long periods. One night, around the back of the hall, he happened to see one of his friends being assaulted by a big fellow who had wrongly accused him of stealing wine from his car. When Baer intervened, the big man grabbed him by the collar of his new shirt. Max retaliated with a swing of his right hand that caught his assailant on the chin and sent him down and out.

Baer's friend thanked Max for intervening and suggested he should take up boxing with a punch like that. A week later, Baer had an opportunity to try out his big punch again at a dance when a cowboy started pushing him around. Max simply lashed out with that big right of his and again his victim was knocked senseless. Baer decided there and then that he was going to be a boxer, and a good one. Packing his bags one day, he said goodbye to his parents and moved to Oakland, where he got himself a job in the Lorimer motor plant where diesel engines were manufactured.

Hearing of Baer's enthusiasm and his wish to become a boxer, his boss J. Hamilton Lorimer, whose father owned the plant, suggested Max join the local gymnasium, learn the rudiments of the game and take it from there. Baer took his advice. Lorimer suggested Max should start off in the amateurs to gain experience but Baer said he wanted to go straight into the professional game 'because I will learn as I go along, and besides, I have the wallop', he mused.

Lorimer arranged for Baer's debut at the Oak Park arena in Stockton against a tough old Native American named Chief Caribou. The date was 16 May 1929. Baer sold over $50 worth of tickets, even giving one to a local boxer and hitchhiker, Kayo Janek, who became a friend and supporter all his life.

Delighted to make a start in the paid ranks, Max celebrated half an hour *before* the fight by drinking several bottles of soda pop and eating a plate of ham sandwiches. It did not affect his performance in the scheduled four-rounder. After Caribou did a traditional war dance in the centre of the ring, much to the amusement of the crowd, the first bell rang and the fight started. The action did not last long. After sounding out Caribou in the opening session, Baer landed his big right in the second round and down and out went the Chief. Max earned $35 for his exertions. He was on his way.

Lorimer signed Baer to a three-year contract and gave him a $3,000 Ford car, as well as assigning a former middleweight named Jim McAllister to teach him the rudiments of the sport. For the remainder of the year, he had no fewer than 15 more fights, his lone loss being a third-round disqualification for a low blow against Jack McCarthy in Oakland.

Baer had earned around $50,000 in the ring, a tidy sum at the time. It was all so easy, and his popularity soared along the west coast. As a boxer with a powerful wallop, he was a top drawing card. As a personality outside the roped square he was adored by the public, especially the ladies who wanted to go out with him or at least be photographed alongside him. The tall, dark and handsome Max was developing the playboy, devil-may-care image and lifestyle that would make him famous throughout the world and eventually contribute to his downfall.

Tragedy struck in 1930. In his 26th fight, after 23 wins, 19 by count-outs or stoppages, Baer knocked out Frankie Campbell in San Francisco on 25 August. The Italian-American, a promising heavyweight, died in hospital five hours later. Baer had forced the pace from the opening round and subjected Campbell to heavy punishment before the Minnesota man collapsed in the fifth round. Baer was arrested and the Californian State Athletic Commission suspended him for 12 months. The newspapers made sensational copy out of the tragedy, with headlines such as 'Baer the butcher', 'Max murderer' and 'Ban this killer for life'.

'They branded me as if I were a blood-thirsty killer,' Baer recalled. 'When I was placed under arrest for manslaughter, the promoter Ancil Hoffman, who later became my manager, posted $10,000 as a bond and gained my release. Of course, it was a tremendous relief when the surgeons announced that Frankie had died of a brain concussion and the court ruled that it was an accident and cleared me of the manslaughter charge. But for the time being, I felt as if I never wanted to see a boxing glove or enter a ring again. My enthusiasm for the game had gone. What I wanted was to get away from California, go somewhere else, anywhere, and try to forget.'

Baer located to Reno, Nevada. He was broke and in debt but friends helped him out. Hoffman bought his contract from J. Hamilton Lorimer in a deal that netted him $5,000. Max kept in touch with Campbell's widow and her young son, and later boxed at a benefit show for the family.

Friends, including the singer Al Jolson, were also encouraging him to return to the ring, reminding him that the Campbell tragedy was an accident, as the court had ruled. Jolson would later lend him large sums of money. Baer made his comeback on 19 December 1930 in his New York debut, four months after the Campbell fight, but lost a ten-round decision to the top ten contender Ernie Schaaf. He was also beaten in three of his next five fights. The old enthusiasm was missing.

Baer's life, inside and outside the ring, seemed to be spiralling out of control. Deeply in debt and needing money to finance numerous liaisons with beautiful women, he sold shares in himself to anybody who wanted a piece of the action. When Hoffman got around to investigating the whole thing, he discovered that Baer had sold 113 per cent of himself to various agents. It took nearly four years to sort out that little matter.

Jack Dempsey, the retired former world heavyweight champion, was brought in to help Max shorten his punches and to get the most leverage out of them. Dempsey also had to warn him to keep away from the ladies while in training. Baer paid no heed to the advice. Whenever he boxed in New York, he was out on the town immediately afterwards. Max simply loved the high life too much.

Ring magazine's Nat Fleischer remembered, 'Baer said New York was the largest and most delightful playground he had yet discovered. The nightclubs got a great play from Max. He was the life and soul of every party thrown in his honour, and there were plenty because the sports, one and all, fell for his sunny, agreeable personality as readily as the girls paid homage to his superb physique and flashing smile.'

During one New York trip, he started a courtship with the beautiful movie actress Dorothy Dunbar and they made the rounds of the nightclubs and speakeasies. The gossip columnists lapped it up. In July 1931, they married. Max was her fourth husband. The marriage lasted less than a year following heated rows about Baer's infidelity.

Despite his wild private life, Baer managed to keep his boxing career on track. By the end of 1931, he had ten fights, winning seven, five by knockout. One of his victims, in January, was the tough New Zealander, Tom Heeney, who had gone 11 rounds with Gene Tunney in the latter's final fight as world heavyweight champion in 1928. Baer knocked him out in three rounds.

Max had it tougher a month later against master boxer Tommy Loughran, a former world light-heavyweight champion. Loughran managed to finish each round near his own corner so that as soon as the bell rang, he simply sat down while Baer had to walk clear across the ring to his own stool. Max never forgot the corner stunt and in some of his later fights he worked it successfully himself. Loughran won a popular decision after ten rounds.

Baer's third and final defeat of 1931 was on 4 July, when he went in against the Spaniard, Paulino Uzcudun, in Reno, Nevada. It was promoted by Jack Dempsey. Max would describe the 20-rounder as the hardest in his career. In addition to having the toughest heavyweight in the business to contend with in the open air, the barometer read 109 degree heat. Max claimed he lost 12lb in the battle.

Newspaper reports called it the worst exhibition they had ever experienced. 'All the two bums did was hold throughout, and the people who paid to get in should have received their money back, plus a bonus for having to sit through the hugging and tugging match,' said the *San Francisco Examiner*.

Back in New York in 1932, Baer went on a winning spree with two victories over King Levinsky, a return with Tom

Heeney, a win over Tuffy Griffiths and victory over Ernie Schaaf. In their first fight two years earlier, Schaaf had beaten Max on points. This time, Baer was determined to reverse the result. The scheduled ten-rounder was close all the way but during the late rounds Baer came on strongly and pounded his opponent with hard blows to the head.

In the final round, Max connected with a series of heavy punches, again to the head, and Schaaf slumped to the canvas, only to be saved from a knockout by the bell. He remained unconscious for two hours after he was carried from the ring. The following year, Schaaf died after being knocked out in 13 rounds by Primo Carnera but it was believed his death was primarily due to his defeat by Baer in Chicago.

Back in California, Max found himself involved in a series of lawsuits. He was sued by ten women at the same time. One ex-waitress demanded a quarter of a million dollars on the grounds that he had been engaged to her prior to his marriage to Dorothy Dunbar. The new love of his life turned out to be another glamorous Broadway star, June Knight. Together, they made a lovely couple as they toured the nightspots. While Baer was having the time of his life, his manager Ancil Hoffman was trying to arrange a match with the former world heavyweight champion Max Schmeling.

The German had just lost a controversial points decision and his title to Jack Sharkey and was anxious to get a chance to win it back. By the same token, Hoffman knew that a victory over Schmeling would mean a sure chance at Sharkey for his title.

The fight was scheduled for 8 June 1933 at the Yankee Stadium. The German was installed favourite, having destroyed all-time great Mickey Walker, the former world welterweight and middleweight champion, in eight rounds in his previous fight.

Baer knew he had to defeat Schmeling to qualify for a world title fight with Sharkey. He was in the best condition of his career. Before an attendance of over 60,000, Baer turned in the best performance of his career to date, possibly ever, by stopping the German in the tenth round. After dominating the previous nine rounds, Baer went on the attack in the tenth, swinging and hooking to the head and body until Schmeling was beaten to the floor. He arose at the count of nine and Baer charged in, determined to finish him off.

Knocked into a corner, the German was now helpless, his arms dangling by his sides, as Baer continued to rain blows on him. Bearing in mind the tragedy in the Campbell fight, Baer muttered an appeal to referee Arthur Donovan to intervene. Donovan hastily stepped between the two boxers and led Schmeling to his corner. The time was 1:51 of round ten.

By now, Primo Carnera was world heavyweight champion, having taken the title from Jack Sharkey on a controversial knockout in six rounds. Baer now set his sights on the Italian and inside 12 months found himself in the ring with the title at stake. Several months before the bout, Baer and Carnera had starred in a Hollywood movie called *The Prizefighter and the Lady*, in which they were required to fight each other.

Max was cast as the hero and therefore scripted to win but Carnera's people had the story changed to allow them to fight to a draw. Jack Dempsey collected a cheque for $10,000 as the referee and Myrna Loy, one of the leading actresses of the day, also starred. But the movie was banned in Nazi Germany because of Schmeling's defeat by Baer.

During the production, the flamboyant personality of Baer overwhelmed the more subdued manner of Carnera, which gave Max a psychological advantage when they met for the world title in June 1934. Max stopped Primo in 11 rounds to become the new heavyweight champion of the world. He would lose the title exactly one day short of a year later when James J. Braddock came off the dole queues to win a 15-round decision in one of boxing's biggest upsets. Baer would soon get a chance to rehabilitate himself in a match against the new and unbeaten sensation Joe Louis.

The Baer Necessities

When Mike Jacobs announced that he had matched Louis with Baer at the Yankee Stadium on 24 September 1935 under the auspices of his organisation, the 20th Century Sporting Club, there was an immediate demand for tickets. The promoter confidently forecast a new million-dollar gate, the first since Gene Tunney retained his world heavyweight title by outpointing Jack Dempsey at Soldier Field, Chicago eight years earlier almost to the day.

Louis went into four weeks' training at Pompton Lakes, New Jersey determined to get into the best possible physical condition for a fight he considered crucial. His sparring partners were instructed to copy Baer's aggressive style, particularly his damaging right-hand shots.

An impressive victory over Baer would enhance Louis' reputation and assuredly move him into contention for a fight with champion James J. Braddock.

Baer prepared at Speculator in Hamilton County, New York State and expressed full confidence in his ability to inflict the first loss on Louis' unblemished record. He knew he had been careless in his training for the Braddock fight, and conceded he underestimated the veteran New Jersey boxer. 'That will never happen again,' he told newsmen at his camp.

Over at Pompton Lakes, Paul Gallico, one of America's foremost sportswriters, could not refrain from feeding off the overwhelming prejudice of the day. In his usual blatantly racist style, Gallico told his readers in the *New York Daily News*, where he was sports editor, 'Louis is the magnificent animal. He lives like an animal, fights like an animal, has all the cruelty and ferocity of a wild thing. What else dwells within that marvellous, tawny, destructive body? Is he all instinct, all animal? Courage in the animal is desperation. Courage in the human is something incalculable and divine. It acquits itself over pain and panic.'

Louis and his team knew this was certainly not the case. Blackburn advised him not to read the papers and concentrate on the upcoming fight. Joe ate well at the camp but desperately missed his mother's home cooking. He rarely ate out if given the choice of a restaurant or having his mother cook up his favourite meal.

By arrangement with Jacobs, Louis would get married a few hours before the fight, shortly after the morning weigh-in, which took place at the offices of the New York State Athletic Commission. Baer was late and Louis nonchalantly read a newspaper while waiting for him. Stepping on to the scales, Joe weighed 199lb and Max 210lb. Afterwards, they shook hands and Baer poked a finger in Louis' ribs and, always the prankster, cracked, 'See y'later, kiddo.' Louis smiled before both left with their teams.

At 8pm, two hours before the fight was due to start, Louis arrived at the ground-floor apartment on Edgecomb Avenue, on Harlem's Sugar Hill, that Marva had sublet for the wedding. The streets around were so jammed with fans waiting to cheer on the happy couple that Marva and her sister came into the building through a fire escape. Louis found his 19-year-old bride-to-be and her brother, Reverend Walter C. Trotter, who would conduct the ceremony, waiting for him. There, before a few close friends, Joe slipped a four-carat diamond ring on his bride's left hand. They were now man and wife. Joe told her he hoped she would like his wedding presents – a new Lincoln car and a six-room apartment on Chicago's Michigan Avenue. A police escort, with sirens screaming in the warm night air, conducted Louis to the Yankee Stadium.

Marva took her courage in both hands and quietly followed. The possibility of seeing Joe get hurt frightened her and made her knees weak. But she was his wife now and felt that she should be near him on this very important occasion, to share in his joy if he won or to provide solace if he lost. On reaching the stadium, a police officer escorted her to a ringside seat behind the press rows.

Making their way to their ringside seats were representatives from the worlds of commerce, politics and the arts. Fans pointed out movie stars such as George Raft, James Cagney and Edward G. Robinson, the cream of the Warner Brothers lot, who were exchanging small talk with the likes of Cary Grant, George Burns and Gracie Allen. This was a night to see, and be seen. It was not a night, either, to start a row, not with four past world heavyweight champions in attendance such as Jack Dempsey, Gene Tunney, Jack Sharkey and Jack Johnson, as well as reigning title-holder James J. Braddock.

When a reporter asked Braddock for his opinion on the likely outcome, the New Jersey resident was non-committal. 'Let's wait and see,' he said with a smile. Overhearing Braddock's remark, Johnson, a noted critic of Louis, quipped, 'I think it has to be Baer. He's the harder hitter, that's for sure.'

America's top sportswriters were at their typewriters ready for the action. Grantland Rice, considered the doyen of newspapermen where sport was concerned, was there for his paper, the *New York Herald Tribune*. Beside him was Frank

Graham of the *New York Journal American* and near him was Damon Runyon, later to become a top short story writer but now a syndicated columnist for the William Randolph Hearst newspaper chain.

O. B. Keeler of the *Atlanta Journal* was near *Ring* magazine's Nat Fleischer. Nat, in his usual centre-row seat, was a walking encyclopaedia on the noble art and was the man writers turned to if any facts needed to be checked out.

America's busiest boxing announcer, Joe Humphries, who had officiated at scores of big fights, including some of Jack Dempsey's most famous title bouts in the 1920s, pulled down the overhead microphone. 'We'll be brief because you want action,' he started, 'and I'm here for that purpose, to give it to you. The main event... 15 rounds... the principals... the sensational Californian and former world heavyweight champion... Max Baer,' an announcement that drew cheers from the big crowd. 'His worthy opponent,' he continued, 'the new and sensational pugilistic product... the idol of his people... from Detroit, Michigan... Joe Louis,' which drew more cheers.

After referee Arthur Donovan called the two boxers together for the usual pre-fight instructions, they went back to their corners. Jack Blackburn said to Louis, 'Go out there and box him, "Chappie". He can't box like you. When he starts to throw that long right hand, you beat him to the punch. That'll break up his rhythm. But keep up your boxing. Your time will come for the knockout.'

It worked out just like the trainer predicted. Louis jabbed and threw the occasional hook as Baer moved around, seeking to get into range for his big right. The opportunity never came. Max was aggressive but most of his punches went around his opponent's head and he looked frustrated. He had started laughing at his own clumsiness by the third round. This was not the killer puncher of the Schmeling and Carnera fights. He wore the look of someone who would much rather have been somewhere else than inside this roped square. Was he seeing the ghosts of Frankie Campbell and Ernie Schaaf before him?

This is how Clem McCarthy, broadcasting to over 130 radio stations across the land, described the fourth round, 'They are out there in the middle of the ring. Neither makes a move for about five seconds, then Louis jabs him with a left, another left, then a right swing that catches Baer on the jaw and they go into a clinch. Another right and a left to the jaw and Baer is down. The count is four... five... six... seven... eight... nine. Baer is on one knee and it's all over. Joe Louis is the winner.'

When asked in the dressing room about taking the count while apparently making no effort to rise, and shaking his head from side to side, Baer said, 'Yeah, I could have struggled up one more, but when I get executed as I was being then, people are going to have to pay more than $25 a seat to watch it.'

Louis said little in the dressing room except, somewhat predictably, that he was delighted to have won and was still on track for a title fight with James J. Braddock. In his autobiography 40 years later, he elaborated, 'I had beaten the Great Lover. I'd knocked out my second [former] world heavyweight champion. I've always considered the Baer fight my greatest. I've never had better hand speed. I felt so good. I knew I could have fought for two or three days straight. I knew in my head that this was the turning point. He was a popular ex-champion and a good puncher. All my fights had meant nothing until Baer. I said to myself then, "Maybe I can go all the way."'

Mike Jacobs had reason to be happy with the outcome. The fight drew a crowd of 88,150, marginally short of the 90,000 he had predicted. But boxing had another magic million-dollar gate. Receipts came to $1,000,832, the highest since the Dempsey–Tunney return fight eight years earlier almost to the day. In addition, Jacobs sold the radio rights to a car company for a reported $27,500.

The 'savage', 'animal' and 'killer' descriptions of Louis were soon back, as if they ever went away. Typical was the report by Paul Gallico, sports editor of the *New York Daily News*, who would later become an acclaimed fiction writer. 'Louis went from tenderness to terror, and there is no figuring, or knowing, or even believing a man like that,' he wrote. 'Here was the coldest concentration ever a man displayed. And I wonder if his new bride's heart beat a little with fear that this terrible thing was hers. If Baer had offered more resistance, and there had been no rules, Louis would have killed him with his hands and never so much as blinked an eye, or altered the shape of his parted lips.'

Shirley Povich of the *Washington Post* focused on another familiar issue, the racial angle. Before the fight, Povich, a male whose first name was a common one for boys where he grew up in Washington DC, wrote, 'They say that Baer will surpass himself in the knowledge that he is the lone white hope for the defence of Nordic supremacy in the prize ring.' After the fight, he softened his tone somewhat. 'Never did the public as a whole show a greater tolerance for the black man. If they did not care to see Louis beat Baer and thus pave the way for the return of the title to the black race, then at least they did not kick up a great fuss about it.'

Harry Salsinger of the *Detroit News* concentrated on Louis' performance rather than on other issues. 'Louis, a boxer still two years removed from his peak, is being pronounced as a greater fighter than past champions like John L. Sullivan, James J. Corbett, Bob Fitzsimmons, James J. Jeffries and Jack Dempsey,' he wrote.

'Nothing like this has ever happened before. No heavy-weight champion in history was ever considered as anything but a good prospect after 18 months of professional boxing. Louis should continue flattening the heavyweights of the world, and by the time he retires he undoubtedly will be remembered as the greatest fighter of all time by acclamation.'

Mike Jacobs, meanwhile, was anxious to see out 1935 with another win for his promising heavyweight contender. Following consultations with Roxborough, Black and Blackburn, he came up with Paulino Uzcudun, one of the leading contenders for champion Braddock, over 15 rounds. Considered the greatest boxer ever to come from Spain and the youngest of nine siblings, Paulino Uzcudun Eizmendi was a former butcher who was known as the 'Basque Woodchopper'.

A rugged fighter who fought out of a crouch, Uzcudun possessed a powerful left hook that had accounted for many of his 51 wins in 70 fights, including three draws. Uzcudun's promoter was Francois Descamps, who had guided the great French war hero Georges Carpentier to the light-heavyweight championship of the world and was greatly respected in boxing circles.

Under Descamps' management, Paulino won the European heavyweight title in the early 1930s and took on the best and toughest fighters of his time, on both sides of the Atlantic. The Spaniard was afforded only one opportunity at the world heavyweight championship, but was outpointed over 15 rounds by Primo Carnera in Barcelona in October 1933.

Trainer Whitey Bimstein, who had accompanied Uzcudun to the fight in Spain, gave an account in an interview that told of a scene more reminiscent of a movie. 'I remember one day we were at a sidewalk cafe,' he said. 'Just as I started to put my lips to a glass of vermouth, a shot splintered the glass. Believe me, I got back to the hotel rapidly. The Spanish Civil War was on at the time, and it was nothing to walk along the streets covered with hundreds of dead, and you couldn't tell when the fighting would break out anew.'

Against this chaotic backdrop, Paulino's shot at the title took place. Just prior to the fight, Carnera balked at the choice of Spanish-made gloves, chosen by the governing boxing commission. The champion, who had insisted upon American gloves, stated loudly, and in Spanish, that he would not fight. The commissioner, according to Bimstein, removed himself from the room, and 'about a dozen soldiers walked toward Carnera'. Primo backed up hurriedly and conceded the choice.

'As for the actual fight, Uzcudun went the 15 scheduled rounds and when the verdict was announced in favour of Carnera, the revolution started all over again,' Bimstein said. 'A riot, replete with gunplay, commenced. Myself, Uzcudun, the other seconds and as many as about 300 others took refuge under the massive ring until troops restored order. Even with this, the rioting continued in the streets all night. It was just incredible, and an occasion I can never forget.'

Mike Jacobs called a press conference to announce he would stage the Louis–Uzcudun fight at Madison Square Garden on 13 December 1935. It will be remembered that the Liverpool-born promoter James J. Johnston had an exclusive deal with the Garden for boxing promotions. Additionally, Johnston had previously rejected Louis over fears that an appearance by the black boxer would be boycotted. 'No blacks against whites here,' he said.

The situation had now changed dramatically. Louis was one of the world's most formidable heavyweights, an exciting young boxer with 22 straight wins. When Jacobs approached Colonel John Reed Kirkpatrick, chairman of the board of Madison Square Garden Corporation, with a view to featuring Louis on a big promotion, Kirkpatrick could hardly disagree. Louis was boxing's number one attraction, a top money-maker who could add prestige to the Garden, which was, to all intents and purposes, the world's premier boxing arena.

Kirkpatrick sanctioned the Louis–Uzcudun fight, the first time the Garden had been leased to a rival promoter. It was a decision that effectively hailed the beginning of the end of Johnston's position as boxing's leading promoter. Having already staged three world heavyweight championship fights at the Garden, Johnston would never again be in that exalted position. Jacobs had Louis, and both had the Garden. Nothing else mattered. Uncle Mike was the new kid on the block, even though he was still two years away from achieving his dream of promoting a world heavyweight title fight. But he was getting there.

Blackburn worked for long hours on Louis, teaching him how to open up Uzcudun's crouching, peek-a-boo style, which consisted of keeping his gloves close together in front of his face as he came in. It was a precursor taught by Cus D'Amato when managing world heavyweight champion Floyd Patterson and later light-heavyweight king Jose Torres. 'Get under his guard with uppercuts, "Chappie", and that will break up his defence,' instructed Blackburn. Louis promised to follow instructions even if the Spaniard was probably the toughest fighter around then, in any division.

Louis went into hard training at his camp at Pompton Lakes. Blackburn brought in sparring partners whose styles resembled that of Uzcudun, their gloves up close to their faces. By the night of the fight, Joe was confident he could handle Paulino's crab-like defence.

In the first two rounds, though, he failed to penetrate that peek-a-boo style, though he had a points lead on his better boxing. Louis was becoming frustrated and perplexed at his inability to get a straight shot at Uzcudun's chin. Blackburn told him to be patient. It was not until the fourth round that he was able to make a breakthrough. Paulino committed a palpable blunder by widening his gloved hands about six inches to prepare for a left hook. This was Joe's moment.

In a flash, Louis launched an overhand right that landed flush in Uzcudun's face, driving two of his teeth through his bottom lip as the blood spurted. The blow sent the 200lb fighter sailing across the ring and down, his head bouncing off the canvas. Although Paulino managed to struggle to his feet at the count of nine, he looked all in and referee Arthur Donovan intervened. The time of the round was 2:32.

It was the first time Uzcudun had failed to finish in 71 fights in a 12-year career. In his dressing room, he fell over in a heap. Louis said in his quarters, 'I never threw a better punch.' To which Blackburn added, 'Or a harder one.'

Among the ringsiders was the German contender Max Schmeling, the former world heavyweight champion. Jacobs had been planning to match him with Louis in a big outdoor fight at the Yankee Stadium in 1936. To drum up publicity, Mike invited him to the Uzcudun fight as a special guest and had him introduced from the ring. After the fight, Max told reporters he was impressed with Louis' performance and the manner in which he achieved his early victory. But he said he felt he could end the Detroiter's unbeaten run, now extended to 23-0.

Legend has it that Max said, 'I see something' during the fight, and when asked by reporters what it was, he refused to disclose what he had discovered. In fact, the Uzcudun fight only revealed what Max already knew – a glaring flaw in Louis' defence. Joe was wide open to a right hand, which happened to be Schmeling's best punch.

'A few days after the fight my trainer Max Machon and I left for Germany, and my contract for the Louis fight, although yet to be officially signed, wasn't the only thing in my luggage,'

Schmeling revealed in his autobiography. 'One whole suitcase held nothing but film. Machon had managed to get copies of all the films of Louis' earlier fights. I wanted to have slow-motion copies made in order to study, in as minute detail as possible, every aspect of every fight with military precision, or I didn't have a chance. Machon and I agreed to tell no one about the films. I didn't even tell my close friends who drove to meet us in Cherbourg.'

In any event, it was no secret in boxing circles that Louis' defence had the defect, although nobody had been able to capitalise on it. One of his sparring partners, Frank Wotanski, had admitted the flaw to reporters. Jack Miley of the *New York Daily News* had often referred to it as well. Jack Johnson, the former world heavyweight champion, also noticed it. Jack Blackburn was aware of the flaw but insisted that Joe's speed and powerful punching more than compensated for anything he may have lacked – 'however minor', as the trainer pointed out.

In truth, in view of the euphoria surrounding Louis' rapid rise, and the fact that America was desperately seeking an exciting young heavyweight to inject new life into the somewhat stagnant division, the gap in Joe's defence went generally unnoticed.

The Louis–Schmeling fight was finally announced for 19 June at the Yankee Stadium. Could the German fulfil his boast that Louis was ready to be brought down, and that he was the man who could do it? Or would Louis consolidate his position as the world's number one heavyweight contender?

Schmeling was born in Klein Luckow, north of Berlin, on 28 September 1905, the son of a coastguard sailor, and given the imposing Christian names of Maximillian Adolph Otto Siegfried. The family moved to Hamburg when Max was one year old. It was while living in that ancient city that the youngster cultivated a love for sporting activities, especially track and field, soccer and wrestling. From the very start, he displayed tremendous endurance, a quality that later became evident in his ring career.

Shortly after leaving school and starting work in an advertising agency, Max went to the local cinema with his father to watch the newsreel of Jack Dempsey knocking out the Frenchman, Georges Carpentier, in the fourth round in Jersey City in July 1921. The fight made a lasting impression on the 16-year-old Max, and in a back room at his home, using his father's socks as boxing gloves, he would spar and shadow box for hours.

Max told his parents he wanted to be a boxer but would have to leave home if he wanted to make progress. They gave their approval if that was what he really wanted. Setting off one morning for Berlin, where boxing was very popular, he visited gyms and talked to boxers, especially old-timers who told him tales of great champions like John L. Sullivan, James J. Corbett, Jim Jeffries and Jack Johnson.

Max worked at various jobs and managed to send some money home before moving to Cologne, where he joined the Muhlhelm Amateur Boxing Club. He made steady progress and in 1924, at the age of 19, he reached the finals of the German national championships as a light-heavyweight. At ringside that night was Arthur Bulow, editor of the magazine *Boxsport,* who recognised the lad's talent and encouraged him to continue in the sport. 'You've got genuine talent, Max, and I can predict even now that we'll be hearing a lot more about you,' Bulow said.

Encouraged by Bulow's remarks, Schmeling spent most of his evenings after work in the gym, learning his craft, endlessly practising the basics of footwork, methods of attack and defence, balance and body movements. He was developing a style that would characterise his career, studying his opponent and waiting for the opportunity to let go his big punches, mainly his right hand.

While working in the gym one evening, he was approached by Hugo Abels, a roller blinds maker and part-time boxing manager. Abels suggested Max should turn professional as he had all the qualities needed to make the grade in the paid ranks. Abels would act as his manager, with Bulow as an advisor. Although Schmeling felt he was not yet ready to leave the amateurs, Bulow convinced him otherwise. 'We got lots of letters to our magazine and many of those readers mention you very favourably,' he said.

Schmeling made a successful debut as a professional in Cologne on 2 August 1924 with a stoppage in six rounds over Kurt Czapp. By the end of the year he had nine wins, all inside the distance. His lone loss was in four rounds to the experienced Max Dieckmann in Berlin. In 1925, Schmeling had ten fights, with six wins. By this time, Bulow and Schmeling's manager, Hugo Abels, had agreed that Max should join the stable of Max Machon, a leading trainer who operated out of Berlin and was well respected in the sport. Machon would stay by Schmeling throughout the boxer's career. Bulow would continue for the foreseeable future as Schmeling's advisor.

Schmeling continued to progress in 1926 with four wins and a draw. The fights that gave him the most satisfaction were two against Max Dieckmann, who had beaten him in four rounds two years earlier. Schmeling drew with Dieckmann in February but in August he had learned enough to put him away in the first round with a powerful right to the chin. In the process, Schmeling had the satisfaction of winning the German light-heavyweight title.

If 1926 was a good year for Max, 1927 was even better as far as boxing was concerned – 15 fights, 15 wins. One of his victories was a stoppage in 14 rounds over Belgium's Fernand

Delarge for the European light-heavyweight title in Dortmund. However, it was also a year tainted by tragedy for the Schmeling family. After a sightseeing trip to Paris before going on to London to watch Mickey Walker retain his world middleweight championship by knocking out Scotland's Tommy Milligan in ten rounds at Olympia, Schmeling returned to Berlin, where his mother and 14-year-old sister Edith joined him.

One day, while taking Edith for a ride on his new Harley-Davidson motorcycle, Schmeling was involved in an accident in which his sister was killed. Max was devastated by the incident but he had to put it behind him and carry on with his boxing career. A successful defence of his European title came in November, when he clashed with Hein Domgoergen in Leipzig. Domgoergen's manager, Willie Fuchs, had been so confident of his boxer's chances (he had lost only three of his 84 bouts) that he suggested a winner-takes-all. Max won on a knockout in seven rounds and collected the combined purse of 20,000 marks.

Gipsy Daniels, one of Britain's busiest light-heavyweights in the 1920s, had lost a ten-round decision to Schmeling in Berlin in December 1927, but sought a return. They met again, this time for Max's European title in Frankfurt in February 1928, and the Welshman sensationally won by a knockout in the first round. Schmeling claimed that making the 175lb limit had drained him of his strength, leaving him vulnerable to attack. Daniels sportingly decided not to claim the title but Max had already decided he was moving up a division. It turned out to be a wise move. Two months later, he outpointed Franz Diener over 15 rounds to capture the German heavyweight championship in Berlin, despite injuring his thumb in the first round.

The injury proved to be a major setback. A bone had been splintered and caused Schmeling and his mentor, Arthur

Bulow, to cancel several important fights in the coming months, including defences of his European and German championships. Max decided to relinquish both titles after Bulow suggested they head for the US and seek an opportunity to campaign for a world heavyweight title fight. Gene Tunney, the reigning champion, was talking about retirement and it seemed the right time to make the move.

In early May, Schmeling and Bulow sailed to New York, where the fighter had an operation on his hand before getting down to serious work in Madame Bey's training camp in New Jersey. The wealthy Bey, who was born in Istanbul, was a keen fight fan and created a home for her boxing clientele where they could train for their sport. The boxers who stayed at her camp followed the rules that she expected her boarders to obey.

There was no alcohol, up by 6am, breakfast at seven, supper at five in the afternoon, lights out at ten, no swearing and no women. She was strict in running her business but had personal, matriarchal relationships with the many famous boxers who trained there, calling them her 'boys'. She spoke seven languages – English, Armenian, French, German, Greek, Italian and Spanish.

One of the boxers who trained there was the Frenchman, Andre Routis, the world featherweight champion. Routis advised Schmeling to contact a well-known boxing manager named Joe Jacobs. 'If anybody can move you on in America, it's Jacobs,' said Routis. The son of Hungarian Jews, Jacobs was one of boxing's greatest characters, a cigar-chewing bundle of energy who held the belief that you shouldn't use ten words when 100 would do, even if it did mangle the English language. A master stroke-maker and opportunist, Jacobs was always on the lookout for another meal ticket, and had agents looking around for anybody he might be able to turn into a champion.

Schmeling made contact with Jacobs, who agreed to work with Max as the boxer's four-year contract with Bulow was due to expire soon. When it did, Jacobs became Schmeling's official manager, with Max Machon retained as trainer. Schmeling's debut in New York was at Madison Square Garden on 23 November, when he knocked out Boston's Joe Monte with a perfect right to the chin in the eighth round.

With world champion Gene Tunney already talking of imminent retirement, America's two leading organisations, the New York State Athletic Commission and the National Boxing Association, set up an elimination tournament to decide the number one contender – either to face Tunney if Gene changed his mind about retirement, or to meet for the vacant title if Tunney stepped down.

On 26 July 1928, Tunney easily defeated the New Zealander, Tom Heeney, in 11 rounds at New York's Polo Grounds. It was Gene's last fight. Not long after, he announced he was finished with the ring and planned to marry the love of his life, the heiress Polly Lauder. Schmeling and the Boston boxer Jack Sharkey had proven to be the best of the contenders. They were matched for the vacant title on 11 June 1930 at the Yankee Stadium, where a crowd of 79,222 paid a gross gate of $749,935 to see the first ever German to contest boxing's premier title.

Sharkey learned to box in the US navy. While he was a fine boxer and possessed a knockout punch, he was inclined to be erratic with his punching. Jack entered the ring as favourite, and for three rounds had a points lead. In the fourth round, after being forced to the ropes, he crouched and delivered a terrific left hook to the pit of Schmeling's stomach. Max grimaced and slumped to the canvas, writhing in pain. As his seconds carried him to his corner, Jacobs yelled, 'Foul, foul.'

In the commotion that followed, Arthur Brisbane, editor of the Hearst newspaper chain, demanded that referee Jim

Crowley immediately disqualify Sharkey and proclaim Schmeling the winner – or he would have the Walker Law, which had banned boxing in the past, repealed. To add to the confusion, neither the referee nor one of the judges, Harold Barnes, had actually seen the alleged foul punch. But the other judge, Charles F. Mathison, agreed with Schmeling and Jacobs. 'I saw Sharkey land the blow, and it was definitely low.'

Crowley had not started a count but went over to Schmeling's corner, where the German was slumped on his stool, his face still grimacing in pain, to see what was happening. Jacobs was still yelling, and demanding Sharkey be disqualified. Crowley then consulted with the judges and went back to Schmeling's corner and raised his hand as the winner. It was the first time the heavyweight championship of the world had been won in such a manner.

Max was welcomed home a national hero and a film of the fight was shown as the main feature in German cinemas. Adolf Hitler's Nazi party used it to support their propaganda campaign for the so-called Aryan Master Race. Schmeling tried to keep a low profile and disassociated himself from any political connections. In any event, he was busy wooing the Czech-born actress Anny Ondra, who was enjoying a successful career in German movies.

Basically a shy man in private, Max wanted to get engaged but was reluctant to put it to Anny, so he asked a friend, boxing promoter Paul Damski, to do it for him. After several refusals, she relented and soon she and the boxer became a glamorous item. They would be married on 6 July 1933 and remained together until her death in 1987.

Meanwhile, back in the US, and to add to an already muddled situation, the New York authorities refused to recognise Schmeling as world champion and wanted a quick return. This did not happen until two years later, when public opinion demanded a rematch to decide the *real* world champion. Schmeling and Sharkey had their eagerly awaited rematch at the outdoor Long Island Bowl in New York on 21 June 1932.

A crowd of 61,863 turned out to see if the title would return to America or stay in Europe. Schmeling was a 6/5 favourite, with the odds against a knockout by either man at 3/1. Nevertheless, Schmeling and Jacobs expressed fears that the appointed referee, Gunboat Smith, an ex-boxer, was in fact a close friend of Sharkey and, like Jack, had been in the navy. Jacobs protested to the New York Commission.

'My man is at a great disadvantage here,' he told chairman William Muldoon. 'It ain't fair. I demand a neutral referee.' Muldoon said Smith's friendship with Sharkey would not influence the course of the fight in any way as he was a fair official and would call it as he saw it. Jacobs stormed out of the office in an angry mood, throwing his lighted cigar into a waste paper basket.

It turned out to be an eventful fight over 15 rounds. Sharkey sustained a badly cut eye in the early rounds and seemed to have trouble coping with the German's attacks. Schmeling carried the fight to Sharkey, manoeuvring his opponent cleverly and landing the most effective punches. The decision was split, with referee Smith and judge George F. Kelly voting for Sharkey and the second judge, Charles Mathison, calling it for Schmeling.

This is how Nat Fleischer described the fight in his book *The Heavyweight Championship*, 'The majority of spectators, myself included, thought that Sharkey had lost to Max and sided with the German in his contention that the officials erred in awarding the crown to his Boston opponent. The loser made most of the fight and inflicted most of the punishment. He was up against a cool, clever boxer who was none too easy to hit, and he made the most of it under the circumstances. It was difficult to say which one looked more bewildered and amazed when the verdict was rendered – Sharkey the winner or Schmeling the loser.'

No sooner had announcer Joe Humphries said, 'The winner and new champion' than a storm of booing broke out, with many in the crowd yelling, 'Robbery!' Jacobs, seething with anger, yelled in the radio microphone, 'We wuz robbed!' Grantland Rice told his readers in the *New York Herald Tribune,* 'This is the worst decision in the history of the heavyweight game. I gave Schmeling eight rounds, Sharkey four and three even.' Edward J. Neil of the Associated Press also favoured Schmeling. 'It seemed that Max had earned the right to retain his title even if not by any great margin,' he said.

David E. Egan, writing for the *Boston Sunday Advertiser* and arguably biased, said he saw the fight in Sharkey's favour. 'Sharkey fought one of the most intelligent battles of his speckled career and beat the German with one of the prettiest exhibitions of boxing the ring has seen for many years,' he said.

In Max's dressing room, Schmeling took the loss of his title surprisingly well, although Jacobs was furious. Max tried to grin as he answered questions. 'If someone beats me, I don't care. I say the better man wins and that is all right,' he said. 'But how can Sharkey beat me by running away all the time? Never did he hurt me. I can feel that he knows I beat him but they give him the decision. But I will fight Sharkey again. I have plenty of time.'

Sharkey said, 'I won the title and won it handily. Now I will defend it. I will be a fighting champion. I was not hurt.' Alas, a third match never materialised. A year and eight days later, Sharkey lost the title to Primo Carnera on a knockout in six rounds.

With the coming of 1933, Schmeling's image in America began to take a decided turn. On 30 January, Adolf Hitler swept to power in the German parliament, the Reichstag, with torchlight parades in towns and cities all across Germany marking his appointment. His Nazi party became the most powerful political force in the land, and its ideologies, voiced by the Fuhrer, overflowed with anti-Semitic tendencies. Major American cities such as New York had large Jewish populations, who worried over what the party could mean for people of their religion in the future.

Schmeling, because he was German, was viewed as an extension of Hitler's plans for world domination. When he was slated to fight the heavy-hitting contender Max Baer at the Yankee Stadium on 8 June 1933, he immediately became the 'bad guy' in the eyes of fans. Baer came into the ring wearing the Star of David on his shorts, although he did not practise the Jewish faith even though his father was Jewish. Promoter Jack Dempsey played up the religious angle and suddenly the fight was viewed as Baer defending his faith against the prejudice of the Nazis, represented reluctantly by Schmeling.

Thrown off of his game in part by the adverse publicity but also because of Baer's wild, brawling style and frequent fouls, including backhand punches and rabbit blows, Schmeling was thrashed before nearly 60,000 onlookers. With the German taking a heavy battering against the ropes in the tenth round, referee Arthur Donovan moved in quickly and stopped the fight. The time was 1:51 of the round.

The Baer defeat, combined with a follow-up loss to contender Steve Hamas on a knockout in nine rounds in Philadelphia and a draw with Paulino Uzcudun in Barcelona, both in 1934, left many wondering if Schmeling was still a world-class fighter. The sceptics were silenced in 1935 when, in return fights, Max knocked out Hamas in nine rounds in Hamburg and outpointed Uzcudun over 15 rounds in Berlin.

Both victories impressed promoter Mike Jacobs enough to invite him back to America to meet Louis. The winner was promised a shot at Braddock's world title. As a warm-up, Jacobs matched Louis with Charley Retzlaff at the Chicago Stadium on 17 January 1936. Retzlaff, a native of North Dakota, possessed a tremendous amount of courage and a hard right hand. Of his 71 fights, he had lost only eight with two draws and was expected to provide a good test for the unbeaten Louis.

In the first round, Retzlaff started fast, catching his opponent with quick left jabs to the face and following with a right cross to the head. Louis retaliated with a barrage of blows that sent Retzlaff down. After he climbed to his feet, Louis moved in fast and floored him again with a hard left hook. This time, Charlie failed to make it up in time and was counted out. It was one of Louis' quickest wins, with the timekeeper's clock showing that just 85 seconds had elapsed since the opening bell. For his short night's work, Joe collected a cheque for $23,065.

'We were rather disappointed in the length of time it took Joe Louis to dispose of Charley Retzlaff in what was laughingly termed a "fight" at the Chicago Stadium last night,' wrote Eddie Bachelor in the *Detroit News* the next day. 'We had assured our large and trusting public that Retzlaff would not last out the first minute. So when the "fight" dragged on to one minute and 25 seconds, we felt that the Detroiter either didn't have his mind on his work or else is beginning to slip.'

There was an element of truth in what Bachelor said. Louis' sensational wins inside the distance were getting to be so much the expected thing that reporters felt the only news that could break the connection with a Louis fight would be a close contest or a losing one for him. They reported the Retzlaff fight much as they had other Louis fights. What else was there to say? Joe was enjoying the same aura of invincibility that Mike Tyson would have 50 years later going into his fight with Buster Douglas, when Mike was knocked out in the tenth round in Tokyo. Tyson was a prohibitive 42/1 favourite, the longest odds in heavyweight championship history to date.

As for the Louis–Retzlaff bout, the *New York Times* was the only newspaper in the country that gave a novel twist to it. On the day of the battle, most newspapers informed the public that the fight was to be broadcast from 11pm to midnight on station WJZ. The contest, had it gone the scheduled distance of 15 rounds, would have taken just an hour. The *Times*, however, had a different listing. It said, '11.00, WJZ. Boxing, Joe Louis–Charley Retzlaff. 11.15, Male Quartet.' In a sense, the newspaper reported the fight before it happened. It did so, too, with terseness, a considerable amount of accuracy, and a good deal of humour.

Following the Retzlaff bout, Louis decided to take a break and return to his Chicago apartment and Marva. With the Schmeling fight arranged for 18 June at the Yankee Stadium, he could afford to relax and spend quality time with his wife. Marva had seen little of him since their wedding day, what with long training sessions and the fights themselves. They would make up for lost time.

In the months and weeks leading up to the Schmeling fight, America's newspapers carried regular reports, especially when both boxers went into hard training at their respective camps. The German worked out at Napanoch, a resort about 95 miles outside New York, while Louis prepared in his regular quarters at Pompton Lakes, New Jersey. There was tension in the air, notably the growing hostility towards Nazi Germany in the United States. The Third Reich's Nuremberg Laws of 1935 had deprived Jews of both property and legal rights. Several months earlier, the Reichstag had re-introduced conscription and created a new air force.

The moves amounted to a public rejection by Germany of the Versailles Treaty that ended World War One but had strictly limited the country's military strength. Hitler boasted he was seeking an army of 500,000, five times larger than was allowed by the treaty.

The Nazi hierarchy claimed the conscription was a response to Britain's recent announcement of re-armament, but it was an open secret that Germany had already begun a recruiting programme. Nazi troops were occupying the Rhineland, which was traditionally German territory anyway. Joseph Kennedy, the US ambassador to Britain and father of the future US president, praised the Third Reich and said the party would do good for Europe.

It was into this hostile environment that Schmeling found himself dragged, one that he had always tried to avoid. The Nazi party was angry with Max over his association with his manager Joe Jacobs, a Jew. The official party newspaper *Fraenkische Tageszeitung* made a front-page attack on Schmeling and Jacobs for what it described as 'a despicable insult to our Fuhrer'. Jacobs had been pictured before Max's fights in Germany with Hamas and Uzcudun, giving the Nazi salute while holding a massive Havana cigar in the fingers of his extended right hand.

'Herr Hitler has been grossly insulted, and Schmeling should discharge the Jew immediately in the interests of Germanhood,' said the editorial. Hans von Tschammer, the Imperial Sports Minister and a top-ranking Nazi, followed this with a letter to Schmeling demanding 'that you disassociate yourself from your Jewish connections. The Jew has greatly offended our beloved Fuhrer.'

Max decided, at great risk, to go over Tschammer's head and approach Hitler himself in an attempt to sort out the problem. He requested an urgent meeting with the Nazi leader, and was invited to tea at Hitler's private residence at Obersalzberg in the Bavarian Alps. Max's wife Anny would accompany him.

'What are you going to do about this associate of yours, Herr Schmeling?' said Hitler, frowning.

'Joe Jacobs is a very good man, Herr Fuhrer,' explained the boxer. 'He is efficient, orderly, honest and trustworthy. He has helped my career like no other, and together we can bring honour to Germany. I would be very reluctant to let him go.'

Hitler sat quietly for a few moments before changing the subject completely, asking how married life was for Max and Anny and even discussing movies. After about an hour, Hitler just rose, shook hands with Schmeling and his wife and wished them luck. The partnership between the boxer and his manager was never discussed again, either by the German leader or the Nazi party.

On the morning of the fight, a cable expressing good wishes arrived from Hitler, although party members would say later that he felt privately that Louis would win. Joseph Goebbels, the Nazi Minister for Propaganda, seemingly felt the same way but wished Max good luck. Another newspaper brought out by the party, *Volkischer Beobachter,* which dealt mainly with sport and leisure activities, assigned their representative, Amo Hellmis, to cover the fight. It devoted several pages to coverage of the boxers in their training camps, complete with photographs.

It rained heavily on the evening of the fight and it was postponed 24 hours to 19 June. The extra day did not help the gate, which barely reached the half-million-dollar figure that Mike Jacobs had hoped for. Receipts came to $547,531. The official attendance was just under 45,000, less than half as many who attended the Baer fight at the same venue. It was clear that the paying public did not consider it was going to be much of a fight. After all, Louis had won all his 24 fights, with only four going the scheduled distance. Among his victims were two recent world champions, Baer and Carnera.

Schmeling, on the other hand, was considered a veteran and had already been stopped by Baer in ten rounds. Since the Baer fight, he had only managed to win three of his five bouts. Moreover, he was approaching his 31st birthday and ten years older than Louis. The German would enter the ring a heavy underdog, with the betting at 8/1 on the Detroiter. There seemed no way that Max could win. Paul Gallico wrote in the *New York Daily News*, 'Warning: to my friend Max Schmeling – stay in Germany. Have no truck with this man. He will do something to you from which you will never fully recover. You haven't a chance.'

Many leading newspapers had not even bothered to send their top sportswriters to the fight, with executives assigning their junior reporters to gain experience of big boxing occasions. Three weeks before the fight, Jimmy Cannon was called into his office at the *New York Journal American* by the sports editor Eddie Frayne.

The Louis–Schmeling fight would clash with the New York Yankees' baseball visit to California. Which event did Cannon want to cover? 'Schmeling is all washed up, ed,' said Cannon. 'I think I'll travel with Joe DiMaggio out west.' Stopping off in Detroit to join up with some other writers heading west, he listened to the radio broadcast of the fight in his hotel room.

Schmeling, at 192lb, entered the ring first to a mixture of boos and cheers. A minute later, Louis climbed through the ropes, not unexpectedly to cheers. At 196lb, he was a little lighter than Blackburn had wanted him to be, but the old trainer was not worried. The boxers and their handlers huddled around referee Arthur Donovan as he gave them the usual pre-fight instructions, a microphone above his head sending the words out to the crowd. As Donovan spoke, Louis was looking at the floor. Schmeling kept staring at Louis. The boxers shook hands and went back to their corners, where they had their mouth guards put in.

Blackburn's strategy was for Louis to use his left jab to keep Schmeling off balance before bringing in his right hand. Joe followed instructions, moving around the German, who had his left shoulder protecting his face, his right hand cocked alongside his chin, his left acting like a prod. By the second round, Max's left eye was closing as a result of Louis' right-hand shots, which followed the left jab. In the closing minute of the third round, Schmeling landed a glancing right to the head that dazed Joe momentarily. Max was beginning to put his plan into action. In his head were the words, 'Louis can be brought down with a right.' Back in the corner, Blackburn warned, 'Keep that left hand up, "Chappie", this guy can be dangerous.'

There was high drama in the fourth round. A stiff left hand from Louis drove Schmeling back a few paces but suddenly Max stepped forward and hit Louis with a right cross to the face. The American staggered momentarily as Schmeling moved in fast. A left hook followed by another right, this time a vicious hook, thudded into Joe's jaw and he sank to the canvas. Vainly trying to support himself by the top rope, he landed on the seat of his trunks.

The Yankee Stadium erupted in a cacophony of sound as the crowd rose to their feet. This wasn't in the script. The famed 'Brown Bomber', the invincible wonder boy who was going to bring the sport to new levels, was on the floor for the first time in his two-year professional career.

Back in the hotel room in Detroit, Jimmy Cannon heard commentator Clem McCarthy's hoarse, excited voice over the airwaves yelling, 'He's down. He's down.' Turning to another newspaperman, and just barely hearing McCarthy's voice above the din, Cannon said, 'What did I tell you? It's all over. Schmeling's on the floor.' It was only when it became clear that it was Louis who was down and heading for a sensational defeat that Cannon regretted missing one of the biggest sport stories of the decade.

Louis climbed to his feet, weak and uncertain, as the count reached three. Above the shrieks of the crowd, Blackburn had been shouting, 'Stay down, "Chappie", stay down,' but Joe did not hear him. He did not hear anything. All he felt was a terrible throbbing in his head. He was heading for certain defeat, and he knew it. So it went, round after round, Schmeling giving and Louis taking. Max complained to the referee in the eighth round that many of Louis' blows were going below the belt, resulting in warnings by Donovan, but the Detroiter simply did not know where his punches were landing, or whether he was in a fight at all.

In the 12th round, Schmeling drove his man to the ropes with a left-right combination. Louis fought back but he was noticeably weak and his punches carried no power. Max seemed determined to finish his opponent. A cracking right cross to the head turned Louis around so that he was facing the ropes. Like a drowning man, he grabbed at the top strand but his knees buckled and he started to slide down. He grabbed instinctively at the middle rope but all his strength had left him and he slithered to his knees. He tried to get up but that last destructive punch had frozen his brain. He could only manage a half turn before pitching forward on to his face.

As Donovan counted off the fatal seconds, Louis showed no signs of rising, and at ten Schmeling leapt high into the air in jubilation. He had achieved the impossible. He had destroyed the seemingly invincible 'Brown Bomber', just as he said he would. His secret weapon had been his big right hand, and

Louis had been open to a right hand. That was the 'something' he had seen.

Louis, his face badly swollen, both his eyes practically closed and his thumbs badly sprained, kept asking Blackburn in the dressing room, 'What happened?' Blackburn replied in a soothing voice, 'You just got tagged, "Chappie". And when you get hit right, that's it. There isn't any more.' Louis said he couldn't remember much about the fight. He thought he had been knocked down for the first time in the second round, not the fourth. 'When the referee counted, it came to me faint, like somebody whispering,' he said. 'It didn't make any difference anyhow. I lost, and I've no excuses. Tell Max that. Tell him too I'm sorry I hit him with some low blows. I didn't know what I was doing and that I didn't intentionally hit him low.'

Over 30 years later, Louis held the same views. 'What I would like to clear up is, yes, the better fighter won on the night,' he said in an interview with this writer on a visit to Dublin. 'The newspapers made a big issue of me hating Schmeling because he was a German and the Nazi party was on the rise and all that,' he said. 'It was the same for our second fight but really, in the end, it was all for publicity, dreamed up by my promoter Mike Jacobs, and Mike was always looking for a good angle. Max and I were always good friends.'

It was Julian Black, Louis' co-manager, who elbowed his way through the crowd and into the winner's dressing room. Shaking Schmeling warmly by the hand, he said, 'You were great, Max.' When a reporter brought up the question of low blows from Louis, Max said, 'You couldn't blame him. He didn't know what he was doing. Anyone could see that.' Later in an article in the *Saturday Evening Post*, Schmeling seemingly changed his mind and accused Louis of deliberately fouling him.

As if the shattering defeat was not bad enough, Joe discovered that his stepfather had been paralysed by a stroke two days before the fight. The family had decided against telling him as they were afraid the bad news would affect his concentration. Within a few weeks Pat Brooks died, and Louis was distraught.

Arrangements had been made for Schmeling to broadcast to Germany. The crowd in the dressing room became silent. His German sentences were short but spoken in a tone of exuberance. At the end of the broadcast, he looked at the Americans who were crowded around him, dropped his voice and said, 'Heil Hitler.' A short time later, he was in possession of congratulatory telegrams from Joseph Goebbels, the Nazi Propaganda Minister, and the Fuhrer himself.

The German reaction to Schmeling's stunning victory was predictably ecstatic. Hitler cabled a personal message, 'Most cordial felicitations on your splendid victory.' He also sent flowers to Max's wife. Goebbels had previously perceived that the fight had no real significance to the Third Reich and had predicted a heavy defeat for Schmeling. Now he cabled, 'I know you have fought for Germany. Your victory is a German victory. We are all proud of you. Hearty greetings. Heil Hitler.' The party's press bureau enthusiastically embraced Schmeling as 'a great example of the New Youth, the Master Race', and declared 'his great victory was a triumph for the Fuhrer and all Germany'.

The American press, in general, praised Schmeling for his stunning win and consoled Louis by saying he was game, complimenting him for his great courage in lasting 12 rounds with the fierce-hitting German. Henry McLemore, who wrote about boxing for the Hearst newspaper chain, was the only reporter who picked Schmeling to win. 'I just thought he had the equipment to pull off a shock victory, that's all,' he said. 'Louis hadn't really been tested.'

The white press, especially in the Deep South, were quick to consign Louis to mediocrity. O. B. Keeler of the *Atlanta Journal* wrote a column under the heading, 'You can have the "Brown Bomber"' and went on to say that Louis, 'the pet pickaninny', was just another boxer who had been built up.

Bert Wahrman of the *Richmond Times-Despatch* asked which sportswriter would be the first to change Louis' name from 'Brown Bomber' to 'Brown Bummer'. Even Jack Dempsey jumped on the bandwagon. The former champion, who had spent a great deal of the previous year sponsoring 'white hopes' to oppose and beat Louis, went on record as saying, 'Schmeling exposed the fact that Louis has a glass jaw and consequently cannot take a punch. All you have to do is to walk into him and bang him with a solid punch. I don't think he'll ever whip another good fighter.'

A week after the fight, Schmeling was invited to fly home on the Hindenburg zeppelin. An official gave up his berth so that the new German hero could travel in style. After a 61-hour flight, the craft landed in Frankfurt to tumultuous cheers from the waiting crowd. From there, Schmeling journeyed on to Berlin, where a beaming Hitler invited him, along with his wife, mother and several close friends, to lunch at the Reich Chancellery. The Fuhrer embarrassed Schmeling by making a long speech of congratulations.

The mood eventually relaxed. At one point, Hitler said it was a shame he could not have seen the historic fight but Max told him that a film of the bout, and several copies, were at customs and could be collected at any time. Promoter Jacobs had given Schmeling full rights to overseas distribution of the film because he did not think the fight would last long enough to make them saleable. 'It'll be all over in a few rounds,' Jacobs had confidently told his associates.

Hitler, a movie buff as well as a boxing fan, watched the film with Schmeling the next day. Max would recall the Fuhrer slapping his thigh every time a solid punch landed on Louis.

'Schmeling,' he said at one point, 'have you read what I wrote in *Mein Kampf* about the educational value of boxing? Boxing is a man's sport. That why I tell my officials that boxing should be introduced into the sports curriculum.'

Hitler ordered that the film, instead of being shown as a newsreel in cinemas, should be made into a full-length documentary by adding footage of Schmeling and Louis in training, and of Max's big homecoming welcome. Released under the title *Max Schmeling's Victory: A German Victory*, it was one of Hitler's favourite films and played to full houses for several weeks.

The Third Reich was in buoyant mood. The Olympic Games opened in Berlin on 1 August, just six weeks after Schmeling's win. As far as the track and field events were concerned, with some 5,000 athletes from 53 countries taking part, the Games were a big success. Records were broken but the Nazi government turned the Games into a political event. Hitler intended them to be a showcase for German strength and ability.

Star of the Games was the American sprinter Jesse Owens, who had broken five world records in one day in America the previous year. In Berlin he won four gold medals, the 100 metres, 200 metres, the long jump and the 4x100 metres relay. This was bad news for Hitler because, apart from being a non-German, Owens was black. The Nazis believed that the so-called Aryan race was superior and that blacks, like Jews, belonged to a lesser breed. As the big crowd cheered Owens, who won worldwide admiration for his sportsmanship and good humour, as well as his fabulous talent on the track, the Fuhrer hurriedly left the stadium.

In any event, Schmeling was the real hero in Germany. He would bring honour to the Rhineland and win back the heavyweight championship of the world. He was now the number one contender for Braddock's title. Germany, with the help of the world's boxing commissions, would make sure he got that opportunity. As for Louis, what next? His aura of invincibility had been shattered as if a rock had been thrown through a glass window. Could he come back from such a crushing defeat? That would depend on Louis himself, his team and promoter Mike Jacobs.

Round 6

Fairytale rise for the 'Cinderella Man'

Mike Jacobs was in discussions with Johnny Buckley, who managed the former world heavyweight champion Jack Sharkey, about the possibility of a fight with Louis. The promoter was prepared to put it on as soon as possible in a move aimed at re-establishing the 'Brown Bomber' to something resembling what he had been before the Schmeling fight.

There was no guarantee that Louis could defeat the experienced Boston contender but at least the boxing world would know where Joe's true credentials lay, and if he could come back from his heavy loss. In any event, Jacobs felt that a Louis–Sharkey fight would be a big attraction. With both teams agreeing on the match, Jacobs set about drawing up contracts with his officials at the 20th Century Sporting Club. He announced the date and venue, 18 August 1936 at the Yankee Stadium.

An experienced campaigner, Sharkey had been around since the Jack Dempsey–Gene Tunney era of the 1920s. He had won the world heavyweight title from Max Schmeling on a disputed decision over 15 rounds in June 1932, losing it a year later when he was knocked out in controversial circumstances by Primo Carnera in six rounds. Now, three years later, he felt he still had the ability to win back his old title – but first he had to get by Louis, which would be no easy task.

'Sure, it may be tough but I outsmarted Schmeling, and Schmeling knocked out Louis,' Sharkey confidently told reporters at his training camp at Orangeburg, New Jersey. Sharkey was conveniently forgetting that it was four years since he won the title and now, aged 34, he was 12 years older than Louis.

Joe's site at Pompton Lakes, New Jersey was closed to the public and only members of his immediate party and press were allowed in. Mike Jacobs felt that Louis needed his full confidence back after the Schmeling loss and that too many onlookers seeking autographs and requests to pose for pictures might prove a distraction from the important job in hand.

An attendance of 27,380 paid $159,000 into the coffers of the 20th Century Sporting Club to see the bout. Louis started fast, jabbing and hooking the advancing Bostonian, who seemed to be having difficulty reaching his opponent with any meaningful punches. Sharkey had no better fortune in the second round as Louis was now seeking a knockout. Sharkey started bobbing and weaving but a stiff jab to the face left him open to a combination of hard hooks and uppercuts.

Sharkey landed a left jab to Louis' face but the Detroiter countered with a heavy right to the chin and Sharkey went down for a count of nine. When he got to his feet, Louis went back on to the attack and dropped his man for the second time with left and right hooks, this time for a count of eight. Jack went back to his corner with a bad cut over his left eye. The end looked near.

There was no escape for Sharkey in the third round. A volley of punishing lefts and rights sent him down for the third time, his body hitting the lower rope as he fell on his face. The veteran slowly hauled himself to his feet at nine before Louis moved in with a vicious left hook to the body, followed by an equally hard right to the head and a final left hook to the chin. Sharkey slumped to the canvas. Game to the end, he tried to rise but was unequal to the task as referee Arthur Donovan counted him out on all fours. The time was 1:02 of round three. Sharkey announced in the dressing room that he was retiring. 'That's it,' he told reporters. 'The finish.' He kept his word.

'The destruction of the Boston fighter was accomplished in a workmanlike manner,' wrote James P. Dawson in the *New York Times*. 'He gave Sharkey one of the worst drubbings of his career. The youth had hammered his way back into the heavyweight picture. The Schmeling experience apparently was but a memory and a dim one at that.'

Dawson noted that few of Louis' knockout victories had been scored more masterfully. 'Louis was once more the "Brown Bomber", the "Alabama Assassin". Indeed, the expression was heard at the ringside that the Louis of this fight would have knocked out the Schmeling he faced last June.'

While Louis intended to keep busy in the ring, he was also playing around, much to the displeasure of his co-managers and trainer. Blackburn blamed a big part of the Schmeling defeat on Joe's extracurricular activity, and had warned him to control his sexual urges.

There was an unwritten law in boxing circles in those days that a boxer should not have sex in the weeks leading up to a fight. Many trainers felt that sex tired out a boxer and that the absence of sex made him feel meaner and more aggressive. A lack of medical evidence over the years has weakened those claims but back in Louis' time 'Thou shalt not make love before a fight' was one of boxing's commandments.

While in the movie capital without Marva early in 1936 to make a movie *Spirit of Youth*, in which he played a dishwasher who becomes heavyweight champion of the world, Louis was never short of female company. On subsequent trips to Hollywood, it was the same story. 'Beautiful women threw themselves at Louis, a big, handsome man, and Joe was not slow to reciprocate,' said the widely read gossip columnist Louella Parsons, the self-styled 'Queen of Hollywood', a title she shared with bitter rival Hedda Hopper.

Mae West, the racy blonde bombshell whose popular catchphrase was 'Come up and see me sometime', was one of his lady friends – and Louis did not delay in answering her call. Sonja Henie, the attractive Swedish ice skater who broke world records in three successive Winter Olympics and later had a successful movie career, was another. A charming blue-eyed blonde with a winning smile and exuberant personality, she met Louis at a Hollywood nightclub and they soon became an item.

The news of Louis' philandering was nothing new to Walter Winchell back in New York. Winchell, whose syndicated column in the *New York Mirror* had over 50 million readers across the nation, often mentioned Louis in dispatches. Having seen Joe in nightclubs and fancy restaurants with various lady companions, including showgirls and wannabee Broadway actresses, he commented, 'How Louis finds time for training is beyond me.'

All these liaisons with female celebrities was naturally kept from Marva, although there was enough evidence in newspapers and magazines to suggest that she knew all about it but decided to say nothing to keep the marriage intact. While training for a fight, Louis would have Marva stay at a local hotel but this did not stop him from bedding down with a variety of camp followers. His affairs never affected his performances when he ducked between the ropes for ring action, although Blackburn always felt he could have been a lot fitter than he was for the Schmeling loss, and put the defeat down to 'too much sex'.

The trainer's job now was to continue what he called the 'rehabilitation' of his contender. The impressive win over Sharkey was a good start. Blackburn and Louis' co-managers agreed that their promising prospect would continue to campaign for a world title fight with Braddock. Mike Jacobs felt the same way, and the first thing the promoter did was to map out a busy campaign for the rest of 1936.

Meanwhile, over in Germany, Schmeling had received news that James J. Johnston, a regular promoter at Madison Square Garden, was in the process of arranging for Braddock to defend his title against Max in September. Johnston would hire the Yankee Stadium for the fight. Braddock had not made any money since winning the championship from Max Baer in the summer of 1935. He had not even been in action since then.

Johnston was happy to accommodate Schmeling. The German was the number one contender following his victory over Louis, and both the New York State Athletic Commission and the National Boxing Association would approve the fight as being for the title. A date was provisionally set for late September 1936.

Schmeling arrived in New York in early August to prepare for the fight only to discover that Braddock had developed arthritis in his right hand and would not be able to go through with the bout. His doctors told him it would be at least six to eight weeks before he could even train. The New York authorities, in consultation with the NBA, had no alternative but to postpone the fight until the following summer. Madison Square Garden was available but Johnston felt that the indoor venue was too small to accommodate the large crowd anticipated for such a major attraction as Braddock vs Schmeling.

It was a fight the boxing world wanted to see more than any other, and would need to be outdoors. In the days before closed-circuit television, promoters made their money from big outdoor championship fights in the summer when the weather was better. Winter was definitely out, so Johnston had no alternative but to plan the fight for 1937, probably in June.

The Louis team, along with Jacobs, also had a return with Schmeling in mind but that would come later. Joe was booked for the Municipal Stadium, Philadelphia on 22 September to meet local favourite Al Ettore, who had a 56-7-2 record. Attore had championship ambitions but they ended after 1:28 of the fifth round from a Louis left hook to the chin. Two weeks later, Argentina's undefeated Jorge Brescia took the full count in round three at the Hippodrome theatre, New York, a left hook again ending it.

Eddie Simms from Florida thought he could do better at the Public Auditorium in Cleveland on 14 December but lasted less than a round. Louis dropped him with a powerful left hook. Simms managed to get to his feet before referee Arthur Donovan counted ten but when Donovan reached out to wipe his gloves clean, the disorientated Florida boxer said, 'Let's go someplace. Let's get out of here. Let's go up on the roof or someplace,' probably thinking he was talking to some woman. Donovan answered, 'That's enough,' and intervened. It remains one of the shortest heavyweight fights on record to this day.

Young Stanley Ketchel had ambitious plans to live up to the deeds of his old namesake, the great world middleweight champion of the early 1900s. Alas, he was put away in 31 seconds of the second round with a left-right combination to the head.

Louis went home to Chicago for Christmas while John Roxborough travelled to New York for talks with Mike Jacobs on the possibility of a title fight with Braddock – conveniently ignoring the fact that Braddock and his manager, Joe Gould, had already agreed to defend his title against Schmeling at the

Long Island Bowl, Madison Square Garden's outdoor arena in New York, on 3 June. The talks did not reach any definite conclusion but further discussions would take place.

Louis continued his barnstorming journey on 29 January with a scheduled ten-rounder against Bob Pastor at Madison Square Garden. It would be his first fight there since the Uzcudun bout 13 months earlier and turned out to be more difficult than expected. A former football star at New York University, Pastor had risen through the ranks of the Golden Gloves around the same time as Louis, although they had never boxed each other. James J. Johnston, Mike Jacobs' arch rival, handled Pastor's affairs.

As Johnston was the boxing promoter at the Garden, he was officially ineligible to manage a boxer. Nevertheless, he did his utmost to rattle Louis and undermine his confidence. Minutes before the scheduled ten-rounder was due to start, Johnston and several armed men burst into Louis' dressing room, accusing the Detroiter of having his fists covered in quick-drying cement. Blackburn allowed the men to examine Joe's hands, with negative results, but the wily Johnston would have another surprise in store.

Louis climbed into the ring before a capacity crowd as 2/1 favourite to win by a knockout. On Johnston's explicit instructions, Pastor was to make Louis look foolish. 'Run, run, run,' he told his boxer. Pastor did just that, making Louis look clumsy in his attempts to nail him as the crowd booed. Newspapermen at ringside would call it a bicycle race rather than a boxing match.

Pastor flicked the occasional jab but generally he kept on the move to avoid any clusters of punches from his sharp-shooting opponent. At the finish, Pastor jumped in the air, arms raised. He had succeeded in staying on his feet for the entire fight and was congratulated by Johnston.

There is little evidence that Pastor, who had entered the ring with an impressive record of one loss and two draws in 24 fights, expected to win using his strange tactics, but he did succeed in making Louis look somewhat amateurish and cumbersome. It was a unanimous decision, with referee Arthur Donovan awarding Louis eight of the ten rounds. The verdict was booed for at least 30 minutes.

Not that the crowd thought Pastor should have won, but it had been such a disappointing fight with so little action. It fed the prevailing belief that Louis would always have trouble with 'smart' opponents like Pastor and Schmeling. As it turned out throughout his career, it was scientific boxers rather than big punchers who provided the most problems for him.

Despite Pastor saying at the time that his sole aim was to stay on his feet, he claimed in an interview 45 years later that he should have been awarded the decision. 'The judges and the referee knew I had won but they couldn't call me the winner because they didn't know what to do,' he said. 'Johnston had Pastor and Jacobs had Louis. They were in a quandary so they made Louis the winner.'

Louis was disgusted with his own performance. 'I felt like a goddamn fool trying to chase that mosquito,' he recalled. '"Chappie" kept telling me to try and trap him in a corner but it was impossible. I never fought anyone like him. I was clumsy. When I reached out to give him a good punch, I might just graze him. I didn't get in one good shot, except a right to his collarbone. But he bumped me with his head and stuck his thumbs in my eyes. That's all the damage he did. He must have run 12 miles that night.'

Less than a month later, Louis was back in action, this time at the Municipal Auditorium, Kansas City where his opponent was Natie Brown from Philadelphia. Six months earlier, the state of Missouri had reversed its long-standing ban on inter-racial boxing matches, a decision that was due in large part to Joe. It was a return fight. Two years previously at the Olympia Stadium in Detroit, Brown had managed to avoid Louis' knockout blows and stayed the full ten rounds to lose the decision.

With New York's leading sportswriters watching Louis in action for the first time, he was determined to impress. It was all over with eight seconds remaining in the fourth round, thereby supporting Blackburn's contention that '"Chappie" never makes the same mistakes twice.' A volley of lefts and rights drove Brown to the boards and as he tried to pull himself up by grabbing the referee's legs, he brought the official tumbling down as well. Stretched out, Brown never moved as the count reached ten.

What followed in Louis' career was a good example of boxing intrigue at its most blatant, with Mike Jacobs the arch plotter. Aware that Braddock, the world heavyweight champion, was under exclusive contract to Madison Square Garden, he set in motion a plot to deprive the Garden of Braddock's services for a title fight with Schmeling, set for the Garden's outdoor arena at the Long Island Bowl on 3 June 1937. Jacobs had earlier tried to persuade Schmeling to give the 'Brown Bomber' a return match. He refused.

Instead, Schmeling and his manager Joe Jacobs signed contracts in New York for Max to fight Braddock under the Garden's auspices, and returned to Germany comforted by the notion that Schmeling would bring the title back to the Rhineland.

The German's team promised that if such an event happened, Schmeling would return to the United States and defend his title against Louis. American observers knew that would never happen. It was feared that once the championship was held by a German, American challengers would have to travel over there, and consequently risk losing it.

Meanwhile, Mike Jacobs called a press conference to announce that Braddock would defend his title against Louis on 22 June 1937 at the Chicago Stadium, and contracts would be signed within seven days. Uncle Mike knew that the New York State Athletic Commission would not recognise the fight on the grounds that Schmeling, the number one contender on the basis of his decisive win over Louis, had earned the right to get first crack at Braddock. But Jacobs was adamant. It was Braddock vs Louis for the title, but outside the jurisdiction of New York.

The Nazi party, not surprisingly, was seething with anger, notably Hitler and his very vocal Propaganda Minister Joseph Goebbels. 'There can only be one official title fight, and that is the one already signed by Schmeling and Braddock for 3 June at the Yankee Stadium,' a fuming Goebbels told the Reichstag. 'Braddock must honour his contract. If he doesn't, I will call on all commissions around the world to strip him of the title and declare Schmeling and another top contender as the rightful participants in a fight for the vacant championship. We cannot stand for any more of this double-dealing with America, who think they own the championship.'

In Jacobs' favour was the fact that support for Schmeling in America was dwindling, especially after newspapers quoted Max as saying that Louis was 'an amateur' and 'a stupid black man'. Schmeling vehemently denied making such comments and claimed they were 'invented' by the Nazi hierarchy to degrade Louis. When Joe read the reports, he said he would make Schmeling pay for those alleged remarks. The whole scenario was developing into a hate campaign against Schmeling and Germany, not helped by Hitler's racial policies and strong rumours of war.

The Madison Square Garden Corporation, supported by promoter Johnston, filed suit in the federal court on 20 February

1937 insisting that Braddock was obligated by contract to defend his title only under the auspices of the Garden. Jacobs' lawyer, Sol Strauss, read out the contract between the Braddock party and the Garden, and reached the conclusion that it was invalid because it tied Braddock to the Garden organisation without any obligations to the venue itself.

'I cannot see any clause in this contract that imposes on the Madison Square Garden organisation, which includes the Long Island Bowl, to say that Braddock must box there, against Schmeling or anybody else,' said Strauss. In Newark, New Jersey, Judge Guy L. Fake handed down a decision that ruled against the Garden. There was an appeal but the Supreme Court upheld Judge Fake's decision. The Schmeling–Braddock fight was off, officially.

Joe Gould was Braddock's manager. He had been insignificant in the fight business until Braddock's unexpected ascension to the heavyweight throne. Boxing writer and author Barney Nagler would call him 'a small, sharp-nosed little man and conspiratorial by nature'. Gould said he was pulling Braddock out of the Schmeling fight because of mounting public opposition. Protest groups confirmed Jacobs' fear of the likelihood of the heavyweight championship being held hostage for propaganda purposes by the Third Reich, which would happen if Schmeling, as expected, defeated Braddock.

For several months, the Non-Sectarian Anti-Nazi League had pressurised the New York State Athletic Commission into banning the Schmeling–Braddock contest or risking a boycott. The league had enough clout in political and press circles to have a significant influence on public opinion, particularly as one of its vice-presidents was Fiorello LaGuardia, the mayor of New York. LaGuardia sent telegrams and letters to the boxing commission and to Jacobs threatening to support the Anti-Nazi League in boycotting the Schmeling–Braddock fight.

Soon, the protest campaign included the American Federation of Labour and various Catholic and Protestant groups. The Jewish War Veterans of the United States, which could count on 250,000 members, also denounced the fight. Jacobs now had the most vigorous allies he needed to support his own Louis–Braddock bout, and there was no way Schmeling's fight with Braddock could conceivably go ahead. Uncle Mike was winning the fight outside the ring. At the same time, he was luring the heavyweight title away from the controlling grip of James J. Johnston and the monopoly of Madison Square Garden.

Johnston was still adamant that the Schmeling–Braddock fight would happen. He was supported by the New York State Athletic Commission. On 3 June, Schmeling fulfilled the terms of his contract by turning up at the commission's offices and stripping down for his physical examination. Dr William Walker declared him to be in excellent shape. Stepping on to the scales, Schmeling weighed 196lb. Having done everything expected of him, Max was called into the offices of the commission chairman Major General John J. Phelan, who read out an official statement.

It read, 'This body, after due and lengthy consideration of the matter, finds James J. Braddock and his manager Joe Gould in violation of the commission's orders and hereby imposes a civil fine of $1,000 apiece on Braddock and his manager. In addition, this board suspends Braddock from fighting in this state, or any state affiliated with the New York Commission, for an indefinite period. Also, any fighter meeting Braddock will be suspended automatically. Gould is also suspended. The forfeit money of $5,000 put up by Madison Square Garden for Braddock should be divided in equal parts by the Garden and by Max Schmeling, who is ready, willing and able to fight tonight.'

After resting at his hotel, Schmeling and his party, along with New York officials, headed for the Long Island Bowl. Arriving there, with the venue in complete darkness, Schmeling changed into his ring gear, climbed into the ring and sat on his stool, a completely bizarre situation that boxing writers and historians would forever call 'the phantom fight'. Returning to his dressing room, Max changed back into his civilian clothes and returned to his hotel. He had fulfilled his obligations and could do no more, even if the whole operation had cost him around $25,000 in travel and hotel expenses.

Meanwhile, Jacobs announced that ticket sales for the Braddock–Louis fight in Chicago on 22 June were brisk. Braddock's manager, Joe Gould, always preferred Louis over Schmeling as an opponent for his charge because Louis would draw a bigger crowd. Jacobs had offered Gould and Braddock a $500,000 guarantee, or half the gate and radio revenues, whichever was greater. Determined to gain control of the heavyweight title and lure it away from Johnston, Jacobs did a deal by also guaranteeing Gould and Braddock ten per cent of his own net profits from heavyweight championship promotions for the next decade should Braddock, as expected, lose to Louis.

Jacobs was paying a high price for Louis' services but stood to profit in the long run. Assuming Louis beat Braddock, Mike would have complete control of the destiny of the world heavyweight title. Schmeling and his party were still protesting through every source about being sidetracked but effectively they were fighting a lost cause. The Louis–Braddock fight was on, with the Illinois State Athletic Commission officially sanctioning it. Max would have to bide his time. 'We will be prepared to take on the winner,' said Schmeling's trainer Max Machon. 'Our man is still the logical number one contender.'

Where was Louis while all this wheeling and dealing was going on? He had been working out at his camp in Chiwaukee, Wisconsin since early May and had already spent a few weeks in the west Michigan resort of Stevensville, 'relaxing and building up energy' as Blackburn described it. Louis wanted to be in the best possible shape of his career, physically and mentally, for the Braddock fight. Nothing could be left to chance.

Louis would be strongly tipped to win the title and become the first black fighter to ascend to the heavyweight throne since Jack Johnson over 20 years earlier. But Braddock would be the sentimental favourite. He was one of boxing's nice guys, a devoted family man who kept out of nightclubs and shunned the bright lights. An underdog all his life, he always considered himself 'a very lucky guy' to achieve what he did.

Braddock's parents, Joseph and Elizabeth, were Irish but moved to the UK and settled in Lancashire before relocating to New York, where Braddock was born, the sixth of seven children – five boys and two girls – on 7 June 1905. They lived in a slum tenement on West 48th Street in what was known as Hell's Kitchen. Braddock's middle name was actually Walter. The 'J' is thought to have been added as something of an in-joke, following the tradition of famous heavyweight champions such as James J. Corbett and James J. Jeffries.

In Hell's Kitchen, fighting with other kids was an accepted part of every youngster's daily routine, so James learned how to use his fists. It was a case of the survival of the fittest. Money was never plentiful in the Braddock household. His father was, at times, a furniture remover, a railway guard and a pier watchman. Subsequently, he moved the family across the Hudson River to Hoboken, New Jersey. James left school at the age of 14 in the eighth grade and worked in a printing shop.

His brother, Joe, who was four years older, was a professional boxer and passed on his love of the sport to James. He was the first to teach him the rudiments of the noble art. Joe had 19 fights and knew his way around the ring. This knowledge came in handy when James decided to try his luck in the amateurs.

'I guess the Braddocks always fought,' James would recall in later years. 'My dad was a handy fellow with his fists back when I was a kid. He used to travel around the country fairs in England and flatten those £1-a-round professionals in the booths. He used to tell us proudly that he once knocked out a horse with a blow straight between the eyes. My uncle Jim, too, was one of the best rough-and-tumble fighters back in Ireland, so I guess fighting came naturally to me.'

It was an old black heavyweight of the early 1900s named Joe Jeannette who was instrumental in giving Braddock his major start. Jeannette, sometimes spelt Jennette, which was his real name, was one of the most admired boxers in history but, like many others, was barred because of the colour of his skin. Racism, promoters' fears of riots and economic considerations made it nearly impossible for black boxers to get bouts against leading white fighters.

As a result, Jeannette fought fellow black boxers regularly. He had 15 fights with Sam Langford, nine with Battling Jim Johnson, seven with Jack Johnson, five with Sam McVey and three with Harry Wills. At the end of his 15-year career in 1919, it was estimated he had fought over 150 times, although Jeannette himself said it was around 400. Jeannette would be inducted into the International Boxing Hall of Fame in New York in 1997.

Jeannette ran a busy gym in Hoboken, probably most famous today as the town where Frank Sinatra, 'Old Blue Eyes', was born. Joe Braddock advised younger brother James to join the gym and pick up some invaluable tips from the great Jeannette. A young hopeful like James could have had no better teacher than Jeannette, who showed him how to punch correctly, use the ring, slip punches, keep up his defence and, more importantly, always be in condition. 'You've got the makings of a champion some day, James,' said Jeannette.

Braddock made steady progress as an amateur, winning the New Jersey light-heavyweight and heavyweight championships. He finished up losing just one of his 22 bouts, 21 on count-outs or stoppages, mainly around the New Jersey area. Remembering Joe Jeannette's early advice, James told his brother he was going to give the professional game a try. 'You've nothing to lose, James, so go for it,' said Joe. 'If you don't like it for whatever reason, you can always go back to the amateurs.'

With the connections that Jeannette and Joe had made with promoters, managers and matchmakers over the years, they came up with an influential sportsman named Alfred J. Barnett to manage Braddock. Barnett knew his way around the boxing scene and arranged for his new charge to make his debut as a light-heavyweight at the Amsterdam Hall in Union City, New Jersey on 13 April 1926.

His opponent was a local, Al Settle. It would be a no-decision bout over four rounds as under New Jersey's laws, official decisions could not be registered. This was in contrast to New York regulations, which permitted official decisions under the state's Walker Law, named after Mayor Jimmy Walker, who helped guide its formation and enactment.

Local experts felt that Braddock might not have an easy time with Settle, and that is how it worked out. The *Jersey Journal,* which had been very supportive during his amateur career, expressed a tinge of disappointment in his performance. 'To say that Braddock's debut was a success would be stretching a point too far,' the paper said. 'He started well but was going very badly as the bout progressed and when the bell sounded, he seemed about ready to drop the verdict to Settle. Officially, it goes into the record books but we ruled it a draw.' Braddock's purse was $10, which Barnett allowed him to keep. That arrangement would hold for two more fights.

Braddock's next bout eight days later was against rugged George Deschner, the 'German Oak', at Ridgefeld Park, New Jersey. Scheduled for six rounds, it didn't last long. Braddock floored Deschner twice in the first round and once more in the second before the fight was stopped. This time the purse was $35. By the end of 1926, and boxing around the New Jersey and New York areas, Braddock had added another 14 wins.

It was towards the end of 1926 that Braddock met the man who would change his life and career forever, and become his closest friend and only advisor. His name was Joe Gould, a New York boxing manager who had served in the US navy and got his start in the sport by putting on boxing shows while on duty. One day, while Braddock was working out in Joe Jeannette's gym in Hoboken, Gould walked in with his promising Brooklyn middleweight Harry Galfund. Gould had been approached by several New Jersey businessmen who were eager to buy Galfund's contract for $2,500, and Gould invited them along to the gym to see him work out.

Spotting Braddock working out on the punch bag, Gould called him over.

'How would you like to earn five bucks, kid, to spar three rounds with my fighter?' he said. 'He'll take it easy on you, I promise.'

'Ok, for five bucks, I'd take on anybody,' said a delighted Braddock.

Neither Gould, Galfund nor the prospective buyers expected the workout to be anything more than that – a workout. Galfund was a brilliant prospect while Braddock was untested against any serious opposition despite his winning run. After two minutes of the first round, Braddock landed a powerful right to the jaw that put Galfund down and out. He was unconscious for two minutes. By then, the prospective backers had walked out.

Gould had seen enough of Braddock to convince himself that James J. had what it took. He paid off Barnett and signed up Braddock the following day. So began one of boxing's most lasting friendships – dapper little Joe, son of a rabbi, and big James J., the kid with lots of ambition. A star was born. Together, they would experience the good days and the bad days, the ups and downs, and remain loyal to each other, even when Braddock hit the big time and could have changed managers if he had so wished.

Early in 1927, Braddock caught the eye of America's most influential sportswriter, Damon Runyon. 'I should have mentioned a young man in Jersey, James J. Braddock by name,' he wrote in the *New York Journal American*. 'I have seen Braddock on a number of occasions and I think well of him. However, I believe he is only a light-heavyweight as yet, though certain to get bigger in another year. James J. Braddock has considerable natural class, and a bit of a punch. His manager is taking him along with great care, for Braddock is still 21 and has much to learn. I am inclined to think, however, that he will go far.'

Within two years, Braddock qualified for a world light-heavyweight title fight against Tommy Loughran. Although he did not possess a knockout punch, Loughran, a southpaw from Philadelphia, was a master craftsman who won his fights on skill alone. Also, he had a habit of ending each round near his corner, so that when he bell rang he could sit on his stool for more rest while his opponent had to walk across the ring to take his seat. Max Baer also used this trick.

'After just three years as a professional, I figured it was a hell of an honour to fight for the championship, as far as I was concerned,' Braddock told the author Peter Heller in his retirement years.

On 18 July 1929, Braddock climbed into the ring at the Yankee Stadium as an 8/5 underdog. He opened a bad cut over Loughran's left eye with a solid right in the opening round but the injury seemed to invigorate the champion, who used his scientific boxing and clever footwork to outfox the New Jersey battler. Braddock was completely frustrated by Loughran's elusiveness and after 15 rounds, the Philadelphian was a clear winner.

The official scoring was never made public but everyone in attendance, fans and the press, knew who the champion was at the last bell. 'James J. was little more than a raw pupil in the hands of a master,' *Ring* magazine's Nat Fleischer would remember in later years. The fight earned Loughran the nickname the 'Phantom from Philly'.

'I knew Tommy was a good boxer,' said Braddock after the fight. 'I was more or less a boxer-puncher. I figured that I had to fight him rather than box him, but he was always too clever. I knew I was outclassed long before the finish. He beat me so easy with his boxing ability. He was a guy you could never hit with a good, solid punch.'

Still, Braddock had his biggest payday to date, with his share of the purse amounting to $17,000. It was a small fortune at a time when the average annual income was $750, and for farm workers, just $235. In one evening, Braddock had earned more than the average worker would make in 20 years. He was still just 24 yers old, and had an impressive record, 33-4-0. He made plans to marry Mae Fox, a beautiful brunette he would eventually spend the rest of his life with. There was enough money in the bank, and the rest was tied up in sold stock investments.

Braddock took a long time to get over the Loughran loss. The heavy defeat seemed to knock a lot of the drive and ambition out of him. He told Gould he wanted to quit boxing and go back to the docks. Gould advised him to move up to the heavyweight division, as there was little chance of getting a return bout with Loughran for the title. Braddock had no better luck in the heavier class, losing six of his next nine fights. By now, America was in deep trouble.

On 24 October 1929, the stock market crashed, bringing to an end the excesses and optimism of the Jazz Age and the Roaring 20s. A prolonged, speculative boom in stocks and shares, fuelled by borrowed money, came to a violent end. By the end of November, investors had lost more than $100 billion in assets, triggering the worldwide economic slump that would come to be known as the Great Depression. The crash did not have an immediate effect on Braddock's finances. True, like many others, he lost some on the stock market but his capital was mainly invested in a taxi company and a bar.

He could only win two of his six fights in 1930, the same in 1931 and two out of eight in 1932, his last fight that year being a stoppage loss against Lou Scozza in San Francisco in November, when a nasty gash over his right eye ended the bout in the sixth round. The defeat seemed to make it clear that Braddock was through as a headliner.

The big fellow, however, supported by Gould, kept plugging away, winning here, losing there, before finally breaking both his hands against Abe Feldman in September 1933, when the fight was stopped in the sixth round and declared a no-contest. Completely discouraged, and becoming something of a stepping stone for promising young boxers, or 'an opponent', Braddock announced his retirement from the ring. Gould did not disagree.

America was still in the throes of the Great Depression, with long queues outside relief offices. Braddock had by now married Mae Fox and had two young sons and a little daughter to support as well. Every morning, he would walk down to the docks looking for work. If he was lucky, he might get the odd eight-hour shift. He hoisted freight parts from the ships on to trucks. Other times he worked on the coal docks all night for 60 cents an hour.

At this stage, the Braddocks were living in the basement of an old tenement house. The rent was $25 a month. James J's wages averaged $19 a week when he was working regularly, but for most of the time he was on relief. When there was no work, he would sit on a bench outside James J. Johnston's office at Madison Square Garden while Gould went inside pleading with the promoter to get his boxer a fight.

'He's more or less retired,' said Gould one day, 'but if my guy can get one more fight for a good purse, we'll take it and then he'll go back into retirement again – this time for keeps. He's fed up with boxing anyhow.' Gould always got the same reply – nothing doing yet but if something turned up, Johnston would be in touch.

Fate stepped in on the morning of 12 June 1934. Johnston was promoting Primo Carnera's defence of his world heavyweight title at the Long Island Bowl two days later. He was now looking around for someone to meet John 'Corn' Griffin in one of the preliminary bouts as the original opponent had pulled out.

A soldier based at Fort Benning, Georgia, Griffin was a promising heavyweight who had attracted a lot of attention, with some reporters calling him 'the new Jack Dempsey'. He was a heavy hitter with both hands and as one of Carnera's chief sparring partners, he had often belted the Italian giant around the ring. All his manager Charlie Harvey needed now was a 'suitable' opponent to enable Griffin to show off his true potential in front of many of New York's leading sportswriters.

After running through a list of likely suspects, Johnston told Harvey in his office, 'There's a guy out in New Jersey named

James J. Braddock. He's more or less retired but I'm sure I can get him to fight Griffin in a special five-rounder before the main event. Agreed? That's fine.'

Leaving the office, Harvey permitted himself a smile while Johnston picked up the phone to call Gould and offer him the Griffin fight, which he readily accepted. What had they got to lose anyhow? Meanwhile, Harvey reckoned he had a real soft touch in Braddock and would use 'the old longshoreman', as he called him, to push Griffin further up *Ring* magazine's ratings. As it happened, Harvey was nearly right. After a fairly tame first round, with both boxers sizing each other up, Braddock was sent sprawling from a vicious right cross to the point of the chin in the second round. Struggling to his feet a second before the ten count, he managed to hang on until the bell.

In the third round, Braddock spotted an opening and fired an overhand right that landed flush on Griffin's chin. The army man slumped to the canvas, out to the world. He was carried to his corner and only woke up in the dressing room and asked his manager, 'What round is it?' Harvey barked, 'It's all over, you idiot. You were knocked out in the third round by that has-been!' Johnston walked into Braddock's dressing room and handed Gould a cheque for $250.

'No kidding, that $250 looked bigger than the big purses I had collected in other days,' Braddock remembered. 'More than that, I felt in my bones that it was the break I had been waiting on for so long. Joe Gould and I were the happiest men in the United States that night. The dark clouds that had hung over us so long were blowing away. We were both convinced that I had hit my stride again. I had whacked Griffin hard without hurting my hands. I felt we were going to be in the big money at last.'

Braddock and Gould stayed on to see Carnera knocked out in the 11th round after being down 12 times. Boxing had a new heavyweight champion of the world in Max Baer – and now he had a hard-punching contender on his hands. James J. Braddock, the supposedly washed-up fighter, was back on the sports pages, and this time as a winner. He now had the motivation to train more rigorously. He had the support of his wife, Mae, and a good manager who believed in him. His injured right hand had fully responded to treatment, so another retirement was out of the question.

The offers came in fast, and Gould accepted a ten-rounder with the talented John Henry Lewis in New York on 16 November 1934. Lewis, a future world light-heavyweight champion who had jabbed Braddock silly two years earlier, had designs on the heavyweight championship. This time Braddock, entering the ring as a 5/1 underdog, fought with a new dash, dropping Lewis in the seventh round and winning on points.

Braddock next went in against big Art Lasky, a promising Californian who was being considered as the next challenger for Max Baer. He had lost only four of his 44 fights, with three draws, and was a 3/1 favourite not only to beat Braddock but finish him off in six rounds. They met at Madison Square Garden on 22 March 1935. Conceding height, reach and nearly 15lb in weight, James J. dominated the action, outboxing and outfighting the Californian all the way. The veteran seemingly could do no wrong and after 15 rounds won a unanimous decision.

Braddock's purse was $4,100, more than he had earned in the previous two years combined. There was no more need to stand in dole queues. In fact, he went to the New Jersey Department of Welfare to repay the money he had been given over the previous 18 months.

Damon Runyon became so fascinated with Braddock's amazing rise from obscurity to leading contender for the heavyweight championship of the world that in his report for the *New York Journal American* the next day, he referred to Braddock as the 'Cinderella Man'. It was a nickname that stuck.

The New York State Athletic Commission and the National Boxing Association both approved of a Braddock–Baer fight for the title. As soon as the match was announced for the Long Island Bowl, New York on 13 June 1935, Baer was installed as a 10/1 favourite, later shifting to 15/1. Nobody outside Braddock's camp at Loch Sheldrake, near Paradise, Michigan was giving him any sort of a chance.

Paul Gallico of the *New York Daily News* wrote, 'I am telling you that Baer will knock Braddock out inside three rounds, and the referee will have to look sharp because Jimmy is game and gets up, and if Baer hits him when he is groggy and can't get his hands up, Baer may injure him permanently.' Dave Walsh of the International News Service wasn't any more flattering. 'Looking at this fight from where I operate from, it will be surprising to me if we don't all end up in a police court,' he wrote.

When Baer was asked for a comment, he smiled and said, 'It's a joke. He's made it to the number one contender's spot but that's as far as it goes. When I heard the fight was arranged, I had the biggest laugh in years, and I'm still laughing. All I can say is that, personally, Jimmy's a swell guy but I'll just have to take him to the cleaners.' Braddock said, 'The man who is in better shape will win this fight and as for me, I'm in the best condition of my life. Baer won't be able to take it easy with me because I won't let him. I intend to give the public all that is humanly possible to give.'

A flaming red sunset greeted the crowd as they filed into the Bowl on fight night. The turnout was a disappointing 35,000. Few people thought Braddock had a chance and many stayed away. But those who attended were about to get the shock of their lives. Celebrities from all walks of life were introduced from the ring, including two former greats in Jack Dempsey and Gene Tunney, as well as title contender Joe Louis. There were also a number of underworld figures spotted among the crowd.

From the first bell, Braddock waged a smart, determined fight, outboxing the champion. *Ring* magazine's Nat Fleischer claimed that Baer had trained in a slapdash, careless manner, with the result that he was far from in his best physical condition.

'A good puncher himself, Braddock did not make the mistake of trading blows with so dangerous a clouter,' remembered Fleischer. 'Instead, he boxed masterfully on the defence, steadily piling up points by consistent use of a left jab, and cleverly blocking or ducking under Baer's ponderous swings. Even when Baer did manage to connect, his punches seemed to lack their one-time potency.

'At no time during the 15 rounds did Baer even remotely resemble the devastating demon of the Schmeling and Carnera battles. He fought listlessly most of the way, and his poor physical condition was evident when he did try to uncover an offensive. His rallies were few and short lived.'

There did not seem to be any dispute as to the winner, and Braddock did not have to wait long for the scores. Referee Johnny McAvoy called it 9-5 for Braddock with one even, and judge Charley Lynch made it 11-4 for Braddock. Judge George Kelly caused a surprise by scoring it even, 7-7-1, but gave the decision to Braddock because Baer had hit low and used some backhand punches. It was a fairytale rise for the 'Cinderella Man'.

Two years later, on 22 June 1937, Braddock climbed into the ring at Comiskey Park, Chicago for the first defence of his title. The man in the opposite corner was Joe Louis.

Night of revenge

As champion and challenger made their way to the ring, there were cheers from the crowd of just over 45,000. Under his red-trimmed blue bathrobe, Louis wore purple trunks with the initials JL embroidered on them. As a tribute to his Irish heritage, Braddock wore a green satin robe with a white shamrock on the back. At the morning weigh-in, both boxers had scaled 197lb. Louis was a 2/1 favourite.

Spectators stood on seats and craned their necks to get a glimpse of celebrities from movies, including Al Jolson, James Cagney, Jack Benny, George Burns and Gracie Allen, Edward G. Robinson, Cab Calloway, Bing Crosby, Clark Gable, George Raft, Bill 'Bojangles' Robinson and Mae West.

Introduced from the ring were boxing stars past and present such as Jack Dempsey, Gene Tunney, Battling Nelson, Willie Ritchie, John Henry Lewis, Sixto Escobar and Barney Ross. A notable absentee was Louis' severest critic, Jack Johnson. After referee Tommy Thomas gave instructions to the principals, they went back to their corners to await the first bell. Jack Blackburn whispered to Louis, 'Tonight, "Chappie", you come home the champ.' Braddock, sitting on his stool across the ring, made the sign of the cross with his gloved right hand.

Braddock took the fight to Louis from the start, jabbing before going into a clinch. Braddock tried a right cross but Louis narrowly avoided it, snapping out his left hand, once, twice, three times. Suddenly, coming out of a clinch, Braddock landed a chopping right to the chin and the challenger sank to the canvas as the crowd roared. Louis was up at the count of two and backed away to clear his head. 'He got up so quick, I guess I was surprised,' Braddock remembered. 'By the time I got to him, he had recovered. I went into the attack and tried to land another shot but he was moving away, and I guess that's where I lost the fight.'

Louis recalled, 'Blackburn told me later that I should have stayed down and taken advantage of the count. But I guess I was in a hurry. I just got up and went at it. The knockdown made me mad. He was a good right-hand puncher but my head was always clear. Before the bell, I staggered him with a left hook and a right cross.'

Braddock had a good second round too, keeping the pressure on Louis, but he sustained a bad cut over his left eye shortly before the bell. By the third round, Louis was beginning to take control of the fight with snappy left jabs and stinging hooks and uppercuts. By the fourth, Braddock's energy seemed to be running out and he was missing more than he was landing.

'After that, I got hit by more punches than in my prior 87 fights,' he remembered. 'Because I never got hit so much, I never was cut up so bad. I got 23 stitches in my face that night. He hit me in one of the later rounds and drove one of my teeth through the mouthpiece and straight through the lip.'

It was obvious to all that the fight had turned irrevocably in Louis' favour. Joe Gould scrambled up the steps leading to the ring as Braddock staggered to his corner at the bell ending the seventh round. 'I'm throwing in the towel,' said Gould. 'If you do, I'll never speak to you again,' said James J. 'I'm the champion and if I'm going to lose, I'll lose it on the deck.'

It was all over in the eighth. A left hook shook Braddock and he fell into a clinch. Louis pushed him off and unleashed a barrage of blows that put the soon-to-be former champion on the canvas to be counted out. The final right cross was described by Peter Wilson, Britain's most travelled boxing writer and reporting for the *Daily Express*, as 'the hardest single punch I have ever seen land on another'.

In Braddock's dressing room, the loser said little except paying respect to Louis' terrific power and wishing him a long reign. Thirty-six years later, in an interview with author Peter Heller, he elaborated, 'I figured I could lick Louis as I licked others. For four rounds I did all right but from then on, I got hit with more punches than in the other 87 fights.

'But I'm glad I had the opportunity to fight the guy because, as it came out, he's been one of the best in history. Even though I lost, the fans out there enjoyed it. It was action for eight rounds.' In another interview in his retirement years, Braddock said, 'If I had electric light bulbs on my toes, they would have lit up.'

Louis told reporters in his dressing room that Braddock was 'the gamest guy I ever met', adding, 'But I ain't the real champ until I beat Schmeling.'

There was nationwide praise for Louis after the fight. Typical was the view of Dan Parker, sports editor of the *New York Mirror*. 'How wrong everybody had been about Louis. They called him dumb. They said he was a sucker for a right hand. They questioned his courage. After all, a lucky combination of circumstances that could never happen again enabled Max Schmeling to score a knockout over him a year ago. I think it was lucky for Mr Schmeling he wasn't in there instead of Braddock at Comiskey Park.'

Back in New York, even the boxing commission had to face reality. Its chairman, Major General John J. Phelan, duly issued a statement. It read, 'This board does hereby recognise

Joe Louis as the world heavyweight champion on the strength of his knockout victory over James J. Braddock last week. We cannot suspend notice for his having floored Braddock, for the former is not duly licensed with this body. However, should Louis make application for permission to box in this state, he will not be accorded such permission until he promises to make the first defence of his championship against Max Schmeling. Braddock will remain under suspension in this state indefinitely.'

The Louis team and Mike Jacobs formally agreed. The NBA followed New York's edict and declared that Schmeling must come first. But as so often happens in boxing, then and now, internal politics got in the way of fair play. Jacobs had been named the official promoter at Madison Square Garden, replacing James J. Johnston, who was fired as a result of the fiasco surrounding the failed Braddock–Schmeling title fight.

Jacobs soon consolidated his position by leaking information to the press of his three silent partners' involvement in the 20th Century Sporting Club to the Scripps-Howard newspaper chain, Damon Runyon, Bill Farnsworth and Edward J. Frayne. They worked for the rival Hearst group and now they had their conflict of interest revealed to the world. They quickly sold their interest to Jacobs for a paltry $25,000 apiece. 'Uncle Mike' now had the world's number one heavyweight exclusively under contract and he planned to exploit that position as far as possible, with Louis benefiting as a result too.

By this time, Schmeling was back with his manager in Germany attempting to arrange a fight with the British and Empire champion Tommy Farr from Wales for the 'legitimate world heavyweight title', as they put it. Furious at being passed over for a shot at Louis, Max claimed the championship for himself. 'The Chicago fight simplifies the situation,' he told the International News Service. 'It makes my forthcoming fight with Farr the logical world title contest. I have no intention of putting myself in the position of challenger. Louis has got to come to me if he wants to fight. I have already beaten Louis and there is no reason why my fight with Farr should not be for the world's championship.'

Wishful thinking on Schmeling's part? Certainly. Max may have been pushed out of a deserved championship fight, calling the whole business an American conspiracy to keep the title away from him, but Louis was regarded as the official champion, having beaten Braddock in a legitimate title fight. In any event, Louis was prepared to meet Schmeling for what he called the 'real' championship. 'I leave all negotiations and plans to my managers and Mike Jacobs,' he told the press. 'If they tell me I've been matched with Schmeling or whoever, that's fine with me.'

When Jacobs offered Schmeling a title fight in New York, with the usual challenger's 20 per cent share of the gate, he turned it down and insisted on 30 per cent. Jacobs refused. Schmeling went ahead with plans to meet Tommy Farr in London. Promoter Sydney Hulls set up the fight for the White City Stadium on 30 September. Hulls successfully applied to the British Boxing Board of Control to have it recognised as being for the world heavyweight title. It was generally expected that it would be approved but the board announced it could only be a final eliminator, with the winner meeting Louis for the title.

Jacobs' mind was now working fast. He promptly despatched his lawyer, Sol Strauss, to London to offer Farr's management double what they were getting from Hulls. Jacobs' offer for a Louis title fight in New York was a $60,000 guarantee, plus 25 per cent of the radio and movie rights, as well as four round-trip tickets. The Louis–Farr fight was on. It would be staged on 26 August 1937 at the Yankee Stadium.

One of eight children, Thomas George Farr was among Britain's toughest fighters. Born into a poor Welsh coalmining family in Clydach Vale, overlooking Tonypandy in the Rhondda Valley, there was only one real option for a poor boy in the area. In common with other children, he left school at an early age to help support his family by working down the mines. Yet his hatred of the work was so profound that he soon quit for a series of low-paid jobs and the constant nightmare of unemployment. He worked in various posts, including making deliveries from a handcart for local shopkeepers.

It seemed almost inevitable that Farr would get involved in boxing. All around him in the local towns and villages, there were clubs and gyms. Travelling boxing booths constantly passed through and set up in fairgrounds. Other famous Welsh boxers like Jimmy Wilde and Jim Driscoll had started in the booths, which were considered good breeding grounds for future champions. Farr also got encouragement from his father, George, a burly 240lb Irishman from County Cork who had engaged in some bare-knuckle fighting to earn extra money for the family.

Tommy decided to try his luck in the professional ring and made his debut a week before Christmas 1926 with a points win over Jack Jones in Tonypandy. Allied to his toughness and grit, Farr was also a clever boxer and made steady if slow progress with his bobbing and weaving style. He won the British and Empire heavyweight titles in March 1937 and 12 months later achieved his finest victory when he outpointed former world champion Max Baer at Harringay Arena, London.

The gritty Welshman followed up his stunning win with a third-round knockout of German's scourge of British heavyweights, Walter Neusel, again at Harringay, in June. The two victories convinced Mike Jacobs that the Welshman, rather than the uncooperative Schmeling, was the man to climb into the ring to face his pride and joy, not to mention his biggest money-maker, Joe Louis. Farr would be aiming to become the first British-born heavyweight to win the world title since Cornwall's Bob Fitzsimmons was champion back in the 1890s.

As the fight night drew near, Louis was installed as a 10/1 favourite but by the time of the weigh-in, the odds had dropped to 7/1, in some cases 4/1. Farr was first on the scales and weighed 207lb, followed straight away by Louis, who balanced the bar at 198lb. When Louis noticed scars on Farr's back, a legacy of his days down the mines, he asked how they got there. 'Oh, they're nothing,' replied Farr. 'I got those from fighting with tigers back in England.' 'Gee,' said Louis turning to Blackburn, 'this guy must be as tough as hell.'

Both boxers were given a stern lecture by commission chairman John Phelan about fouling, and warned that if either man butted or used any other illegal tactics, he would be disqualified and his purse withheld. Farr took offence at being spoken to in this way. 'I've never lost a fight for butting or any foul,' he snapped. 'I'm a fair man, both in the ring and out of it. I won't foul Louis and nobody need be looking out for it.'

Just as Phelan was about to leave, Jacobs rushed over to him and they engaged in a hurried conversation. Then, to everybody's amazement, the promoter announced that due to overnight rain, the fight would be postponed four days, to 30 August. This caused great surprise as all indications were that the weather would be fine and settled, and there were still nine hours to go. The truth soon came out.

Ticket sales had been slow despite daily publicity and Jacobs feared he would lose money on the night. The extra few days would allow things to pick up. As it happened, the delay made hardly any noticeable difference.

The attendance of just over 32,000 was still below the figure anticipated by Jacobs when the fight was first announced. Had

Farr, the first Welshman to fight for the world heavyweight title, any realistic chance? Nobody outside the Farr camp thought so. Six rounds, if he was lucky, agreed the ringside experts. Probably less, said some. Both boxers were lighter at the second weigh-in, Louis coming in at 197lb and Farr at 204.

When Harry Baloch introduced Max Schmeling, who was among the boxing celebrities in the ring, the crowd cheered. The cheers must have had a hollow ring in the German's ears. Max had learned that Mike Jacobs controlled the sport, not the paying public or the boxing commissions, or even newspaper opinion. Schmeling would have to wait his turn, and at the whim of the promoter. All the boxers, including Max, wished both principals luck. Jack Johnson continued his animosity towards Louis. Ignoring Joe, he went across the ring and shook Farr's hand.

After referee Arthur Donovan issued last-minute instructions to the champion and challenger, they returned to their corners to await the bell. Farr started fast, poking out his left jab and going into his familiar crouch. Louis got his own left jab working. Towards the end of the round, Louis cracked a right cross on Farr's chin but the sturdy Tonypandy man took it unflinchingly. This was not going to be an easy title defence for the champion.

To American fans accustomed to Britain's reputation of sending over 'horizontal heavyweights', notably Phil Scott, who seemed to cry 'foul' at any given opportunity, Farr was a revelation. He stood up to Louis' best shots while always fighting back, even when his face was a mass of cuts and bruises as the fight progressed. But Louis' better all-round work seemed to be deciding the issue. Still, Farr was always in there fighting, driving the champion to the ropes in a thrilling eighth round. Louis was landing his best shots but could not put the challenger on the canvas.

Farr was giving Louis little chance to launch sustained attacks, bobbing and weaving, and was never reluctant to mix it with the champion. As Louis remembered it, 'From the ninth round to the 12th, I just kept sticking and sticking with my left. I caught him with some good uppercuts but the 12th was almost over and I just spent the last two rounds trying to protect my lead.'

Farr acknowledged Louis' superiority in his autobiography. 'I had my moments, few though they were,' he said. 'In the 14th round, Louis was on top but try as he would, he could not land a sleep producer. In the 15th, Louis came at me at the double. I stood my ground and having flicked him with a right hand, parried his right. Stalking Louis as he backed to the ropes, I held my own at in-fighting and we finished the fight to a tornado of cheers.'

Referee Donovan caused something of a surprise by walking to Farr's corner and shaking his hand, leading him and everybody else to believe he had won. This was not the case. Donovan was merely congratulating him on 'a good show'. When Harry Baloch announced the scores, Donovan gave Louis 13 rounds, one to Farr and one even, a decision that drew boos from the crowd. The two judges were more realistic. William McParland had it nine rounds to six for Louis, and Charles Lynch called it eight rounds to five for Louis with two even.

In the dressing room, Louis had his badly bruised right hand in a bucket of water. He had injured it while breaking Farr's nose in the fourth round and would have it in a plaster cast for two weeks. 'Farr was one of the toughest men I ever fought,' Louis said. Farr had no complaints. 'He hits harder than anybody else I ever fought but I still would like to fight him again,' he said through puffed lips.

Louis now wanted Schmeling. The NBA and the NYSAC were demanding a Louis–Schmeling fight, seeing that Max

Louis with trainer Jack Blackburn, centre, and promoter Mike Jacobs

Louis awaits an opening against Max Baer

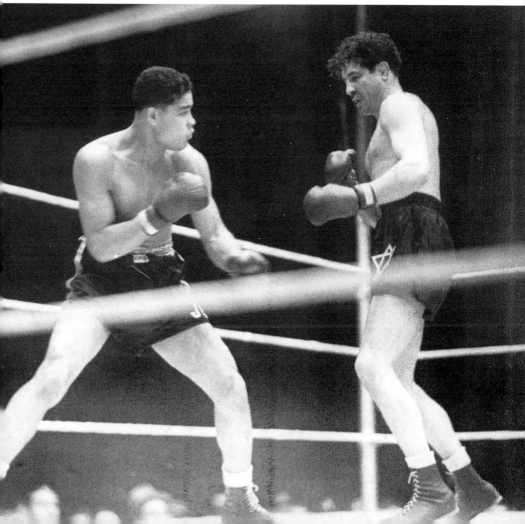

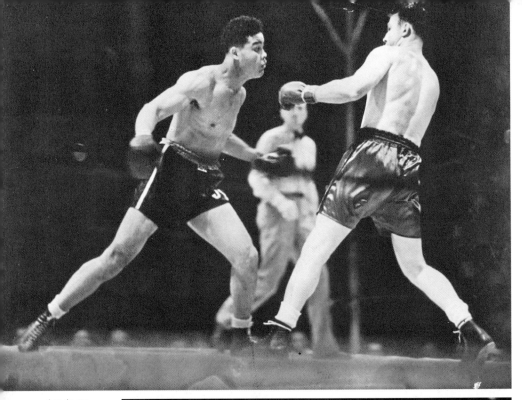

Louis on
the attack
against Jack
Sharkey

Tommy
Farr breaks
through
with a left
against
Louis

Author
Thomas
Myler feels
Louis's
famous
right hand

It's all over
as Louis
stops Max
Schmeling
in one
round

Louis reads about his quick win in the New York Daily News

The champ tells his young admirers how it's done

Tony Galento has Louis on the boards in the third round

Louis served his country with distinction during the Second World War

Billy Conn takes the full count against Louis in the 13th round

A sweeping left hook knocks Tami Mauriello off his feet for a one-round knockout

Louis knocks Jersey Joe Walcott against the ropes just before the finish in round 11

Ezzard Charles, right, on the attack against a fading Louis

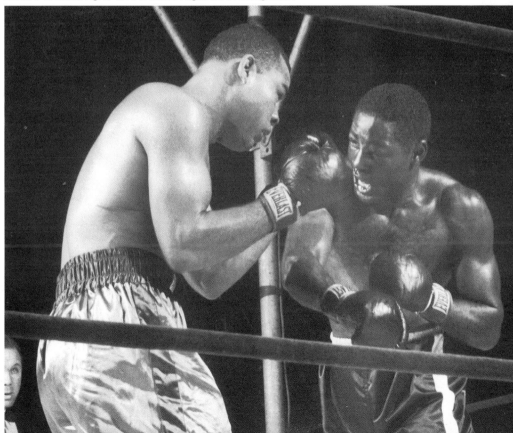

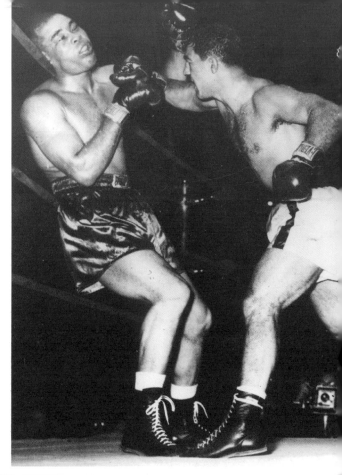

It's all over as Rocky Marciano pounds Louis to defeat in eight rounds

Old champ meets new champ, with Joe Frazier, left, and mentor 'Yank' Durham

was the number one contender. Jacobs told both organisations he would put the fight on in the summer of 1938. 'This is the fight the public want to see,' said New York commissioner John Phelan, 'and Schmeling must get his opportunity to challenge Louis, one he thoroughly deserves. After all, he is the leading contender and has been for a long time.'

In early September, Jacobs announced that the Louis–Schmeling fight would be held at the Yankee Stadium on 22 June 1938. Louis was on 40 per cent of the gate, with Schmeling settling for 20 per cent. Both were on an equal percentage of the radio and movie rights.

Louis had two warm-up championship fights. The first was at Madison Square Garden on 23 February against Nathan Mann of New Haven, Connecticut. As a 15-year-old in the spring of 1930, Mann was working on a heavy punch bag used by his father, a keep-fit fanatic, when he was spotted by Bill Reynolds, a delivery man from the local bakery. Pulling into the driveway, Reynolds watched the kid for a few minutes and saw 'a power puncher with a world of potential', as he put it later. Reynolds, a former boxer who now ran a gym, invited the youngster to drop by. Eight years and 46 professional fights later, of which he won 39 and drew three, Mann was climbing into the ring to face Joe Louis.

A capacity crowd of 20,000 passed through the turnstiles to see two of the youngest contestants ever to fight for the world heavyweight title – Louis was 23 and Mann 22. Mann had beaten leading contenders Bob Pastor and Arturo Godoy within the previous year, but he stood little chance against Louis. After putting Mann on the canvas four times, the 'Brown Bomber' finished his opponent off in the fourth round with a left hook to the jaw. The time was 1:36 of the round.

Just over a month later, Louis ducked between the ropes at the Chicago Stadium to meet Harry Thomas, a tough veteran from Eagle Bend, Minnesota. It was April Fool's Day but Louis had no intention of fooling around. After two rounds that he won without any trouble, he staggered Thomas with a hard right. Groggy, Thomas started for his corner and made it to his stool several seconds before the bell rang.

Spectators thought that referee Dave Miller would disqualify Thomas but Louis asked Miller to let the fight continue as he wanted the fans to get their money's worth. In the fifth round, he dropped the Minnesota contender with a solid left hook for the full count, with just ten seconds remaining on the timekeeper's clock.

Schmeling, meanwhile, had three tune-up bouts, the first against the same Harry Thomas in Max's final fight of 1937. The German stopped his opponent in eight rounds at Madison Square Garden just before Christmas. Thomas liked to recall that he must have created some kind of record by boxing a former world heavyweight champion and a reigning one in just over three months.

Returning to Germany to celebrate the holiday at home, Schmeling had two fights in Hamburg, convincingly outpointing South Africa's Ben Foord, a former British and Empire champion, on 30 January and stopping Steve Dudas from New Jersey in eight rounds three months later. Max now felt ready for the biggest fight of his career, the return bout with Louis.

On his arrival in New York, Schmeling told reporters at the dock, 'I will beat Joe Louis again because I have placed in his mind a sense of fear. Always now, in the ring, he anticipates danger. Fear is something he never knew before. It caused him to talk more than usual. He has been trying to explain our last fight for two years now and he is still no nearer the solution. Heil Hitler.' Wilbur Wood of the *New York Sun* said: 'Suppose Louis knocks you out this time. You're a hero in Germany.

Will there be any change in the way your country looks at you?' Schmeling was serious for a few moments. 'No, no, of course not,' he said. 'What difference would it make? It's just a prize fight. Nothing else.'

Yet, as Schmeling realised privately, the wider symbolism of the fight threatened to overwhelm him. He was now regarded by many Americans as an official representative of Adolf Hitler. As he walked around New York, Max was distressed when people flashed contemptuous Nazi salutes at him. In interviews, he tried to defend his countrymen by saying, 'Germans are the fairest people in the world', but he remained something of an enemy.

The Nazis were already over-running Europe after ignoring Hitler's pledge to the British prime minister, Neville Chamberlain, for 'peace in our time'. America, torn emotionally by fear, was already against Schmeling even before the first bell rang. They found a meaning in a title fight that transcended its actual value and rendered Max a symbol of Nazi arrogance. Even before official contracts were signed, the Anti-Nazi League to Champion Human Rights was making plans to picket Mike Jacobs' office.

Louis trained at his familiar camp at Pompton Lakes, New Jersey. He said little in interviews, even when newspapermen reminded him that in the German, he would be confronting a very dangerous opponent. Louis' response was, 'Schmeling has got to be good. He knocked me out, didn't he?'

Up at Speculator in Hamilton County, New York State, Schmeling worked out under the supervision of his trainer and confidant Max Machon. Arno Helmers, an official Nazi broadcaster, sent stories back to Germany that New York governor Herbert Lehman was a conspirator in a plot to ensure Schmeling's defeat. How this was to be achieved was never detailed. The basis for the story was that the governor was a Jew.

When Nazi reaction to Helmers' hoax was reported back to America, it added fuel to an already raging fire. Promoter Jacobs was rubbing his hands with glee and his blue eyes grew wider. Ringside tickets, priced at $40 each, were selling even beyond his wildest dreams. By fight night, 22 June, exactly 12 months to the day since Louis beat Braddock to win the title, tickets were selling for as much as $200 each, in some cases $500. Some were so close to the ring that they could see the tense muscles of the champion and challenger. At the weigh-in earlier, both scaled 197lb.

The crowd's reaction to Schmeling's entrance had not been unexpected. Over 20 policemen surrounded him as he made his way to the ring with his handlers while being bombarded with fruit, crushed cigarette packets and paper cups. He had to pull a towel over his head to protect him from the debris. Dressed in an old grey bathrobe, he climbed into the bright ring to boos and catcalls. Louis followed soon afterwards in the same blue and red robe he had worn the first time he fought Schmeling. In sharp contrast and not surprisingly, Louis, a 2/1 favourite, was cheered to the hilt.

Watched by a crowd of 70,043, who contributed $1,015,012 to the gate, Schmeling came out of his corner trying to use the same style that had earned him victory in the first fight, with a straight-standing posture and his left hand prepared to begin jabbing. Louis' strategy, however, was to get the fight over early. Prior to the fight, he mentioned to his trainer 'Chappie' Blackburn that he would devote all his energy to the first three rounds. Louis told Jimmy Cannon of the *New York Post* that he predicted a knockout in one round.

After only a few seconds of feinting, Louis unleashed a barrage of jabs, hooks and uppercuts, including a right to the German's body that had Max audibly crying in pain. After sending Louis to his corner and conferring briefly with

Schmeling, Donovan told the boxers to resume the action, after which Louis went on the attack again, immediately dropping the German to the canvas.

Schmeling climbed to his feet at the count of three before Louis resumed his barrage, this time focusing on Schmeling's head. After connecting with three direct shots, Max sank to the canvas again, arising at the count of two. Schmeling had little defence at this point as Louis connected at will, sending Schmeling to the floor for the third time in short order, this time near the ring's centre.

Schmeling's trainer, Max Machon, threw a towel into the ring in token of surrender, but under New York rules a fight cannot end in this way. Referee Donovan snatched it off the canvas and flung it backwards. He counted up to five before sensing the futility of it all and waved his hands wide. It was all over. Louis was still champion of the world. Two minutes and four seconds had elapsed since the first bell. Newspapermen agreed that Louis had thrown 41 punches, of which 31 had landed solidly. Schmeling, by contrast, had been able to throw only two, one of which missed.

'Louis was a big, lean copper spring,' wrote Bob Considine of the *Washington Post* in his highly descriptive style, 'tightened and retightened through weeks of training until he was one pregnant package of coiled venom. Schmeling hit that spring. He hit it with a whistling right-hand punch in the first minute of the fight – and the spring, tormented with tension, suddenly burst with one brazen burst of activity. Hard, brown arms, propelling two unerring fists, blurred beneath the hot white candelabra of the ring lights. And Schmeling was in the path of them, a man caught and mangled in the whirring claws of a mad and feverish machine.'

When Schmeling got to his feet, he made his way through the happy little crowd in Louis' corner. Putting his arm around his conqueror, he managed a smile. No words were spoken. In the dressing room packed with over 40 reporters, Louis said, 'Yes, it sure feels good to be the undisputed champion now.' Asked if he was hurt at any time, he said, 'No, never. The right he threw just grazed me.' Was he always confident of beating Schmeling? 'From the moment I signed the contract in Mike Jacobs' office, I felt I was going to win. I've been telling folks at my training camp for the last few weeks that I'd do it in one round.'

Max was taken to the Polyclinic Hospital in Manhattan, where he was detained for ten days. It was discovered that Louis' punches had cracked several vertebrae in his back. Schmeling's trainer, Max Machon, complained that Louis' initial volley had included an illegal kidney punch, and even refused visitors, including the press, friends and Louis himself. The claim of foul resounded hollowly in the media, however, and Machon eventually chose not to file a formal complaint.

'I don't remember being led out of the ring,' said Schmeling in his autobiography almost 40 years later. 'Suddenly I was lying in my dressing room with the ring doctor bent over me. Then I was in an ambulance, being taken to the hospital. As we drove through Harlem, there were noisy, dancing crowds. Bands had left the nightclubs and bars and were playing, and there was dancing on the sidewalks and streets. The whole area was filled with celebration, noise, and saxophones, continually punctuated by the calling of Joe Louis' name.'

The Nazi hierarchy, having already banned newsreels of the fight, had now effectively disowned their one-time hero. Schmeling would reflect in later years, 'From the distanced perspective of age, I have to believe that the defeat had its positive side as well. A victory over Louis would have made me forever the "Aryan Show Horse" of the Third Reich.'

Schmeling and the Nazi authorities were growing further apart. On the night of 9 November, a little over four months after the Louis fight, more than 7,000 Jewish shops in German cities and towns were wrecked and looted, as well as hundreds of synagogues burnt down. The night of terror came to be known as Kristallnacht, or crystal night. The following day, Schmeling provided sanctuary for two young Jewish boys to safeguard them from the Gestapo, the German secret police.

The Louis–Schmeling fight had racial as well as political undertones. Much of black America had pinned its hopes on the outcome, seeing Louis' success as a vehicle for advancing the cause of African-Americans everywhere.

In consulations with his co-managers and promoter Jacobs, Louis decided to take a six-month break from boxing after the Schmeling fight. He needed relaxation from the rigours of training. He organised a softball team made up of youngsters from East Detroit. Known as the 'Brown Bombers', he toured the country with them, staying in expensive hotels and paying all the bills. The tour proved to be a costly venture and when the season was over, he had lost $50,000. He had, by then, also taken to riding show horses with his co-manager, John Roxborough, and purchased a 440-acre farm neat Utica, Michigan. It was called Spring Hill Farm.

It was one investment made by Louis that did not result in a financial loss. In 1946, the state of Michigan bought the property and turned it into a public park. Out of the proceeds, Louis received the $8,500 he had invested in the land.

But in 1939, the money was going out as fast as it came in. His wardrobe included over 100 suits and he bought new cars for Marva, his mother and sister Vunies. Joe and Marva already had a couple of cars in their large garage. He was also footing the bills to put Vunies through Howard University and paying the mortgages on houses bought for other members of the family. He opened a fried chicken restaurant in East Detroit, an ill-fated venture as it turned out. It cost Joe $25,000.

Louis was also as easy target for people with hard-luck stories, and there were many. Mannie Seamon, an assistant trainer who would become Louis' full-time coach after the death of Blackburn in 1942, recalled, 'They should have called him "can't say no Joe" because he was his own worst enemy. He liked fun and laughter, and guys clowning around, and he paid for it all. Anyone could give him a hard-luck story and as soon as it was over, he'd reach into his pocket and pay. Age failed to make him any wiser when it came to handing out money. As he grew older, he tossed away even larger amounts on good times.'

Louis was spending money, too, on an assortment of girlfriends away from the eyes of Marva, although as in the past, there was evidence that she knew all about his philandering, preferred to say nothing and tried to keep the shaky marriage together. 'Shortly after establishing himself as a figure of note with the Carnera bout, he began a lifelong career of consorting with women,' said Louis' biographer Gerald Astor. Quoting an acquaintance from this period, the writer said, 'Louis would come into town, go up to a club in Harlem and the manager would bring out all the girls in the show. Joe would pick out one and spend a day or so with her in the Hotel Theresa.'

There was always an urgent need for ready cash, and the quickest way of earning it was between the ropes. Planning to return to action in the New Year, Louis was determined to be a fighting champion. Indeed, in the 29 months from January 1939 through to May 1941, he defended his title 13 times, a frequency unmatched by any world heavyweight champion since the Queensberry Rules were drafted in 1867.

The pace of the title defences, combined with his convincing wins, earned Louis' opponents from this era the collective nickname, the Bum of the Month Club. Despite the disparaging tag, most of the group were top-ten heavyweights and the best around, but the nickname stuck.

Louis' first ring appearance after the Schmeling fight was against John Henry Lewis, the former world light-heavyweight champion, at Madison Square Garden on 25 January 1939. The fight created a bit of boxing history. It was the first ever world heavyweight title fight between two black boxers in the United States, and only the second all-black championship bout among the big boys anywhere in the world since Jack Johnson boxed a draw with Jim Johnson over ten rounds in Paris on 13 December 1913. Lewis was also the first black American to win the light-heavyweight title.

Lewis was a capable fighter, clever and with a hard punch in both hands. Gilbert Odd, the British historian and author, described him as 'a gentlemanly person who possessed boxing brains and fistic ability to a high degree'. Born in Los Angeles, Lewis' great-great uncle was Tom Molineaux, the celebrated American bare-knuckle fighter of the early 1880s. Lewis moved to Phoenix, Arizona when his father got a job as a trainer for the University of Arizona track and field teams. Lewis senior also opened a gym in Phoenix and a young-age John Henry and his brother were put to work in the gym, fighting 'midget boxing' exhibitions. Later, the three Lewises toured the south-west in such exhibitions.

Given this early training, Lewis was well prepared to turn professional at the age of 14 as a welterweight in 1928. Three years later, he won the Arizona middleweight championship. In 1932, Lewis received wide attention by winning a points decision over future world heavyweight champion James J. Braddock in San Francisco. Within three years, he was world light-heavyweight champion.

Lewis' first two defences were against English challengers in 1936. He outpointed the British middleweight champion

Jock McAvoy in New York over 15 rounds and then beat the skilful light-heavyweight Len Harvey, who would win three British titles in a distinguished career, over a similar distance at Wembley. While there were no arguments about his win over McAvoy, who could never get past the American's rapier left jabs, the Harvey fight was closer. Lewis had had to bring out his best to earn a narrow though deserved victory over the Cornishman.

Lewis returned home to make three more successful defences of the title but lack of financial reward, as well as the absence of any logical contender, prompted him to move into the heavyweight division. 'No light-heavyweight champion has ever won the big title,' he told promoter Mike Jacobs. 'Why not me?' Jacobs knew Lewis had little chance, even though he had been victorious in 100 of his 115 fights, with five draws. It was a big payday he was after, and a Louis fight would bring that in.

The promoter got his publicity people working overtime to sell the fight, which looked a one-sided match, on paper at least. He was worried, too, that the fans might not turn out in large numbers, so he kept prices low. He was told that a heavyweight championship fight between two black men would never be a big crowd-puller, and was even advised to forget about the whole thing. Even in bouts involving black against white, the critics said that most of the crowd came to see the black man beaten. On this particular point, Jacobs disagreed. 'They don't come to see Louis licked,' he maintained tersely. 'They just come to see Joe.' As it happened, a crowd of nearly 20,000 packed Madison Square Garden to see the fight.

Prior to the bout, rumours were circulating in gyms around New York that as Louis and John Henry had been close friends for some time, the 'Brown Bomber' would let Lewis last the full 15 rounds and Joe would be content with the decision. The rumours made their way into some newspapers. Nobody who had followed Louis' career believed them on the basis that Joe always wanted to get his fights over as quickly as possible, and the Lewis fight would be no exception. There were also stories that Louis had been told that the vision in Lewis' left eye was less than efficient, and that he would be advised to finish off the challenger as early as possible.

At the weigh-in, Lewis looked drawn and nervous as he stepped on to the scales, balancing the bar at 180lb. Louis weighed 200lb. The fight itself was over before many fans had even settled into their seats. Latecomers missed it altogether. Louis knocked his opponent down three times with hooks and uppercuts before referee Arthur Donovan intervened at 2:29 of the first round.

Louis would reveal the truth behind the fight in later years. 'I wasn't happy about that fight,' he recalled, 'but I knew John Henry was on the way out. At least by getting into the ring with me, he'd had the glory of fighting for the heavyweight championship of the world – and he made a good dollar.'

Jack Roper was next for the chopping block. A rangy if awkward southpaw from Louisiana and based in Hollywood, California, Roper entered the ring at Wrigley Field, Los Angeles as a 10/1 underdog, having lost 39 and drawn 11 of his 111 fights. Roper lasted nine seconds less than John Henry Lewis. Louis had his opponent down three times in the first round, the last count reaching ten. Roper's comment to a radio announcer in the dressing room is remembered more than the brief fight. Asked what happened, Roper said, 'I zigged when I shoulda zagged.'

Over in Orange, New Jersey, a brawler with a 76-23-5 record, who ran a local bar known as The Nut Club, was making all kinds of noises about being 'the best heavyweight in the world, including Joe Louis'. Possessing a wicked left hook, Tony Galento, born Dominic Antonio Galento, was a no-holds-barred fighter who never let the niceties of the ring rules or sportsmanship interfere with his aim to knock out his opponent in the shortest possible time. In the 2003 book, *Boxing's Most Wanted: The Top Ten Book of Champs, Chumps and Punch-Drunk Palookas*, Galento was named the fourth-dirtiest fighter of all time.

Tony went through nine managers, including former great Jack Dempsey. When Mike Jacobs offered Galento a title fight with Louis, he was managed by Joe Jacobs, seventh in the list and who had looked after Max Schmeling, now eliminated as a championship contender. 'Me fight Louis?' said Galento. 'Why not? Bring him on. I'll moider da bum.'

Joe Jacobs boldly forecast he would have his second world champion in Galento. Mike Jacobs announced that the championship fight would be held at the Yankee Stadium on 28 June 1939. Not only was Louis expected to win but he was an 8/1 favourite to stop the New Jersey challenger, who was on an 11-fight winning streak at the time.

The promoter did not have to encourage his publicity men to get to work on Galento. Tony did most of it himself. Jacobs helped out by having the challenger pose for photo opportunities as Tony guzzled drink from bottles, even kegs. When officials from the New York State Athletic Commission complained that his beer drinking was discrediting boxing, Galento impudently posed while drinking from a milk bottle as manager Jacobs was trying to snatch it from him.

Known as 'Two-Ton Tony', he got his nickname from one of his early managers. Asked why he was nearly late for one of his fights, he replied, 'I had two tons of ice to deliver on my way here.' He was reputed to do his roadwork after he closed the bar at 2am. When asked why he trained at night, Galento replied, 'Cos I fight at night.' He was also known to refrain from showering to encourage body odour, a strategy to distract his opponent. When he fought Max Baer, the former world heavyweight champion commented, 'Galento smelled of rotten tuna and a tub of old liquor being sweated out.'

Philadelphia promoter Herman 'Mugsy' Taylor, who had promoted several of Galento's earlier fights, told Bob Considine of the *Washington Post* a week before the fight: 'This fellow honestly thinks he is going to win. Hell, he knows he can't move around like Louis or box with him, but he can punch, and punch hard. He has a good chance against Louis, believe me.'

Galento, who was 5ft 9in, usually weighed in at about 235lb for his fights. He achieved this level of fitness by eating whatever and whenever he wanted. A typical meal for Tony consisted of six chickens and a side of spaghetti, all washed down with a half-gallon of red wine or beer, or both, at one sitting. When he did go to training camp, he foiled his trainer's attempts to modify his diet, and terrorised his sparring partners by eating their meals in addition to his own.

He was reported to have eaten 52 hot dogs as a bet before facing heavyweight Arthur DeKuh, and was so bloated before the fight that the waistline of his trunks had to be slit for him to fit into them. Galento would claim that he was sluggish from the effects of eating all those hot dogs, and that he could not move for three rounds. Nevertheless, he knocked out the 6ft 3in DeKuh with one punch, a left hook to the body, in the fourth round.

Galento trained at Asbury Park, New Jersey, where he constantly belittled Louis and made derogatory remarks about Joe's wife Marva. Asked by a reporter at the camp what he really thought about his chances against the world heavyweight champion, he repeated his oft-quoted claim, 'I'll moider da bum. Look, if you and your colleagues drop into my bar in Orange, you'll see a banner above the counter that says as much, "Bring on Joe Louis. I'll moider da bum" and that's it.

I telephone Louis every day and tell him so.' Asked if he was fit, he said in all seriousness, 'I haven't been drinking for two whole days.'

Another reporter decided to test Galento on his literary knowledge. 'What do you think of Shakespeare, Tony?' he asked. Galento thought for a moment and said, 'Shakespeare? Shakespeare? Listen, if he's one of dem foreign heavyweights, I'd moider him too.'

On fight night, close to 35,000 poured into the ballpark to see Louis' third defence of the title. Newspapermen were convinced that anything could happen once the bell sounded, although defeat for the 'Brown Bomber' was considered unthinkable. Most people, according to a poll conducted by the American Institute of Public Opinion a few days previously, wanted Louis to win.

Yet there was a general recognition of the fact that because of Galento's brawling, unorthodox style, and as he knew no fear, the bartender could well cause a big upset. Tony had a dangerous left hook and a powerful right hand, as well as possessing almost overflowing confidence to bring the title back to New Jersey, where Louis' predecessor James J. Braddock came from.

No sooner had referee Arthur Donovan called the principals together for pre-fight instructions and the bell had sent them on their way, the crouching Galento was on the attack. Moving under Louis' left jabs, Tony landed a strong left hook to the head followed by a hard right uppercut to the chin that stunned the champion momentarily. But Louis quickly shook off the effects before Galento was able to follow up his advantage.

At the bell, Blackburn said to Louis, 'You lost that round, "Chappie", but you'll get him. Keep up the jabbing while you wait for the right opening.' Following instructions, Louis dominated the second round, hitting Galento with fast, hard combinations and opening cuts around his eyes and mouth. Towards the end of the round, a short left hook to the chin actually lifted the challenger off his feet before he went down. It was the first time Galento had been on the canvas in 105 fights. He was up before a count could be administered as his supporters cheered.

In the third round, Louis was again hitting Galento with combinations when the challenger suddenly caught him with a wild left hook followed by a roundhouse right – and this time Louis went down. There was a deafening roar from the crowd, which up to now had done everything with their chairs except sit on them. They knelt on them, stood on them, even lifted them up and down in their excitement. For they were witnessing one of the most exciting brawls in heavyweight history. Louis was up at the count of four and took no chances by resuming his jabbing up to the bell.

By now, it seemed anybody's fight. Louis came out of his corner for round four determined to finish off his dogged and dangerous challenger. Jabbing and hooking as he moved around, Louis battered down the game New Jersey battler with a fusillade of powerful lefts and rights that rendered him helpless. Referee Donovan had seen enough and waved his hands wide. It was all over. Galento had done his best but it wasn't good enough. Just 31 seconds remained in the round.

After the fight, Galento was inconsolable and blamed his corner for convincing him to change his style, and to fight cleanly for once. Whitey Bimstein, from Manhattan's Lower East Side and one of the best-known trainers and cut men in the business, recalled, 'He is sitting there on his stool, with blood pouring from his eyes, his nose and his cheek. He won't let me touch the cuts. He won't let me take off his gloves. He pushes me away every time I try to do something for him, and bellows, "You guys wouldn't let me fight my own fight. I'd have knocked that mug cold."'

Louis told newspapermen in the dressing room, 'He hit me real good. You've got to hand it to him. Maybe he looks funny, with his bald head and rotund shape, but he's not afraid. I'm convinced he would go in there with anybody and be confident of winning.' Rubbing his chin reflectively, he added, 'Yeah, he sure can hit.'

Louis and Galento appeared together on *The Way It Was*, a sports nostalgia programme broadcast in January 1976. The show was lively, due almost exclusively to Galento's still-direct and colourful style of engagement. When Louis was asked by veteran fight commentator Don Dunphy if he still had any ill feelings towards Max Schmeling, who had once knocked him out, he said they had not truly been adversaries but indeed 'good friends'.

Louis then pointed at Galento and stated, 'But that little fellow, he really got me mad. All those mean things he said about me while training for our fight.' Louis furthered this statement by revealing that his anger by fight time was such that he had decided to 'carry' Galento and drag the fight out in order to 'punish him for those nasty things he said'. After suffering the knockdown, however, Louis said he changed his mind, 'Galento hit too hard. So I decided I wanted to knock him out as quickly as I could.'

Blondes, brunettes and redheads

The day after the Galento fight, Louis called into Mike Jacobs' office to collect his purse of $114,000 before expenses, taxes and his team's share would be deducted. 'Who have you got next, Mike?' Louis asked. Jacobs ruffled some papers, pulled out a sheet and said, 'There's Bob Pastor for one.' Five months before he won the title, Louis had to go the full ten rounds with the New Yorker before winning the decision. That was in January 1937 at Madison Square Garden. Pastor avoided being knocked down by constantly moving, rarely standing still.

'Pastor's people have been pestering me ever since for a return match but for one thing or another, I never got around to setting it up,' Jacobs went on. 'OK,' nodded Louis. 'Make the arrangements. I'll give him a title shot.'

Since the first fight, Pastor had put together an impressive record that now stood at 38-4-4. He was a leading contender in *Ring* magazine's top ten ratings. He had remained on his feet throughout the first fight by 'running backwards', as one observer put it, but he claimed he did so on the instructions of his manager James J. Johnston. 'This time it will be different,' he told newspapermen. 'I feel I can trade punches with Louis and bring him down, just like Schmeling did.'

The match was scheduled for 20 September 1939 at Briggs Stadium, Detroit. It was scheduled for 20 rounds instead of the normal 15, with Jacobs explaining, 'Just to be a little different.' When this information was relayed to Louis, he cracked with a smile, 'If I can't catch him in that distance, I ain't no good as champion.' Pastor's reaction to the longer distance was, 'It makes no difference, 15, 20, 30 rounds – I'll have him on his back long before the scheduled finish.'

It would be the first appearance for the 'Brown Bomber' in his hometown since he became champion two years earlier. Louis set up camp at Northville, just outside Detroit. It was often visited by friends and local newspapermen who had known Louis in his early years, when he was just another ambitious youngster.

One afternoon, W. W. Edgar of the *Detroit Free Press* dropped into the camp. The newspaper had sponsored the novice tournament in which Louis won his first amateur trophy. Edgar had known Joe since then and had interviewed him several times. On this particular day, he found chief trainer Jack Blackburn in the camp's dressing room. Louis was busy chatting to other reporters elsewhere.

Edgar and Blackburn, old friends, began chatting about Louis and other boxers. 'You know,' said Blackburn, 'one time you asked me if Joe could beat all the other heavyweight champions who went before him, you know, Dempsey, Johnson, Jeffries, Corbett, old John L. himself. I said, "Sure he could." Then you asked me if I thought he could have whipped Sam Langford when Sam was in his prime. This is the same Sam Langford who was deprived of a title fight because of the colour of his skin, and I kinda hinted that Sam might have beaten him.

'I couldn't exactly say it directly because I was training Joe. But you know, I fought Langford and I knew how good a fighter he was. I didn't think I would ever see a fighter who could take the measure of old Sam. But Mr Edgar, I take it all back now. "Chappie" will knock him out. Be sure of that.'

This time Pastor altered his strategy. Instead of moving protectively, he would carry the fight to Louis. He realised that as the fight was scheduled for 20 rounds, it was a long time to run without getting tired. That was enough to convince him on a change of plan. Bob would stand his ground, attempt to get inside and score a dramatic knockout before the champion got into his stride.

On a windswept fight night, a crowd of 32,199 came out to see the action. The Barrow family had ringside seats. Marva stayed at home with his mother, listening to proceedings on the radio. Lillie rarely tuned into the radio to hear her son's fights but Marva persuaded her to do so this time. Usually, after a fight, the announcer Harry Baloch would bring a microphone over to Louis and ask, 'What have you got to say, Joe?' Louis would say, 'Hello mom, I had another lucky night.'

Pastor came out fighting and this played into Joe's hands. Three times in the opening round, he was sent to the boards after being caught by powerful left hooks and hard right uppercuts. Pastor was put down again in the second round, this time by a smashing right cross to the head. This convinced Pastor that his plan was not working and he agreed with his corner to revert to his old hit-and-run style, one that had served him so well in the first fight.

Having lost the first two rounds, the skilful Pastor fared better as time went on and he was leading on points at the close of the tenth round. Trouble lay ahead in the 11th. After referee Sam Hennessey broke both boxers following a clinch, Pastor was moving along the ropes when Louis landed a powerful right to the jaw that sent the challenger down on his back for the fifth time. He struggled to his feet in time before a similar blow dropped him again. As he tried to regain his feet, he looked decidedly wobbly before Hennessey intervened after 38 seconds of the round.

Chatting to former world champion James J. Braddock the next morning over breakfast in his hotel, Pastor said, 'I would have won except for being blinded by blood flowing into my left eye.' Braddock did not agree. 'No Bob, he was hitting you too hard,' said James J.

Looking back on the fight in later years, Pastor gave credit to Louis for being the better man. 'When I got back to my corner after the bell rang to end the sixth round,' he remembered, 'I asked my second, Freddie Brown, "What round is it coming up? Is it the second?" Brown said, "No, it's the seventh, and you're doing well." Oops!

'Really, I was out on my feet for the first six rounds, but I came back according to reports and won the seventh, eighth, ninth and tenth rounds. Then, Louis came back and as I tried to hold, he put me down. I got up but he put me down once more before the referee stopped it. Which was nice, because he probably saved my life. Yes, Braddock was right. He was hitting me too hard. He was a terrific puncher.'

Madison Square Garden was the location for Louis' first fight of 1940. On 9 February, he climbed between the ropes for his fifth appearance at the iconic Manhattan venue. The man in the opposite corner was Arturo Godoy from Chile. A rugged, confident fighter, he was proclaimed by promoter Mike Jacobs in publicity material as 'the most exciting heavyweight to come out of South America since Luis Firpo sent the great Jack Dempsey tumbling through the ropes in a riotous championship back in 1923'. With a solid 54-9-7 record, Godoy boasted he would bring the world heavyweight title to Chile and become a national hero. Most of the crowd of 15,657 fans who paid out $88,491 to see the fight seemingly did not think so, with Louis confidently expected to retain his title for the ninth time and step down from the ring with his 41st win in 42 fights. Godoy, who smiled perpetually from the opening bell, fought out of an exaggerated crouch, his knees bent and his upper body arched forward, so that his elbows were almost touching the canvas.

Puzzled by the South American's unorthodox style, Louis was at pains to get a clean shot at Godoy's chin, or any part of his body for that matter. It was clear that the Chilean, despite his pre-fight boast that he was going to topple Louis, was more content to stay the full 15 rounds and avoid a knockout than defeat the champion.

Every round that passed was virtually the same as the previous one, with Godoy either hugging Louis in the clinches or moving from side to side in that odd style of his. Referee Arthur Donovan looked as frustrated as Louis at the lack of open action and repeatedly ordered the challenger to 'make a fight of it', telling him, 'No more bear-hugging, Godoy.'

Twice in the 13th round, Godoy planted a wet, resounding kiss on Louis' cheek. At the final bell, the South American, looking pleased with himself after lasting the full distance, jumped up and down in the ring as Louis stared at him incredulously.

Godoy's manager, Al Weill, who would later handle world champions Lou Ambers, Marty Servo and most notably Rocky Marciano, raised Arturo's right hand more in show than anything else. There was only one victor. Announcer Harry Baloch pulled down the overhead microphone. It was a unanimous decision: 'The winner and still world heavyweight champion... Joe Louis.'

Two weeks later, both Louis and Godoy were interviewed on a radio programme. 'Champ, the next time we fight, you had better watch out,' said Godoy. 'My five husky brothers back home are looking for a world champ in the family.'

'You mean you want to fight me again?' queried Louis.

'Sure I do,' replied Godoy.

'Listen, Arturo, if you want to fight me again, you'd better bring those five brothers into the ring with you.'

As time proved, Godoy might well have taken Louis' advice. Meanwhile, Jacobs had other ideas. Out in Iowa, a local heavyweight named Johnny Paychek had built up an impressive record, winning 44 of his 50 fights, and was being touted by Jack Dempsey as 'boxing's new white hope'. Paychek looked a worthy opponent for the champion, and Mike Jacobs set up the fight for Madison Square Garden on 29 March 1940.

The newspapers were continually referring to Louis' challengers as members of the 'Bum of the Month' club. The phrase, a derogatory term, was taken up by many fans. Bums? They were actually the best around but some were pretty poor, and certainly not in Louis' class. Then again, who was? Paychek's followers were convinced that Johnny was the man to end Joe's three-year reign.

Unfortunately, the general boxing public did not think so. A little over 12,000 fans, the smallest attendance ever for a Louis title defence, paid $62,481. Answering the bell for round one, Paychek moved cautiously out of his corner, 'looking more scared than any pugilist I can remember', noted Nat Fleischer in *Ring* magazine. With the first punch of the fight, Paychek was on his knees from a short left hook to the chin, his right hand holding the middle rope. He waited until the count had reached nine before getting to his feet and managed to hold on. Louis shook him off but a hard right to the head dropped him for the second time. Once again, Paychek took a count of nine and survived before the bell rang to end the round.

The end was clearly in sight. It was just a question of how much time it would take in the second round, what with Paychek's retreating and holding tactics. The answer was not very long. The challenger fired a long right to the head that missed before Louis countered with a right cross of such power that Paychek fell backwards and landed flat on his back, whereupon referee Arthur Donovan counted him out.

When his seconds brought their bemused contender to his corner, one of them emptied a full bucket of water over him. His manager, Harold Steinman, was flabbergasted. 'Johnny can do much better than this,' he said. 'Much better.'

Fleischer was scathing in his report. 'Whatever fighting qualities Paychek exhibited in his other bouts I don't know because I never saw him in action prior to the Louis affair, but I do know, and so do the sparse crowd who witnessed it, that this performance was pathetic. Fighting is Paychek's business and why he should have gone into the ring on the verge of collapse is beyond understanding.'

Paychek's summary defeat did not diminish him in the eyes of his conqueror, or his family. His grandson, David Levien, said, 'If boxing historians remember his name at all, it was because of what one reporter wrote at ringside, "Did you ever see a ghost walking? I did." Johnny did not talk much about his fights. He was more willing to talk about his training regimen. Five miles of roadwork, ten rounds of shadow-boxing, bag work, skipping rope, the medicine ball for the stomach, two or three more rounds of sparring, and more in the weeks leading up to the fight. This was every day.

'My grandfather was representative of the many journey-men who fell before Louis' fists during Joe's prime. Losing to Louis was no disgrace. As far as I'm concerned, if one has to fight, elects to follow that road, become a contender and fights for the championship of the world, and if one has to lose heavily, then it might as well be against Joe Louis. My grandfather's journey took him closer to greatness than most men ever come. He was certainly no bum.'

Louis never considered his opponents during that period as 'bums of the month'. 'They were hard-working professionals trying to make a living,' he explained. 'I knew the hard training they went through, and I knew the dreams they had. It was no different from me.

'I respected every man I fought. It's no easy job climbing those steps and getting into a ring. You've got to have a special kind of grit.'

Arturo Godoy was now the *Ring*'s number one contender, having gone the full 15 rounds with Louis seven weeks earlier. Mike Jacobs knew he had been clamouring for a return fight and following consultations with the Louis team, the championship match was set for the Yankee Stadium on 20 June. 'This time, Godoy won't get a chance to get into that ridiculous style of his,' Louis told Blackburn. 'He'll last maybe seven or eight rounds, I guess.' Blackburn nodded approvingly.

Leading up to the fight, Louis' mind was not wholly devoted to boxing. After going into training at Greenwood Lake, he took a few days off to visit Washington and see his sister Vunies graduate from Howard University and receive her diploma. He thought it was wonderful to have a college graduate in the family. He gave Vunies a Packard car as a graduation present and told her that if she wanted to do graduation work in history at Michigan University that he would be glad to arrange it. Vunies decided she would. Joe returned to Greenwood Lake refreshed after his short break.

There was only mild interest in the match. Another quick victory for Louis? Just 26,000 fans turned up at the sprawling ballpark to see how it all worked out. Soon after referee Billy Cavanaugh called the two men to the centre of the ring for last-minute instructions and the bell rang, Louis decided to take charge. Godoy still came forward in that peculiar crouching style but the champion was able to get through his defence with stinging left jabs and short, sharp right hooks and uppercuts.

By the seventh round, Louis had a commanding lead. Godoy's face was cut and bruised. Every time his head bobbed up, Louis was able to score with shots from both hands. In the eighth, a sharp right uppercut dropped the Chilean and he took a count of nine. On rising, Louis went in again and knocked his man down for a second count, this time with a smashing left hook, before Cavanaugh yelled, 'That's enough' and showed the outclassed and bemused challenger to his corner.

Instead of following instructions, Godoy rushed across the ring and threatened to hit Louis, who was preparing to leave. Joe's co-manager, Julian Black, and trainer, Jack Blackburn, wrestled with Godoy until he had calmed down before he was escorted down the ring steps by a police officer. When Louis was asked in the dressing room what he intended to do if Godoy had swung a punch at him, he replied with a grin, 'Oh, I wasn't going to do anything about it. I had a lot of protection in that ring.' Once again, Louis had done better in a return fight.

If Louis was active in the ring, with no less than 11 title defences in three years, including five in the previous 12 months, he was also active in his love life. In between fights, and without his wife Marva, he would visit the Cotton Club in Harlem. One night, in the company of a playboy pal named Dickie Welles, he was introduced to the glamorous Hollywood movie star Lana Turner and started a hot relationship.

Known as 'The Sweater Girl', the stunningly beautiful blonde actress had a reputation for being flirtatious and was said to have had steamy affairs with several of her leading men, including Clark Gable and Spencer Tracy. One of Turner's most quoted comments was, 'I find men terribly exciting, and any girl who says she doesn't is an anaemic old maid.'

Louis told his pal Welles that he did not really love Turner, even though they met often. 'Lana's busy movie career kept getting in the way of our relationship,' he once told Welles. Such was not the case with a glamorous dancer named Ruby Dallas. He met her at the Cotton Club and they fell head over heels in love. Louis also fell for the charms of Lena Horne, the black singer.

Horne was a dynamic performer of striking appearance and elegant style, and Louis would visit her when she was performing at the Blackstone Hotel in Chicago. He would often accompany her on the piano and retire to her quarters afterwards. Lena later became an established star of many Hollywood musicals and whenever Louis was out west, he would make sure to pay her a visit. One of her big hits was the song 'Stormy Weather' – but her relationship with the world heavyweight champion was always calm and smooth.

Louis explained away his affairs in later years. 'A big movie star would see me, the heavyweight champion of the world, and wonder how I am in bed,' he said. 'I see a big, beautiful movie star and wonder how she was in bed. We would find out very easy. Many were one-night stands. But we both knew to keep it cool. Neither of us could afford to be found out in America in those days.' On another occasion, he compared his capacity for having affairs to alcoholism. 'I got drunk with all these beautiful women.'

Shirley Povich, an established writer and columnist with the *Washington Post*, explained, 'We respected an athlete's private life. We overlooked their peccadilloes, though we knew about them. Joe was a womaniser, a lot of us knew about that, or heard the rumours, but we didn't write anything about it, just like we didn't write certain things about Babe Ruth and other sports figures. These were the policies of the time. I personally didn't feel any hypocrisy. There was no conflict there. The feeling was that it was none of the public's business.'

Whether Louis was away in New York or Hollywood or anywhere else, it was always the same. Even during training, he would often slip away for his misdemeanours. Playing in celebrity golf tournaments, or making personal appearances, it made no difference. Marva was always expected to stay at home, doing her duties as the faithful wife.

The celebrity marriage had been heading for the rocks for years but they stayed together. Marva always knew about her husband's affairs but tried not to make a big issue of it, hoping Joe would change his wandering ways. He never did. They stayed married, though they lived apart most of the time. She rarely saw her husband more than once a week while he was in training.

On fight nights, women flew in from cities around the country, checking in to Harlem rooming houses or hotels and then sitting in select seats at ringside. According to one Louis biographer, Richard Bak, 'Joe was an equal opportunity lover, bedding down waitresses, actresses, models, cigarette girls, singers, showgirls and society mavens of every race, shape and creed.'

In 1943, Marva would give birth to a daughter, Jacqueline, named after Jack Blackburn, but this event did little for the shaky relationship. Louis was still living a bachelor's life. For appearances' sake they stayed together before Marva finally served him divorce papers.

The divorce came through in March 1945. Surprisingly, they were remarried in 1946, and in 1947 Marva gave birth to a baby boy, Joe Louis Barrow Junior. But Louis Senior could still not leave other women alone. One evening in 1949, Marva got a tip-off that her husband was in a certain hotel room with a woman. She walked into the bedroom and discovered it was true. Marva divorced him again, this time for keeps.

Tired and weary of his unrelenting womanising and his long absences from home, both of which would also mitigate against their two young children, it was finally all over. Louis tried to make her change her mind but she was adamant. Joe did not contest the action. Marva subsequently married a noted medical practitioner, Dr Albert Spalding.

Marva would remember in later years that she thought fame had a lot to do with Joe's free and easy life, with women throwing themselves at him at every opportunity. 'Eventually you tire of it,' she said, 'the crowds knocking your hat off and pushing you out of the way to reach him. Fame is the most difficult thing that can happen to a relationship. Your life is not your own. You always have to be up and on the scene. Joe was very proud, too. "Oh Marva, you can't wear that," he'd say. "Change your clothes." You see, you represent them, and they want you to be tops. At least, Joe did.'

***

For his fourth and final fight of 1940, Louis returned to the ring on 16 December to meet Al McCoy, the heavyweight champion of Canada and New England. The match was set for the Boston Garden and it would be the first ever world heavyweight title fight in that city. John L. Sullivan, the 'Boston Strong Boy' and probably the most famous Bostonian in sporting history, had fought in the city but never as world heavyweight champion.

McCoy was a French-Canadian whose real name was Florin Alfred LaBrasseur. His mother was Irish. He was a big favourite in Boston and local fans were looking forward to the fight. Nobody gave the challenger much of a chance of lasting six or seven rounds, let alone winning, but the opportunity of seeing their man up against the great Joe Louis was enticing.

It was not an exciting fight. McCoy was understandably cautious, knowing Joe's reputation, and contented himself with moving around and firing the odd left jab. Louis himself was rusty, showing the effects of his six-month lay-off, but he shook up McCoy with jarring left hooks and strong right uppercuts in the opening rounds as if to show who was boss. By the end of the fifth round, McCoy was well behind on points. His left eye was completely closed and he was looking the worse for wear when referee Johnny Martin intervened. In the dressing room, Louis told reporters, 'It was a lousy fight. I'm mighty sorry I couldn't do better. I'm sure I must have looked bad in there.' McCoy said, 'I did my best but Louis is a great champion.'

John Lardner, in his *Newsweek* column, summed up the opinions of most sports writers when he defended the fight. 'McCoy wanted the fight. His manager wanted the fight. His promoter wanted the fight. And the public wanted to pay to see him fight,' he wrote. Two days later, Louis got his call-up papers to register with his draft board at Camp Upton, Long Island. He was now Private Joe Louis Barrow, with an allowance of $12 a day. He would get passes from the army authorities to continue his boxing activities.

At the beginning of 1941, as he did every year, Nat Fleischer, editor and publisher of *Ring* magazine, would study the performances of boxers who had fought over the previous 12 months. In consultation with his staff, Fleischer would select the Boxer of the Year and award him a gold medal. The practice began in 1926, when Gene Tunney won the award. In the following years, it went to champions including Max Schmeling, Tommy Loughran, Barney Ross, Henry Armstrong, Tony Canzoneri and Louis himself, in 1935, 1937 and 1938. Louis won it again in 1940.

Jacobs announced that Louis' next opponent would be James Clarence 'Red' Burman at Madison Square Garden on 31 January 1941. It was the third year of his Bum of the Month campaign, a reference Louis still resented. Joe was now going for his 45th win in 46 fights, and his 13th successful defence of the title. Lucky number for Burman, from Baltimore, Maryland?

221

The challenger thought so, with a 73-16-2 record to back him up. He had fought Tommy Farr on two occasions, defeating the Welshman in New York in March 1938 and losing the return in London four months later. Both bouts went to points decisions.

Burman put up a spirited performance against Louis, unafraid to mix it with the hard-hitting champion. In the third round, Louis went to the canvas briefly. He claimed that Burman had hit him with a glancing right-hand blow that caused him to slip but Burman always insisted it was definitely a knockdown. Louis opened up in the fifth round and finished his opponent with a solid right to the body. As Burman climbed to his feet at eight, he looked unsteady and referee Frank Fulham called it off with ten seconds remaining in the round.

Jacobs, in association with local promoter Herman Taylor, next lined up contender Gus Dorazio for Louis. With an eye on local fans turning out to see their hero, the promoters set the scheduled 15-rounder for the Convention Hall, Philadelphia on 17 February 1941. A rugged battler from the city's tough south side, Dorazio is often cited as one of the inspirations for the Rocky of movie fame, although Sylvester Stallone, who created the character, always insisted that he based Rocky on Chuck Wepner, a world-ranked heavyweight of the 1970s.

Dorazio was a former Golden Gloves winner and had lost just nine and drawn one of his 61 professional fights. In December 1938, he achieved a notable victory when he decisioned Bob Pastor, who had gone the full ten rounds with Louis over a year earlier. Dorazio had Pastor on the boards for two counts. Jacobs and Taylor felt that Gus might provide good opposition for the champion, although the people who set the odds did not think so. They made him a 15/1 outsider.

A crowd of 15,902 passed through the turnstiles, expecting a good fight, despite the landslide betting figures. It was the largest attendance for an indoor event in the sports history of Philadelphia. Louis got down to work quickly. Jabbing the crouching Philadelphian, he moved around his man and peppered him with an assortment of lefts and rights. Going back to his corner at the bell, Dorazio was marked around the eyes.

At the bell starting round two, Dorazio missed Louis' chin with a long right but Joe opened up the challenger's defence with two fast left jabs followed by a sharp, short right. The last punch staggered Dorazio before he went down on his back. He struggled to rise but referee Irving Kutcher counted to ten. The round had lasted 90 seconds. 'I was sure I could have beaten Louis if I hadn't left my feet after throwing a right hand and he nailed me,' said a badly bruised Dorazio.

It was Louis' 14th defence of the title. No previous heavyweight champion had put his championship on the line so many times, the previous best being 12 by the French-Canadian Tommy Burns shortly after the turn of the 20th century. A few days after the Dorazio bout, Johnson came back into the picture with a proposition to James J. Johnston, the former Madison Square Garden promoter.

Johnston was now manager of several leading boxers at the time, including heavyweight contender Abe Simon. Jacobs was considering Simon as the next challenger for Louis and signed the fight for the Olympia Arena, Detroit on 21 March 1941. A native New Yorker, a year earlier he had defeated Jersey Joe Walcott, who would go on to win the world heavyweight championship in 1951. Simon was also one of the heaviest men to fight for the title. At 250lb and 6ft 4in, he spotted Louis 40lb. Nowadays, heavy fighters like Simon are commonplace but back in the 1940s, they were regarded as unusual.

Simon was trained by Freddie Brown, who would later win acclaim as coach for world champions such as Rocky Marciano, Roberto Duran, Larry Holmes and Rocky Graziano. When the

Louis fight was arranged, Simon's manager was approached by Jack Johnson, who offered his services as Abe's assistant trainer. James J. thought it might be a good idea to have the former world champion help out, and signed him on.

It was a good idea, as well as a nice angle for the press. Sportswriters thought it was symbolic that Louis and Johnson should be in opposite camps, and the publicity-conscious Jacobs made the most of the link, sending reams of press releases all over the country.

Louis did most of his training in Detroit but often worked out on his ranch at Spring Farm. He invited Mike Jacobs, newspapermen and various hangers-on to the farm for dinner one day, and urged them to tuck into the food and drinks on the long table. When Jacobs had finished his meal, he was approached by Johnston, who had gatecrashed the party and remained imperturbable in the enemy camp. 'Come on, Mike,' he said, 'let's show the champ and the boys here some fancy footwork.' With that, he hauled an unwilling Uncle Mike in front of the gathering and as the pair pranced around the temporary wooden floor, there was laughter and cheers all round.

Johnston told Jacobs he was planning to match Simon with his other boxer, Bob Pastor, a two-time victim of Louis, after Abe beat Louis. As it worked out, Johnston did not have to worry about his proposed Simon–Pastor title fight. It never happened. Nor was Jack Johnson's help of any benefit to Simon.

Louis had Simon down for a short count in the opening round. As he lay on his back, ringsiders were surprised to see him grinning widely before climbing to his feet. Asked later about his odd behaviour, he replied, 'It was the first time I had been knocked down cleanly in 42 fights, and the thought struck me. "Abe, what a funny-looking sight a big hulk like you must be to all those people sitting out there."'

Despite the knockdown, Simon put up a good fight, standing up to Louis' heavy punches and keeping the champion off with strong left jabs and hooks. But in the 13th round, Louis caught up with him. Countering one of Simon's long lefts with a crashing right to the jaw, Louis sent the challenger down for a count of eight. He rose but Louis put him down again. On getting to his feet, he appeared groggy and referee Sam Hennessey called it off at 1:20 of the round. Back in his corner, Simon told trainer Freddie Brown, 'Hell, I kept seeing three Joe Louises coming at me.' Brown replied, 'Well then, you should have hit the one in the middle.'

Two weeks after the Simon fight, Louis took on Tony Musto from Blue Island, Illinois at the St Louis Arena, Missouri. Fans did not expect it to last too long, especially after Musto was down in the third round from a sharp right to the jaw. A gritty battler, he managed to stay around for the ninth round, though well behind on points, when referee Arthur Donovan intervened with blood streaming from Musto's right eye.

Next up was Buddy Baer. Born Jacob Henry Baer, Buddy came from Denver, Colorado and began boxing in September 1934, three months after his elder brother Max became world heavyweight champion. Standing a fraction over 6ft 6in and generally weighing over 230lb, Buddy possessed a knockout punch in both hands, particularly his right. In 2003, he would appear on *Ring* magazine's list of the 100 greatest punchers of all time. Baer qualified for the title fight by stopping an earlier Louis victim, Tony Galento, in seven rounds and was, by all accounts, a worthy contender. Jacobs announced the fight for 23 May 1941 and the venue would be Griffith Stadium, Washington DC.

Louis had never boxed in the city before and looked forward to appearing there. It was also the first heavyweight championship bout to be staged in the capital. Six years earlier, he had stopped the elder Baer in four rounds. Could he complete the family double? A crowd of 24,812 paying $195,183 would soon find out. At the weigh-in, Louis had scaled 201lb and Baer 26lb heavier.

There was action straight from the bell. Seconds after Louis scored with two fast left jabs, Baer circled the champion and landed two solid left hooks to the head, the second punch sending Joe reeling through the ropes, where he dangled for a few seconds, his shoulders brushing the ring apron and his legs entwined in the ropes.

Louis managed to scramble to his feet without any help from sportswriters, as back in 1923, when Luis Firpo knocked Jack Dempsey out of the ring and reporters pushed him back. Louis was back inside the ropes at referee Arthur Donovan's count of four, and ready for action, thinking to himself, 'This guy is no so-called Bum of the Month.'

Louis kept Baer at a distance with left jabs until the bell rang, ending round one. Blackburn warned him, 'This guy is dangerous. Soften him up with jabs and hooks.' Baer went on the attack in the second round in an attempt to follow through on his earlier advantage, but the champion had made a good recovery and was landing crisper punches with both hands. Through the next three rounds, Louis began piling up the points with his better boxing but Baer closed Joe's left eye with some sharp rights.

Any chance of capitalising on the injury evaporated in the sixth round when, early on, Louis got through with an assortment of jabs and hooks from both hands before a powerful right cross sent the challenger down for a count of six. As soon as Buddy got to his feet, Louis landed another heavy right. He was anxious to end the bout before the bell rang. Baer went down again and struggled to his feet at the count of nine.

Louis rushed across the ring and landed another desperate right just as the bell rang, knocking Baer unconscious.

Buddy's manager, Ancil Hoffman, and his trainer, Ray Arcel, vigorously protested that the final punch had landed after the bell and claimed that Louis should be disqualified. Referee Donovan rejected the claim. 'This is an outrage,' yelled Arcel. 'Donovan is Louis' friend and lets him get away with anything, even blatant fouls.'

When the bell rang, Baer was still sitting on his stool, with Hoffman standing in front of him, insisting that they were unwilling to continue. When Donovan told Hoffman that he had no right to be in the ring as the fight was officially still on, the manager refused to budge. Donovan then promptly disqualified Baer and declared Louis the winner and still champion as the crowd roared and screamed in excitement.

The controversy raged on for days. Was Donovan right to disqualify Baer for failing to answer the bell for the seventh round? It was clear that Louis had not fouled intentionally, and just as clearly, he was winning the fight anyhow. Some experts felt that Donovan should at least have given Baer some extra time to recover from the Louis punch. Others said that there was so much noise that nobody, least of all Louis, heard the bell. In any event, it was a very unsatisfactory way to end a world championship fight. Consolation for the 'Brown Bomber' was that he was still champion, with a purse of just under $37,000 to soften any possible gloom.

By now, Louis wanted a rest. Inside five months, he had defended his title five times. Training had drained him of his energy. But Mike Jacobs was already talking of a big summer outdoor fight in 1941, with Louis pitted against the classy Irish-American Billy Conn in New York. The promoter had earlier been getting glowing reports about Conn, who was world light-heavyweight champion at the time, from Nat Fleischer of *Ring* magazine.

'Who is this kid, Nat?' he enquired. 'Would he be able to concede weight to Louis and put up a reasonable fight? More importantly, would the public pay to see him against Louis? After all, he's only a light-heavyweight.' Fleischer assured Jacobs that not only would Conn put up a good fight, he might even win. 'Mike, this kid is pretty hot stuff,' Nat replied. 'They call him the "Pittsburgh Kid". He's smart and he can both box and fight. I reckon he's the man for Louis.'

After Fleischer left the office, Jacobs reached for his *Ring Record Book* on a shelf behind him, turned to Conn's record and seemed impressed. Nat was right. Billy had done well in the heavyweight division. After retaining his light-heavyweight title by outscoring Gus Lesnevich for the second time, he had notched seven straight wins over the big boys, including the hard-hitting Lee Savold, known as 'Lethal Lee', and three men who had fought Louis in title fights, Bob Pastor, Al McCoy and Gus Dorazio.

After a phone call to Conn's manager, Johnny Ray, in Pittsburgh the following day, Jacobs announced the Louis–Conn fight for the Polo Grounds in New York for 18 June 1941. It would be the first appearance for both boxers at the famous Manhattan venue. Owned by the New York Giants baseball club, it was where Jack Dempsey had kept his heavyweight title by knocking out Luis Firpo in a sensational clash in 1923.

It was also the location where Harry Greb had turned back the middleweight challenge of Mickey Walker in another thriller two years later. In June 1960, the Polo Grounds would be the venue where Floyd Patterson recaptured the heavyweight title from Ingemar Johansson not long before it was pulled down.

Billy Conn was guaranteed to provide Louis with serious opposition. A skilful Irish-American from the tough East

Liberty neighbourhood of Pittsburgh, he had relinquished his world light-heavyweight championship after three successful defences to take on the heavyweights, and ultimately a shot at Louis.

As a kid, Conn got into plenty of neighbourhood scraps. 'I'm sure it was my fighting Irish spirit that got me through,' he recalled in an interview with this writer in Dublin in 1972. Both of Billy's grandfathers were Irish, from counties Derry and Cork, and migrated to the United States, settling in Pittsburgh.

'My dad William was a keen fight fan and used to bring me around to boxing shows in the city,' Billy recalled. 'He would tell me all about the best Pittsburgh boxer of them all, the great Harry Greb, the "Pittsburgh Windmill", who had lived just a mile away in Garfield. I was only nine when Greb died in 1926 after failing to recover from surgery to repair facial damage caused by boxing and an auto accident. Greb was the boxer I worshipped. I wanted to be like him and bring another world title to Pittsburgh.'

Unlike most boxers, Conn never boxed as an amateur, going straight into the professional game at the age of 16 in June 1934 as a lightweight. As he grew, he graduated to welterweight and middleweight before settling at light-heavyweight. He rarely weighed more than 175lb, the light-heavyweight limit, yet he was able to beat leading heavyweight contenders with his superb boxing skill. By all accounts, Billy Conn was certainly no 'Bum of the Month'.

Conn normally trained in Pittsburgh but due to the importance attached to the Louis fight, he worked out at Pompton Lakes in New Jersey. In a white-framed house surrounded by a picket fence, Conn seemed a world away from the grimy streets of industrial Pittsburgh but the change in surroundings did not alter his behaviour. Billy thrived on having lots of people around. 'The joint is jumping day and night, and it's great,' he said. Never had so many sportswriters chronicled his activities, and he bathed in the attention. 'Ain't it grand,' he said. 'I don't want them to leave. Why, I used to fight before crowds that were smaller than this.'

Louis trained at the Catskills. He had listened for weeks to all the talk coming from Conn. 'That boy just talks too much,' he told the newspapermen. 'I do my talking in the ring, with my fists. Conn will find that out when the bell rings.'

When one reporter told Conn the next day of Louis' comments, Billy replied, 'I don't really care what he comes up with, but his championship days are over when that last bell rings. Louis better realise that, and realise it soon. When you next see him, tell him I said to enjoy what's left of his reign. He's had a good run, four years, and that's enough. Tell him, too, that when I beat him, I'll give him a return fight. Now I can't be fairer than that, can I?'

The day before the fight, a poll conducted by the Press Association news agency showed that 22 of 33 sportswriters picked Louis, virtually all by a knockout or stoppage, some within seven rounds. Hype Igoe, one of America's best and most perceptive writers when it came to analysing a fight, was among the 11 who tipped the challenger to win. 'The classy, cocky Conn has the speed and ability to take the title off Louis, who is past his best,' he told his readers in the *New York American*. 'He will confuse Louis.' As events were to prove, he was right to a degree.

A cartoon in the *New York World Telegram and Sun* by Willard Mullen showed a badly beaten Louis being carried out of the ring by his disconsolate handlers. The bookies, nevertheless, favoured the champion, establishing him as a 3/1 favourite. Trainloads of fight fans from all over the country had been arriving in New York several days before the bout, and many of them were anxious to bet in support of their convictions.

Louis wanted to weigh in as light as possible for the fight. He knew he would be much heavier than Conn and did not want anybody to regard him as a bully for picking on a much lighter man. 'If I can get well under 200lb, that will be fine,' he told Jack Blackburn. He ate and drank sparingly with a week to go.

On the day of the weigh-in, he balanced the scales at 199lb, weighing less than 200lb for the first time in six fights. But he felt it left him weak. He was also very much dehydrated. When Conn stepped on to the scales, the needle wavered between 169lb and 170lb. Mike Jacobs imaginatively announced that Conn, who was being given little chance to win, weighed 174lb.

Round 9

So near and yet so far

Among the crowds making their way to the Polo Grounds on big fight night were thousands of Irish fans who had chartered a special train from Pittsburgh to New York. They called it 'The Ham and Cabbage Special'. Other Irish supporters came from cities and towns all over the nation to cheer on their hero.

This was one night they could not miss. Mike Jacobs looked happy at ringside after being informed by one of his officials that there were still long queues outside. He was in even better form the next day when told that $386,012 was in the coffers, contributed by a crowd of 56,763. Moreover, there were also broadcasting receipts to come.

Conn was first down the aisle, smiling with his arms raised above his head. Louis followed soon afterwards, both arms hanging loosely by his sides and looking serious. Both boxers' heads were covered by white towels, which they removed when they climbed into the ring to thunderous applause. Harry Baloch made the formal announcements before referee Eddie Joseph called the champion and challenger together. 'Let's have a good clean fight, boys,' he said, after explaining the rules as both boxers made eye contact for the first time. 'Now touch gloves, retreat to your corners and wait for the bell.'

From the outset, Louis stalked Conn, and the challenger, younger by three years, backed away. The fears the 'Brown Bomber' had at the weigh-in about being weak and dehydrated had vanished.

He felt good, confident he could handle the cocky challenger. Pulling back from a Louis left hook, Conn slipped to the canvas but was on his feet quickly and indicated to the referee he was all right. It was a quiet round with no significant punches landed by either man.

Conn was moving away from the champion in the second round and Louis was collecting points on his aggressiveness. By round three, Conn began landing with his left jabs as he offset Louis' right counters with his own right. Billy was content to stay away from Louis' heavier punches and pile up points on his boxing ability.

Joe was having difficulty connecting with a solid punch because Conn was constantly on the move. Back in the corner at the bell, Blackburn advised Louis to take charge. 'He's taking the play away from you, "Chappie". Get out there and show him who's boss,' he said. Blackburn's assistant, Mannie Seamon, shook his head knowingly. 'You've got to keep the pressure on him, Joe,' he said. 'This fella is no fall guy.'

Louis followed instructions and over the next two rounds hammered Conn with rights and lefts to the body and occasional blows to the head. The head shots were proving difficult as Conn was a moving target with his guard held high. Louis got the better of the fifth and sixth rounds on his aggressive tactics as Conn was content to keep on the move, jabbing and hooking mainly from long range. The pace Louis was now setting, however, was beginning to sap his strength. In the seventh round, Conn said to Louis in a clinch, 'You've got a fight on your hands tonight, champ.' 'I know it,' Louis replied wearily, 'but it's not over yet.'

Conn won the eighth round clearly, not only on his better boxing and ring finesse but with his harder, sharper punching. He was catching the champion with left hooks to the head and body, and following through with hard rights to the head. Was losing the weight and coming in below 200lb having a detrimental effect on Louis? Coupled with Conn's speed, it looked like it. The ninth and tenth rounds were good ones for the Pittsburgher as he connected with an assortment of blows and was not afraid to mix it, despite his earlier fears.

Louis came on in the 11th round with heavy attacks that drove Conn back but with two-thirds of the scheduled 15-rounder completed, Billy was still on his feet and likely in the lead on the scorecards of referee Joseph and the two judges. The 12th round saw Conn move around less and punch more as he staggered Louis with a powerful right to the jaw. Once disdaining discretion, he even led with his right and caught Louis full in the face. Joe countered with a big right that caught Conn on the temple.

The challenger wavered but instinctively replied with a flurry of punches, and Louis, startled, lost his advantage. When Conn got back to his corner at the bell, he told his trainer Freddie Fierro, 'This is easy. I'm going to take the son of a bitch out in this round. He's there for the taking.' 'No, no, Billy,' pleaded Fierro. 'You've got it won. Stay away from him. Box him, stick and run.'

Across the ring, Blackburn and Seamon were telling Louis that he would have to knock Conn out or lose the title. Legend has it that Blackburn said, 'I'm tired of going up and down these steps. Get out there and knock this guy out.'

The crowd was now in a frenzy. A sensational upset was on the cards. The bell rang. Conn went straight on to the attack, delivering five solid blows to two from Louis. Joe jabbed Conn with two sharp lefts before they engaged in a toe-to-toe slugging match. That was the fatal mistake the cocky Conn made, the biggest error of his career. Louis was always one of the great finishers.

By far the heavier puncher, he saw an opening and, pushing Conn off, fired two rights that caught the challenger flush on the jaw. A heavy left hook to the chin followed immediately. Conn spun halfway around as he fell, as if he were filmed in slow motion, and sank to the canvas, reaching the ring floor with his left glove, straining for balance.

Referee Joseph picked up the count from timekeeper George Bannon at four. Conn vainly tried to regain his feet but he just could not make it as the seconds ticked by. Billy just about managed to reach his feet as Joseph completed the count with only two seconds of the 13th round remaining. Conn's seconds immediately ushered him to his corner before a mad rush of reporters, broadcasters, police and officials entered the ring. It was bedlam.

Louis had successfully and dramatically defended his title for a record 18th time, his 16th inside the distance. But it had been uncomfortably close. After the 12th round, two of the three officials' scorecards had Conn in front, with the third even. Referee Joseph marked his card 7-5 for Conn while judge Marty Monroe also called it for Conn by 7-4 with one round even. The second judge, Bill Healy, saw it even at 6-6. It is a misconception, however, to claim, as has been done, that Conn would have automatically won had the fight gone the full 15 rounds. Billy would have had to win the last two rounds to take the decision and after being in serious trouble in that 13th round, it seemed unlikely that he could have survived the final six minutes.

James P. Dawson of the *New York Times* called the bout 'one of the greatest heavyweight battles of recent years'. In his coverage and analysis, he wrote, 'The struggle was waged in an atmosphere reminiscent of older and better times in boxing. The great crowd saw Conn fight a battle that was true to his style, of necessity, but better than usual, though it proved inadequate. And the crowd saw Louis fight as a champion should, a champion who refused to become discouraged, though he was buffeted about outlandishly at times. Unmistakably Louis has slipped. Even making allowances for style – the contrast in styles was inescapable – the champion is not the champion of old.

'He was not sure of himself last night, a fact that might be explained by the circumstances which found him in the ring with a veritable wraith for speed. But the speed that Louis once boasted himself is gone, the accuracy behind his punch is diminishing. He is becoming heavy-footed and heavy-armed, weaknesses which were reflected as he floundered at times in his quest of the target that was Conn. One thing remains undiminished. He is still an annihilating puncher. His right hand claims a victim when it lands. His left hook jars a foe to the heels and props him for the finishing potion that is in the right hand.'

Caswell Adams said in the *New York Herald Tribune,* 'If Conn hadn't been Irish, he would be boss of the heavyweight division this morning. But being Irish, he wasn't content to coast and dance and pick up the points in the last three rounds. He simply lost his head.' Conn's manager, Johnny Ray, put it another way. 'If he had a Jewish head instead of an Irish one, he would be the champ,' he said.

Generally speaking, there seemed to be more praise in the press for Conn's performance in taking the lead than Louis' dramatic win after coming from behind. But William G. Nunn, boxing writer for the *Pittsburgh Courier,* heaped praise on Louis. 'For our money, Joe Louis is still the greatest champion ever to grace the ring,' he wrote. 'Louis proved against Billy Conn that he had it in him. With the chips all down... with the cards stacked against him... with 50,000 white folks pleading for Conn and 5,000 blacks praying for Louis to win... the winner and still champion, Joe Louis. Thank God.'

Conn's biographer, Andrew O'Toole, said in his 2008 book *Sweet William, The Life of Billy Conn*, 'Billy had done much to differentiate himself from most of Louis' other victims. No, Billy's name wouldn't be added to the "Bum of the Month Club". His spirit, will and Irish courage, if not his tactical sense, separated him from the long line of palookas that had become fodder in the Jacobs gristmill.'

Looking back on the fight in his retirement years, Louis said, 'I knew Billy was winning. He did too. He had looked like the new "white hope" and he had a big cheering crowd. I hurt my wrist punching down on Conn's head in the seventh round. It nearly killed me for three rounds but the pain went away. He made the mistake of coming out in that 13th round and slugging it out instead of keeping up his boxing. If he had kept his cool, he might have been champion but he didn't. But he was one clever fighter, and we'd meet again.'

Conn recalled, 'Yes, I got a bit cocky after having the heavyweight championship of the world all tied up neatly. After the 12th round, I knew I could win the last three and take the title. I thought how much better it would be if I could knock out the great Joe Louis and become champion, although my corner advised me against it. I went out for the 13th round with the idea of knocking Louis flat on the canvas. He was ready to be taken. I remember cocking my right hand for the final punch of the fight. That's all I remember.

'When my assistants got me back to my corner, they told me there were only two seconds left in the round. I told them they shouldn't have stopped it. "We didn't stop it, Billy, you were counted out," said Johnny Ray amid all the noise around us.

"You were counted out." When I finally recovered my senses, I said I was terribly unlucky. I felt I could have won the last two rounds and stayed in front. But there you go. When I met Louis at some function later, I told him, "You know, Joe, if I had won the title that night, I would have held on to it for ten years." Louis replied, "Billy, how could you have held it for ten years when you couldn't hold on to it for another two rounds?" Joe was a really good guy, a real gentleman.'

Mike Jacobs was rubbing his hands with glee after the result. As well as having Louis under contract, the canny promoter had already signed up Conn for future fights, even if the war intervened. Mike knew that a Louis–Conn return match would be a tremendous attraction whenever it was held. He would be proven right.

Two days after the fight, Germany and its ally Italy ordered all American embassies to be closed until further notice. Soon, German armies would march into Kiev, the capital of the Ukraine, to find it peppered with time bombs and stripped of anything they might find useful. The Soviets had destroyed their own water and electricity supplies rather than allow the Germans to use them. A sworn enemy of Russia's communist regime, Hitler had earlier promised he would not invade the country and concentrate on the west but after the fall of France, this was no longer important. New Yorkers had begun training air raid wardens. Soon, Britain would bring in conscription for women.

Jacobs was determined to salvage as much time as he could before losing Louis, at least temporarily, to war service. Jacobs also signed up Conn for future fights. Uncle Mike could visualise a Louis–Conn return as a big money-spinner and he had no intention of letting it slip. In the meantime, he announced that Louis' next opponent would be Lou Nova, the number one heavyweight contender and a former world and

US amateur champion. The match was scheduled for the Polo Grounds on 29 September.

Nova, a 6ft 3in Californian, had lost only two of his 32 professional fights with four draws and had beaten Tommy Farr, who had gone the full 15 rounds with Louis. Nova had the Welshman in serious trouble when he left him hanging on the ropes in the 14th and penultimate round following a sustained attack. Farr recovered but both boxers were near a state of exhaustion at the final bell. The fight established Nova as a potential heavyweight contender. He would go on to score two stoppage victories over the former world heavyweight champion Max Baer.

In training sessions, it was revealed that Nova was a student of yoga, an ancient Hindu practice. He claimed that through his adherence to yoga, he had developed a 'dynamic stance' and 'cosmic punch' that would befuddle Louis and put the champion into 'a dizzy state of confusion, leaving him open to my heavy punches'. The betting people did not buy into the seemingly crazy idea and installed Louis as a 3/1 favourite.

Before leaving his dressing room, Nova did headstands and meditated. When he got into the ring before a crowd of 56,549, he was all smiles and looked extremely confident. In the far corner, Louis was serious. He had said earlier that he was not impressed at all with the talk by Nova about his so-called 'cosmic punch'. When a newspaperman questioned him on the subject after the weigh-in, he replied, 'I figure Nova is going to be tough, sure, but is he sincere about this yoga stuff? I've never come across it in boxing before and neither have you guys, I'm sure. I'm getting in there to give him my regular right over a left hook and knock him out, maybe in eight rounds.'

As both boxers climbed into the ring, the crowd were anxious to know what a 'cosmic punch' looked like. They were hopeful too that the fight would answer the question of whether or not Louis had slipped and lost his edge. There was no evidence of either in the opening rounds as the 'Brown Bomber' stalked Nova, cautiously and deliberately. Where was the 'cosmic punch?' And the 'dynamic stance?'

After dominating the first five rounds, Louis moved in fast towards the end of the sixth round and dropped Nova with a long right-hand punch. He was up at the count of nine, groggy and seemingly helpless when referee Arthur Donovan intervened with one second remaining in the round. The 'cosmic punch' was just an ordinary right cross and the 'dynamic stance' simply did not exist.

In his retirement years, Nova recalled, 'As I sat there in my corner at the finish while my handlers fussed over me, with my quiet and impassive opponent sitting across the ring from me, I was thinking about those fans and not about the title. I was thinking what I'd got hit with was the most beautiful punch I'd ever seen. I could feel everything in Joe's body behind that punch, right from the toes on up. Wasn't that odd? I'd got hit by Joe and I just sat there like a painter, admitting the fine work by another painter.'

Louis received $199,500 for the fight, his biggest purse since he stopped Max Schmeling three years earlier. Discussion after the bout centred not on whether he had slipped as a boxer but on rumours of an early retirement now that he was in the army. He offered to sponsor a Joe Louis Fund for the Department of Race Relations of the Federal Council of Churches.

'Before I retire, I want to have one more fight,' he said, 'and I would want it to be the best of my career. It would be to help my people. The hardest fight I ever had was against prejudice and intolerance. My people know what I mean. They are all fighting their way up, and I want to open the door a little wider for them, and I propose to start with my own contribution.'

The boxing world, particularly Mike Jacobs, was stirred by the news that Louis was thinking of retirement. Sportswriters debated whether Joe would retire simply for the duration of his military career or permanently. The devastating attack by Japanese forces on Pearl Harbor in Hawaii on 7 December 1941 changed the scene dramatically. America was now at war.

With the uncertainty surrounding everything, Mike Jacobs hit on the idea of Louis boxing for charity. The charity the promoter had in mind was the Navy Relief Society, which helped the families of sailors killed in service in the event of America entering the war. He promptly arranged for Louis to defend his title in a return bout with Buddy Baer, who had been disqualified in controversial circumstances in their first fight a year earlier. The date was 9 January 1942 and the venue Madison Square Garden.

Once again, Jack Blackburn was to be in Louis' corner – and for the last time. The veteran trainer, heading for his 60th birthday, was ill in Chicago with an accumulation of heart disease, arthritis and other ailments. But he would be in the ring for the Baer fight. 'I'll put Baer away in the first round so as "Chappie" will only have to climb those steps once,' said Louis. Mannie Seamon, his assistant trainer, was handling most of Blackburn's duties and told Joe that when he had last seen Blackburn about a month earlier, he looked anything but well.

On fight night Mike Jacobs, a master of publicity, milked the occasion for all it was worth. He organised flags hanging from the rafters and on every inch of wall space. 'As I sat in my corner waiting for the bell to ring, I looked around the Garden and the place looked like the Fourth of July,' Louis would remember. A line-up of past and present world champions was introduced from the ring, as well as prominent politicians and important dignitaries. Among them was Wendell Wilkie, the unsuccessful Republican presidential candidate in 1940.

Louis had actively supported Wilkie during the presidential campaign because he felt that Franklin Delano Roosevelt had not fulfilled his promises to help the black race.

Wilkie made a speech to the crowd and a national radio audience, mispronouncing Louis' name and calling Buddy Baer 'Max', confusing him with Buddy's elder brother. Nobody seemed to care. In the carefully written speech prepared by one of his senior staff, he said, 'Joe Louee, your magnificent example in risking your world championship belt for no monetary gain, won literally with toil and sweat and tears, prompts us to say, "We thank you." And in view of your attitude, it is impossible for me to see how any American can think of discrimination in terms or race, creed or colour.'

Finally, the long drawn-out programme of introductions and speeches was over and the crowd of 16,689 sat back in their seats to await the first bell. It started fast. Baer connected with two left hooks to the head but Louis kept his cool and snapped Baer's head back with a succession of fast, hard punches, the final right uppercut knocking Buddy down for a count of nine. On rising, Baer was put down again with a hard left hook to the head and took a count of eight.

After getting up, he was soon in trouble again as Louis connected with another heavy right to the head and the challenger sank to the canvas for the third time. Baer tried to pull himself up by the ropes but he could not make it and was counted out at 2:56 of round one. 'The only way I could have beaten Louis that night was with a baseball bat,' Baer said later.

'One of the most thrilling things that night was that "Chappie" didn't have to walk up the ring steps for a second time,' said Louis in later years. 'I had to do that for him, my good friend. Another thing that pleased me, apart from winning, was that my man, Wendell Wilkie, was there. He'd made a fine speech before the fight and I enjoyed it. I sure wished that he was our president. After the fight, he came around to the dressing room and we talked. I really liked that man. As for the fight, damn, it takes me longer to talk about it than to do it.'

Receipts for the fight were just over $200,000. Louis' share would normally have been $65,000 but after deducting training expenses, the balance was $49,000, which he donated to the Navy Relief Fund. Baer contributed $4,078 as part of his purse while Jacobs handed over $37,229. This was supposedly the promoter's entire earnings but according to Truman Gibson, a close friend of Joe and a high-ranking War Department aide, Uncle Mike held on to his share of the revenues from radio and film rights, which was considerable.

The public applauded the champion's generosity. The press heaped praise on him. Jimmy Powers in the *New York Daily News* said that for a champion to risk a personal asset worth over $1 million for no return was truly a magnificent gesture. Powers pointed to a comparison with Jack Dempsey, who had dodged the draft in World War One and caused further damage by posing as a shipyard worker for a publicity photograph. This showed the former world heavyweight champion wielding a sledgehammer while wearing striped trousers and shiny patent leather shoes. Dempsey would make amends in World War Two, serving as a lieutenant commander in the US Coast Guard.

Back in uniform the next day, Joe could hardly ignore the problems that had arisen in Team Louis. His managers were in deep trouble. John Roxborough and several associates, including Richard Reading, a former mayor of Detroit, and 25 other political employees and gamblers, were convicted before Judge Homer Ferguson, who sat as a one-man jury investigating corruption in Detroit, and in particular the running of an illegal gambling operation. Eighty-eight policemen were also charged as collaborators. They would be jailed in Jackson State Penitentiary, Georgia.

Reading received a sentence of four to eight years. Roxborough, named as the number two man in Detroit's policy racket, was convicted and sentenced to two and a half years. Julian Black faced a charge of tax evasion, which was dismissed, but his business collapsed due to adverse publicity. At the same time, Louis discovered that his own financial affairs had been totally mismanaged and were a shambles. He owed $117,000 in back taxes.

Rather than deal with tax problems, he asked his accountant, Ted Jones, to pay the bill. But Jones advised him to hold out, build up some more taxes and then do a deal with the Internal Revenue Service. 'In that way, you should not have to pay the full amount,' said Jones. 'These guys have no pity on people who don't pay their due taxes, but they are reasonable at the same time. Due to your celebrity status too, and the fact that you boxed free for the Navy Relief Society, they would most likely look on your case sympathetically.' Louis agreed.

The next day, he called Mike Jacobs to ask for a loan against future earnings. Louis had already borrowed $41,146 from Roxborough, who was now behind bars. The promoter wrote out a cheque for $59,805, handed it to him and said, 'Joe, you should never allow yourself to fall behind in taxes. Too, you want to get the right people looking after your money. There are a lot of gangsters out there on the lookout for a quick buck.' Jacobs had already signed an agreement with Billy Conn to promote his future fights, and now it appeared that the Pittsburgh boxer was already $34,500 in debt to Jacobs. 'I may be Uncle Mike to you guys but I ain't no charitable organisation,' he said to Louis.

When Louis picked up his career after the war, it was as much out of necessity as love of the sport. He repeated what he had said earlier, that he planned to retire after the Conn fight in 1941. Jacobs arranged a Louis title defence for the Army Relief

Fund at Madison Square Garden on 27 March 1942. It was a return with big Abe Simon, who had lasted 13 rounds with the champion a year earlier almost to the day. Simon's greatest achievement was to defeat future world heavyweight champion Jersey Joe Walcott in February 1940.

Entering the ring a heavy underdog, Simon had a 36-9-1 record and was confident he would at least be on his feet at the end of the 15th round. With Jack Blackburn still in hospital in Chicago, Mannie Seamon, who had been Louis' assistant trainer for the previous five years, took over Blackburn's duties. As a tribute to Blackburn, Louis promised to knock out Simon in three rounds. At 255lb, he outweighed the champion by nearly 48lb.

Louis started fast, throwing punches with both hands, though some of the blows were wild. He seemed anxious to get it over as early as possible and fulfil his promise to Blackburn. Seamon calmed his fighter down and Simon survived the first round by moving around with jabs and hooks. In the second round, Louis dropped his man with a battery of punches for a count of two. Joe dominated the third and fourth rounds on his aggression but he still seemed over-anxious for a knockout.

Towards the end of the fifth round, a powerful left hook had Simon on the floor and it did not look like he could rise in time, but he was saved by the bell at the count of seven. The minute's rest on his stool was a welcome respite but the end seemed near. In the sixth, Louis came straight out and landed a left-right combination to the chin and Simon slumped to the boards.

As he struggled to his feet, it was too late and referee Eddie Joseph counted him out. After being declared the winner and still champion, Louis used broadcaster Don Dunphy's microphone to say a few words to Blackburn in hospital. 'I hope you're satisfied, "Chappie", this one was for you,' he said. The ailing trainer, listening to the broadcast 800 miles away, bent over to the radio and said quietly, 'I sure am, "Chappie". Good show.'

From his $45,882 purse, Louis deducted his expenses and handed a $36,146 cheque to the Army Relief Fund. The contributions from Jacobs and Simon brought the total to around $55,000.

A few days after the Simon fight, Louis was presented with the prestigious Edward J Neill trophy as Fighter of the Year for 1941 at a dinner in New York. Awarded annually by the Boxing Writers' Association of America, the trophy was first awarded in 1938. It was named in honour of the sportswriter and war correspondent who died of shrapnel wounds in 1938 while covering the Spanish Civil War. This award was renamed for Sugar Ray Robinson in 2009. Previous winners were Jack Dempsey, Billy Conn and Henry Armstrong.

Army and navy officers were present at the dinner. James J. Walker, the former mayor of New York, was the principal speaker. Walker had made a valuable contribution to the development of boxing. In his days as minority leader of the New York Senate, he sponsored the Walker Law, which legalised boxing in the state and provided a model for its regulation by state athletic commissions. In presenting the award to Louis, he said, 'Joe, we are all proud of you, and proud of what you have done for your race. You never forgot your own people. When you fought Buddy Baer and gave your purse to the Navy Relief Fund, you took your title and your future, and bet it all on patriotism and love of country. Joe Louis, that night you laid a rose on the grave of President Lincoln.'

James A. Farley, former postmaster general, presented Louis with a desk set on behalf of the writers. J Edgar Hoover of the FBI gave a speech, as did John Reed Kirkpatrick, president of Madison Square Garden. Former world heavyweight champion

Gene Tunney dropped his usual conservatism and called Louis the greatest boxer he had ever seen.

When Louis met Jacobs later, the promoter thanked Joe for his kind comments. The promoter pointed out that he planned to help Louis' escalating tax problems. He had in mind a return fight with Billy Conn to benefit the Army Relief Fund and he had the full blessing of the War Department.

The match was tentatively scheduled for early October 1942 at the Yankee Stadium. It would have to be fought in daylight because of blackout restrictions. Jacobs estimated that the fight would draw a big gate in view of the closeness of the first bout. As the date approached, ticket sales amounted to $300,000 and the National Broadcasting Corporation had agreed to pay a record $71,200 for broadcasting rights.

Everything seemed in order and both boxers went into training – Louis at Greenwood Lake, New Jersey and Conn at Jacobs' rambling estate at Rumson, New Jersey. America's top sportswriters sent daily reports back to their newspapers and, from all accounts, the fight looked like being a blockbuster. Both champion and challenger were said to be in fine shape and ready to resume their rivalry.

Jacobs came to an agreement with both Louis and Conn that before the charity saw any of the proceeds, they would settle their debts to him. In addition, the promoter would have full control of monies from the sales of the first 20 rows of ringside seats. Uncle Mike, the old scalper, never changed. He was still the hard businessman out to squeeze the last dollar, the last cent, from any of his enterprises. Even under these arrangements, the fight would have produced as much as $750,000 for the Army Relief Fund. There was no adverse comment in the press. After all, the fund was still benefiting greatly.

In mid-September, with just a couple of weeks to go, the Secretary of War, Henry L. Stimson, abruptly called the fight off. Without mentioning Louis, Conn or Jacobs, he explained at a press conference that it wouldn't be fair to the millions of other soldiers who weren't given similar opportunities to pay off their debts while serving their country in time of war. Stimson remained adamant in his decision, even after both Louis and Conn offered to fight for free. He also banned all similar charities from projects to aid both the Army Relief Fund and the Navy Relief Fund. 'Both agencies are well funded,' he said, 'and we will have to leave it at that.'

Louis, Conn and Jacobs would have to wait until hostilities ended before a return fight could be arranged. In any event, both the New York State Athletic Commission and the National Boxing Association 'froze' the titles in the top four divisions, from heavyweight down to welterweight. Activities would be resumed after the war. The champions involved were Louis, Gus Lesnevich, Tony Zale and Freddie 'Red' Cochrane.

Louis settled into war service, boxing nearly 100 exhibition bouts and travelling thousands of miles from coast to coast to visit bases and make propaganda films. The detachment under the command of Captain Louis Krem was known as the Joe Louis Troupe. The champion's sparring partner was George Nicholson and the group included Sugar Ray Robinson and two welterweights. Generally speaking, the tour was a big success, thrilling thousands of soldiers as the boxers went through their routines much to the delight of the rapt, excited soldier audiences.

A trip through the southern states, however, was not all pleasant, and there were several upsetting episodes. At one camp in Virginia, just before Louis and Robinson were scheduled to go through with their exhibition bouts, a general came into the dressing room to speak to them. Sugar Ray, peering out at the assembled crowd, noticed that there were no black troops in the arena. He asked the general as to the reason for this. Embarrassed, the flustered officer explained that black soldiers were not permitted in that area of the camp. Robinson thereupon announced that he and Louis would not go through with the exhibitions until blacks were admitted.

The general went into another room. Several phone calls were made and there seemed to be a lot of confusion. When the general came back, he announced that black *and* white soldiers would be in attendance. After about 30 minutes, when Louis and Robinson slipped into their gear and went outside to take part in their exhibitions, there was a good mixture of black and white troops ready to watch the two great boxers do their stuff.

At Camp Sibert, Alabama, there was another incident. As Louis remembered it, 'One day, Ray and I were leaving camp and went to the bus station and found it crowded. There was one bus for black soldiers and another for white soldiers. I went to a phone booth to call a cab while Ray stayed outside and made out he was hitting a golf ball with the putter I had with me. I came out of the booth just as a military policeman (MP) came over to me. He said to me, "Hey sergeant, you belong on the other side. This side is for white soldiers."

'Ray would remind me later that I looked mad, and I was. I said to the MP, "Why should I go on the other side? I've got a uniform the same as you, the same as the other soldiers, black and white. I don't stand being discriminated against and neither does my friend here." The MP started pushing us and he grabbed the golf club Ray was carrying. Ray was now mad and he started choking the MP. Everybody started yelling and soon a lieutenant came over and quietened us down but took us off to the guard house. The commanding officer soon heard about this. So did the whole camp. Soon we were released, and everybody apologised, including the offending MPs.'

On another occasion in a southern camp, Louis discovered not only separate buses but separate bus stations. He called Washington and spoke to Assistant Secretary Kenneth Royall to tell him of the situation. Royall said that such conditions could not possibly exist but Louis asked him to call the camp concerned. The following day, the situation was rectified. Louis was getting an inside glimpse of what the war was all about, like a lot of the troops he bunkered with.

Some were just kids who had lied about their age to enlist and what they wanted more than anything was to be back home with their families. For others, being in the army was the best thing that ever happened to them – three square meals a day, proper clothes on their back, a bed of their own. The common motivator was the enemy, whether it was Germany or Japan or both. What upset Joe was that some of them would never make it back alive and, if they were black, still had to sleep in separate barracks, could not go to the same movies as the white troops and could hardly get into officers' training schools. It was all a double standard that was not right at all.

In early April 1942, Louis got a call from Provident Hospital in Chicago to say that Jack Blackburn was not well. Joe received a four-day furlough to visit his faithful old trainer. At the bedside, the world champion and his equally famous coach talked of old times and old fights, and of the good times they shared. On his return to camp, Louis received a terse telegram from a friend saying that "Chappie" had died. Blackburn had recovered from his bout with pneumonia, only to succumb to a fatal heart attack after being released from hospital. As the soldiers in the provost office looked away in respect, the heavyweight champion of the world, the great 'Brown Bomber', broke down and cried.

Louis received a two-week furlough to return to Chicago for the funeral. Thousands of people tried to get into the Pilgrim Baptist Church where the Rev. J. C. Austin addressed the gathering. Paying tribute to Blackburn, he told mourners of the deceased's legacy. 'Think not that he has deserted the man who was the best work of his genius,' he said. 'He has not. He will be at the next fight, in the corner, leaning over his man's shoulder as usual and whispering in his ear. He has not gone and left his "Chappie" to carry on alone.'

Early in 1944, Louis was sent overseas with the troupe, which now included Billy Conn. Sugar Ray Robinson was not with them, having been admitted to Halloran Hospital in New York after falling down stairs at Fort Hamilton in Brooklyn and suffering amnesia. The troupe boxed exhibitions in North Africa and Italy. In Italy, they visited the front lines and were granted permission by the authorities to pull the lanyard of a large artillery gun. The next day, the gun blew up, killing several soldiers standing nearby.

In London, they survived 12 successive nights of German bombing raids. Once, heading for Liverpool, the plane's landing gear stuck. For half an hour, the craft circled over the city. Apprehensively, Louis eyed Conn. Neither spoke. Finally the pilot, after a deathly silence, said the landing gear had become unstuck and it was now righted. Conn said to Louis, 'You were always a lucky guy, Joe. I want to stick close to you.'

Private Tom Ephrim, who was a correspondent for *Ring* magazine, sent over regular reports to New York about Louis' European tour. One involved an incident at an English airfield. Joe was in the company of Ephrim and Captain Fred V. Maley, the officer in charge of the tour, when they saw a bomber coming in to land. The plane seemed badly shot up, with only two of its engines running and leaving a trail of smoke in its wake. When it reached the end of the field, it crashed. Louis, Maley and Ephrim raced to the scene and found that all but three of the crew were dead. Joe and the reporter comforted the injured while Maley called for medical aid.

When one of the occupants opened his eyes, he took a long look at the champion and his face burst into a grin. 'Well, I'll be damned!' he exclaimed. 'If it's not Joe Louis himself!' Ephrim reported that the man forgot entirely about his wounds while he talked to the champion.

On another occasion, and reported by Ephrim, Louis visited a hospital on England's south coast and got a massive cheer from the patients. One young man from Tennessee, whose eyes were heavily bandaged, asked somebody next to him what all the cheering was about. 'Joe Louis is here' was the response. 'If that's the case, I want to see Joe,' he pleaded. 'He's my hero. Have the nurse take off my bandages so as I can see my hero.'

When a doctor was called, he told the lad from Tennessee, 'I'm sorry, son, but we just could not do that. Your eyes are very weak, and if we took off the bandages we would endanger your sight.'

The patient remained unconvinced. 'But if I can see Joe, it would do me a world of good just to look at him. Just for a minute,' he pleaded.

The doctor went off and conferred with a fellow surgeon. When he returned a few minutes later, he began to gently remove the bandages as a nurse stood nearby. When the doctor finished, he instructed the nurse to put drops in the soldier's eyes so he could keep them open for a short while. When the imposing figure of the famous boxer appeared before him, he held out his right hand with a cry of joy. Joe grasped it. 'This,' said the soldier, 'is the happiest moment of my life.' If he was able to distinguish the tears that dampened the champion's face, he did not mention them.

Louis returned to the United States on 10 October 1944. When reporters asked him about his future boxing plans, he said, 'I don't know, really. I'm now 30 and that's pretty old for a boxer. But somehow, it doesn't make much difference to me if I ever fight again. I've been thinking of retirement for a long time now, ever since I beat Billy Conn back in 1941. Just now, the war is the real fight. This is one fight we all have to win – and we will win, make no mistake about that. This is a time when you can't think of yourself.'

Joe certainly did not think of himself. He had put all his energy into athletic programmes that he helped to build up and direct, under the supervision of the New York Port of Embarkation, which prepared young men about to be shipped overseas. 'It's a little bit like training boxers,' he explained. I tell them some of the things "Chappie" Blackburn used to tell me. I tell the boys to fight to win but not to forget who they are fighting for. I tell them that even if the whole world looks dirty, to stay clean and right themselves, because you can do that in a war, like in a boxing ring. I'm not awfully smart but I learned some lessons on the way up. I tell them what I can that I figure might help.'

The war in the Pacific ended on 14 August 1945, when Japan unconditionally surrendered after two of their cities were totally obliterated by US fighter pilots dropping a new superweapon, the atom bomb. A week earlier, the first A-bomb, regarded as the most powerful weapon ever developed and code-named Little Boy, wiped out the city of Hiroshima. In spite of the US destroying almost the complete Japanese navy and causing the near starvation of the country's population, the government would not surrender. Three days later, a second A-bomb, called Fat Man, fell on the city of Nagasaki, resulting in an overall death toll in both cities of 129,000 inhabitants, with many more thousands injured.

On 8 May, the war in Europe ended when General Alfred Jodl, chief of staff of the German army, signed the agreements of total surrender in the French city of Reims. In reality, however, the war had been over for several days. Nazi forces in Italy had surrendered on 29 April. Adolf Hitler shot himself in Berlin the following day and Russia's Red Army soon took over the city. The main German forces in the west surrendered to Field Marshal Bernard Montgomery on 4 May.

Louis would soon be ready to resume his ring career, although it would be more out of necessity than love for the game. Regarded as one of the all-time greats, he had been heavyweight champion of the world for eight years, longer than any other title-holder in the division, with 21 defences. He really had nothing left to prove. But his extravagant lifestyle and wild ways had generated monumental debts, including $117,000 in back taxes, with the interest mounting day by day. He was also deep in debt to Mike Jacobs.

For help, Louis turned to Julian Black, whose contract with Joe had already expired. Louis claims that Black turned him down on the grounds that Julian had already loaned him sums of money and was still waiting to get it back, although Black denied this. Louis then cunningly decided to make Marva his co-manager, guaranteeing her Black's normal share, which was 25 per cent. His other co-manager would be a good friend of his earlier co-manager, John Roxborough, real estate investor Marshall Miles. Louis explained to Miles that Roxborough's problems with the law had prevented him from staying on as co-manager.

'I only agreed to manage Louis as a favour,' Miles recalled in 1990. 'I certainly didn't do it as a profitable business enterprise. On the contrary, I just joined the lengthening line of creditors. The only thing I ever did was give him money.'

Louis was still in service at the end of the war but Mike Jacobs had just one thing on his mind, a return with Billy Conn. The promoter could visualise cash coming in by the bucketload. It was the only fight the public wanted to see. During the war, he had promoted big fights with whatever talent was available, including Sugar Ray Robinson, then a welterweight contender.

With the championships 'frozen' from heavyweight down to welterweight, Jacobs was able to call on the services of successive lightweight champions such as Sammy Angott, Lew Jenkins, Beau Jack, Bob Montgomery and Ike Williams. Among the featherweight kings were Willie Pep, Harry Jeffra and Chalky Wright. Mike was not too enamoured with the two lowest weights at the time, bantamweight and flyweight. 'There's no money with the little guys,' he would say. 'The paying public are simply not interested.'

This was true to a certain extent as the bantamweight division in the 1940s was ruled by Manuel Ortiz, a talented Californian of Mexican origin who never boxed in New York. One of the finest champions at his weight of all time, Ortiz campaigned exclusively on the west coast and Mexico, where he was a major attraction. Over an eight-year period, he made a record 19 successful defences of his 118lb title. The flyweight title was mainly dominated by British boxers such as the two Scots, Benny Lynch and Jackie Paterson, and Lancashire's Peter Kane.

With the war now over, Jacobs was ready to pick up Louis' career, and what better way to start than with a return match against the man who had come so desperately close to beating him, Billy Conn. Uncle Mike had invited Truman Gibson of the War Department to his offices in Manhattan to discuss ways of speeding up Louis' official demob. Taking Gibson into the toilet and making certain there were no eavesdroppers, Jacobs made a proposition.

'If you can get Louis out of service, it would be worth $10,000 to you, and I can get Joe to make you his manager,' said the canny promoter. Gibson would recall later, 'Jacobs told me how much money I could make by agreeing to his proposal but I turned him down. I was too busy anyhow. When I told Louis subsequently about Jacobs' offer, Joe seemingly did not appreciate my decision. Joe stopped speaking to me for three years.'

Gibson did manage, through his connections, to help Louis get a high public honour. On 23 September 1945, before over 1,000 spectators at Fort Hamilton, New York, Major General Clarence H. Kells presented the champion with the Legion of Merit, a military award of the US armed forces that is given for exceptionally meritorious conduct in the performance of outstanding service and achievements.

Calling Louis 'a model soldier in training and an inspiration to soldiers everywhere', Kells said, 'Joe risked his career and his life, aiding the recovery of injured troops and entertaining others stationed far from home.' Receiving the award made Louis eligible for immediate discharge. A week later, he was out of the army. Louis was not like other men coming out of service, forced to start from scratch, but he was, although the holder of a block of gold in the title, still saddled with debts he could never pay. The heavyweight champion of the world was bankrupt.

How fit was Louis to resume his career in order to put some much-needed finances in his bank account? Four years of indiscipline had added 30lb to his frame and his razor-sharp edge had been dulled by the exhibitions he had taken part in with opponents who were far from top class. If he was going to take on the top contender Billy Conn, and it seemed inevitable, he would need some hard training. The fight, which Jacobs was more or less demanding, would also go some way to repairing the finances of the challenger, who had his own money problems.

Since their last fight in 1941, Conn had engaged in three bouts, all in 1942, before being called up for service. On 12 January he outpointed Henry Cooper, not to be confused with the British boxer of the same name in later years, won a decision over J. D. Turner on 28 January and outpointed Tony Zale, the reigning world middleweight champion, on 13 February.

On 5 March, Conn paid a visit to the naval recruitment office in New York, and emerged declaring to reporters that he would be joining the navy 'in a couple of days'. Knowing that Gene Tunney, the former world heavyweight champion, was also in the navy, Billy enquired of the man who had twice conquered the great Jack Dempsey. Billy was told that Tunney did not talk to other boxers and would not be available. Conn took an instant dislike to Tunney. Billy was not prepared to meet anybody who looked down their nose at people, and promptly put Gene out of his mind.

The incident effectively deterred Conn from joining the navy, and he opted for the army instead. The next day, he visited the army recruitment office in New York and enlisted. Coming out of the office, he was asked by reporters why he had changed his mind. 'I just changed my plans, that's all,' he said. The navy's loss was the army's gain.

When Conn was demobbed in 1945, he was anxious to get his career back on track, and in particular to have his eagerly awaited return with Louis. Boxing fans wanted it too, having being deprived of heavyweight championship action for four years. The press regarded it as a dream match. Mike Jacobs calculated the hunger of customers for Louis–Conn II as financially insatiable. Announcing the fight at a press conference in late October 1945, the date would be 19 June 1946, with the Yankee Stadium as the venue. Jacobs also set a previously unheard-of price of $100 for ringside seats, which covered considerably more territory than the immediate tier around the ring.

Louis knew he would have to be in the best possible condition for the Conn fight, the 22nd defence of his title and a new record. 'The best way to get back into shape was to hit the road again, so Mike Jacobs and Marshall Miles set up a series of exhibitions for me,' Joe remembered. 'These bouts would also provide some spending money, and goodness knows, I needed that.'

Heading out to the Pacific Northwest, Louis boxed eight times between 15 November and 13 December in cities where local fans had never seen him live – including Sacramento, Portland, Vancouver and Victoria. San Francisco was another stop, and he had only boxed there once before, in 1935 when he stopped Don 'Red' Barry in three rounds. The world champion's shows pulled in big crowds and local promoters were happy, even if they had to pay Mike Jacobs part of the gate receipts 'for Joe's services'.

The exhibitions were either over two rounds or three rounds. Several newspapermen from New York and Chicago travelled with the Louis party. They noted that while the boxer looked sharp, he was still carrying a lot of excess baggage at around 240lb. He would need to lose at least 30lb if he wanted to be in top physical condition, or at least in the best shape that a 33-year-old boxer could possibly be.

After the Christmas break in Chicago, and with the exhibition tour finished, Louis headed for Indiana, where he worked out for several weeks at French Lick, a former French trading post and now a popular resort. By the beginning of March, he was on familiar ground at Pompton Lakes, New Jersey. In public, he expressed full confidence of victory, telling reporters that what he could do before he could do again. Privately, though, he was doubtful of his ability to regain his pre-war sharpness and co-ordination.

Louis had changed considerably in a physical sense, having added inches to his chest and waist measurements, but he buckled down to hard training. Gradually, the old feeling started coming back as he continued regular sessions with his sparring partners. One thing he realised was that he still had the ability to punch hard and fast, and more important, accurately. Yet he estimated he had lost 25 per cent of the speed he'd had since he won the title from Braddock nine years earlier.

Mannie Seamon, who had taken over from Jack Blackburn as Louis' trainer, was confident that Joe would be in top form and in 100 per cent condition. He had Louis doing lots of roadwork every morning before the crack of dawn, and then sparring in the afternoon and taking steam baths. Seamon had been in charge of the champion's corner for the Simon fight and Louis had expressed his satisfaction in him.

A cheerful Russian Jew, Seamon was born Mandel Simenovitch in Chicago and raised in Harlem, New York. He was a boxer in his early teens but after being knocked out in his only two fights he turned to training at the age of 15. Seamon soon gained a reputation as someone who got boxers into fine shape, mentally and physically.

Seamon trained several world champions in the years following World War One, most notably world lightweight champion Benny Leonard. A master boxer and knockout puncher, Leonard is considered by many historians and experts as the greatest 135lb boxer of all time. 'Benny often went to the gym even when he wasn't training because boxing was his life", said Seamon. 'Benny said he discovered new moves and tricks by watching other boxers work out. He was a thorough student of boxing.'

In an interview a year before his death from cancer at the age of 85 in 1951, Seamon said of modern boxers, 'They don't train hard enough, and when they do train, it's not done correctly. A boxer needs a good trainer in his corner if he is going to get anywhere. You don't just work hard. You become a student of the game. That's my advice.'

Seamon first worked in Louis' corner as Blackburn's assistant when Joe was training for his fight with Tommy Farr in August 1937. Blackburn put him in charge of Louis' sparring partners and Seamon remained in that capacity until he took over as the champion's chief trainer following Blackburn's illness and subsequent death in 1942. While nobody expected Seamon to be as good as Blackburn, least of all Louis, who regarded his old trainer as a father figure, Mannie always got the job done. For several of Joe's fights, Seamon often replaced his sparring partners, always with Blackburn's approval. 'Joe wants real hard work when he spars, and he is sure not going to get it by working on slow-motion guys you might knock over with a feather duster,' he said.

Seamon got on well with Louis' manager, Marshall Miles, but was often bewildered by the bawdy humour of the other members of Joe's small entourage. Mannie also had Louis sparring on a ring canvas that was nearly an inch thicker than normal. He explained that training on the slower canvas helped to put some spring into Joe's legs when he stepped on to the ring canvas on fight night.

Always the perfectionist, he took 45 minutes to tape Louis' hands and was careful to have separate towels, labelled A, B and C, for the champion's face, body and legs. He also had the boxer alternately walk or run between five and six miles a day, occasionally picking up loose stones, without stopping. 'It's very good exercise for the back muscles,' Seamon would explain.

Over at Conn's camp at Greenwood Lake, New York, the challenger was working hard in his second attempt to win the heavyweight title. The only problem was he hated country life. He liked the freshness of the open air in the beautiful surroundings but complained when he was working out. 'What are we going to do about all those crickets?' he said to his manager, Johnny Ray. 'They keep me awake at night with all that noise they kick up. If that's what you call country life, then you can have it. Why didn't you let me train in the city, anyhow? There's nothing wrong with my hometown, Pittsburgh.'

Ray calmed him down by saying that while there was nothing whatsoever wrong with Pittsburgh, Billy had to get out in the country, where the air was clearer and healthier. 'We can leave nothing to chance,' said Ray. 'After all, it's not every day that a fighter gets a chance to fight for the heavyweight championship of the world, and this is your second chance.'

Conn's chief sparring partner was Mickey McAvoy. Billy got on well with McAvoy, and it was not because Mickey was an Irishman based in Brooklyn. Conn had known Billy since he first entered the heavyweight ranks in 1940. They developed a strong relationship and regularly played jokes on each other. Though McAvoy's record as a heavyweight boxer in the 1930s and early 1940s was not remarkable, he had built up a substantial reputation as a sparring partner for six previous heavyweight champions in Jack Sharkey, Max Schmeling, Primo Carnera, Max Baer, James J. Braddock and Louis.

McAvoy retired from the ring during the war and drove a truck for a brewery company in New York. After much persuasion, Conn's manager, Johnny Ray, was able to persuade him to take leave of absence and join the Conn team at Greenwood Lake. He proved an invaluable asset.

As well as working out in tough sparring sessions with Billy, McAvoy revelled in sharing stories from his days as a bodyguard in Hollywood and often had the camp in stitches with his humorous tales. 'There are some stories I couldn't tell you guys,' he once said. 'Let's just say we'll leave those to some other day.' Camp members would say that there was a strong rapport between them and they constantly played jokes on each other.

On his last day in camp before heading to New York for the weigh-in, Conn told reporters that all the talk about rivalry between him and Louis was for publicity. 'I like Joe, I really do,' he said. 'I'm not mad at him, not at all. Joe's a nice guy. I just want that title of his, that's all. He's had it a long time now and it's time somebody else took over. I'm 28 but look at Joe. He's an old man. He's 32. They tell me he isn't moving too good. I'm glad to hear that because if he doesn't keep moving, I'm going to have that title. If it goes the full 15 rounds, I ought to be the new champion. I'm pretty sure of that.'

Over at Pompton Lakes, Louis had been working hard, perhaps harder than he had ever worked before. He had to win this fight and he knew it. Nobody was interested in an ex-champion, an also-ran. The game was for winners, not losers. He had felt good in camp, working hard all day and then relaxing at night. After dinner at 5.30pm, he would spend a few hours taking it easy, playing cards or calling his many girlfriends around the country.

Sometimes he might go into town to see a movie. He had a wide choice, whether it was a thriller *The Big Sleep* with Humphrey Bogart, a comedy *It's A Wonderful Life* starring James Stewart, a western *My Darling Clementine* with Henry Fonda, a romance *Gilda* with Rita Hayworth or a Disney animation *Song of the South*.

Mannie Seamon told newspapermen, 'Joe is in fine shape. Remember, nobody can expect him to be the fighter he once was when he polished off Max Baer and Max Schmeling and Jim Braddock, but I want to go on record [and say] that he will be 90 per cent of the Louis he was and I think you will all agree that will be more than enough.'

Louis was asked by Arthur Daley of the *New York Times* how he planned to combat the speed of Conn, who was expected to use the ring and avoid Joe's lethal punches until an opening presented itself for a possible knockout. Joe replied with his most famous remark and one of the best ring quotes of all time, 'He can run, but he can't hide.' This remark is often attributed to the first fight but research shows that Louis also made it before the return bout.

As both boxers left their respective training camps and headed for Manhattan for the weigh-in, excitement was high. Newspapers had been carrying regular reports of the upcoming big fight since it was officially announced the previous October. Soon, it would be a reality.

Round 10

Jersey Joe and trouble

The champion and challenger looked in good shape as they arrived for the weigh-in. They exchanged friendly words. Stepping on to the scales, Louis weighed 207lb, 7lb above what he scaled for the first fight. Conn balanced the bar at 182lb, heavier by 13lb than in 1941. Several hours later, the fans started streaming in to the Yankee Stadium.

Celebrities from all walks of life were in attendance. Past and present boxing champions included Jack Dempsey, Gene Tunney, James J. Braddock, Barney Ross, Mickey Walker, Max Baer, Gus Lesnevich and Fritzie Zivic. Among the celebrities from the entertainment world were Frank Sinatra, Clark Gable, Irving Berlin, Ann Sheridan, George Burns and Gracie Allen.

Interest in the fight, the first major championship match after the war, was high. More than 700 press credentials were issued to journalists in America and around the world. In an earlier poll of boxing writers, 57 picked Louis while 17 went for Conn. The odds favoured Louis at 3/1. The general feeling was that while both were clearly past their best and had been without serious combat for four years, the puncher that was Louis stood the best chance.

A skilful boxer like Conn could hardly afford a long lay-off that would rob him of speed and versatility. The last thing a boxer loses is his punch and there were few harder hitters than the 'Brown Bomber'. No challenger had ever matched Louis toe to toe. History also favoured Louis. He had always done better in return fights.

The first disappointment of the night came with the gate. Mike Jacobs had expected it to hit the $3 million mark, with an anticipated attendance of up to 70,000. The crowd numbered 45,266 but the gate receipts still reached $1,925,564, a figure topped only by the second fight between Jack Dempsey and Gene Tunney in Chicago on 22 September 1927. Jacobs could still afford a smile.

Tension was high as referee Eddie Joseph called the champion and challenger together for their pre-fight instructions and to order, 'Go back to your corners, await the bell and may the best man win.' Louis was first into the attack, stabbing left jabs into Conn's face that drove Billy back a few paces, forcing him to retreat. After a flurry of punches in the middle of the round, Conn said to Louis, 'Take it easy Joe, we've got 15 rounds to go,' making Joe smile.

Conn's plan was to keep away from Louis in the early rounds by using his boxing skill to offset his opponent's aggression and power. He would then pick up the tempo and pile up the points, as in the first bout. But he was finding the hot pace set by Louis was preventing him from doing that.

Louis was continually coming in with both hands as the early rounds went by. Conn, realising he had lost much of his speed, could only dodge and move away from his opponent, who was always coming forward. He could not bring himself to take the necessary risks to win this crucial fight. When Billy did land some hooks to the champion's head in the second round, he could not follow through fast enough and allowed the opportunity to slip by. Conn improved in the third round when he landed a succession of jabs and hooks that actually drove Louis back to the ropes. It was a good round and the only session he won.

In the fourth, Conn failed to capitalise on his strong performance and was soon back to his negative work, landing occasional jabs by moving backwards and going into a clinch at every opportunity. Billy slipped while trying to dodge the champion and the two touched gloves before resuming hostilities. By now, the crowd was booing and calling for more action. One bored spectator was heard to shout, 'Hit him now, Billy, ya got the wind with ya.'

The next two rounds livened up and went to Louis on his aggressive tactics. He was able to catch Conn with left hooks to the head and body. At least he was trying to make a fight of it. Before the bell sounded to start the eighth round, Louis said to Mannie Seamon, 'I'm going to pick up the pace in this round and see if Conn can take it.' The trainer nodded. 'I think Conn's ready for the taking,' he said.

At the bell, Louis moved in on the challenger, who had slowed considerably by now. Two fast left jabs from Joe, followed by a quick right cross, drove Billy back. Louis followed as Conn retreated to the ropes. Conn tried an overhand right cross that missed and he fell into a clinch. Louis pushed him off, landed several jabs and then a hard right to the head that buckled the challenger's knees. The crowd stood up and cheered. A bit of real action at last. Was this the beginning of the end?

Conn tried to hang on but Louis pushed him away and connected with a powerful right cross followed by an equally hard left hook and Conn slumped to the canvas. He struggled to a sitting position and managed to grab the middle rope, getting to one knee, but it was too late. Referee Joseph had already counted him out. The timekeeper's clock showed 2:19 of round eight. Conn's attempt to win boxing's premier and richest title had failed for the second time.

In the dressing room, Louis stood on a bench and raised his hands to gain the attention of the reporters. He was cocky at first. 'Everybody seemed to be wondering whether I would still be as good as I used to be,' he said. 'Seems to be that I am, doesn't it?' After being asked more questions, Louis got tired and more restrained. When queried as to whether he really felt as good as ever, he said with sober honesty, 'I don't know. I wasn't tested.'

Conn, sporting small cuts on the bridge of his nose and under his left eye, told reporters in his dressing room, 'Louis is still a terrific puncher. I didn't have to go in there to find that out, but I figured I could tire him out. You know, play safe with him for a while. The next thing I know, he's knocked me down. I heard the count but I just couldn't get up.'

The fight took a hammering from the press, with Conn bearing the brunt of the criticism. 'If the Louis–Conn fight had been a main event in Madison Square Garden, the customers would have booed it out of the arena,' said Arthur Daley of the *New York Times*. 'Nobody can blame Louis for it. He was always willing to fight.'

Nat Fleischer wrote in *Ring* magazine, 'Conn was a bitter disappointment. He made few offensive gestures. Louis, boxing warily, wasted little motion, stalking Billy relentlessly. Once he had Conn going in the eighth round, Louis wasted no time in finishing him. A furious assault battered the Pittsburgher to the canvas, where he was counted out.'

Covering the fight for the International News Service, Dan Parker reported, 'Conn was scared out of his wits when he entered the ring and acted during most of the fight as if his wits had actually deserted him. Billy backed up far enough to be in the suburbs of Pittsburgh if he had travelled in a straight line.'

Reminiscing in later years, referee Eddie Joseph, who handled the two Louis–Conn fights and had the best view of proceedings, felt that Conn was not in the best condition. 'I don't care what the doctors or anyone else may have said but Billy Conn was not in the best shape for a tough fight, and I knew it as soon as I saw him step into the ring,' he proclaimed.

'Now, don't give me a song and dance about his heart and his pulse and his blood pressure. I knew there was something wrong when I saw those circles under his eyes. I don't know whether he was over-trained or not but I do know he wasn't in shape for a battle against one of the hardest punchers the ring ever saw.'

One consolation for Conn was that he collected a cheque for $312,958, a huge sum in those days. It enabled him to pay his debts to Mike Jacobs and his manager, Johnny Ray. Louis' share came to around $625,000, the largest purse of his career. Out of that figure, his manager, Marshall Miles, received $140,000. The State of New York deducted $30,000 in taxes and Louis paid his overdue debts to Jacobs and his former manager, John Roxborough, coming close to $200,000.

There was also an outstanding tax bill from 1941, approximately $115,000. Louis, one of the greatest and most respected champions in boxing history, came out of his 22nd title defence, the second richest fight of all time up to then, with very little. He also still had to pay tax on the second Conn fight.

Marshall Miles was one of the first people to help get Louis out of what Joe's biographer Chris Mead called 'a quicksand'. Miles contacted Mike Jacobs and asked him to arrange a September title defence against a top contender. Miles would not take his managerial fee, and he persuaded Roxborough to forfeit his cut of the purse. As for Marva, Louis asked her to marry him again. He would try to be faithful this time. She agreed and they remarried several weeks after the Conn fight.

Conn, who was disappointed with his performance, announced his retirement after the fight but soon changed his mind. In September, he said he wanted a third fight with Louis and would give his purse to charity. But Jacobs said that there was no market for it. In the Associated Press annual end-of-year poll, the fight was named 'Flop of the Year'. Conn fought twice more, in November 1948, scoring two knockout wins over fairly obscure opponents before retiring for good.

Jacobs and Miles arranged for Louis to defend his title against the New York contender Tami Mauriello at the Yankee Stadium on 18 September 1946. It would be the challenger's 23rd birthday. A native of the Bronx and of Italian origin, the stocky Mauriello was coming into the fight with an impressive 69-7-1 record. He was on a 12-fight winning streak with victories inside the distance over the likes of Lee Savold, Lou Nova, Lee Oma and Red Burman.

Mauriello had also boxed a draw with Bob Pastor, who had once gone the full distance with Louis. He figured that with his right-hand power, combined with Louis' four-year lay-off during wartime and a nine-year difference in age, he had a real chance of causing an upset.

In his final fight before the Louis match, Mauriello took on the British heavyweight champion Bruce Woodcock at Madison Square Garden on 17 May 1946. The Yorkshireman was one of Britain's sporting heroes in those heady, deprived, optimistic days immediately after World War Two. He had a snappy left jab, a hard right, a big, honest heart and plenty of charisma. Bruce was the dominant European heavyweight of his generation, and was Britain's hope for the world title. The old country had not had a world heavyweight champion since the 1890s with Bob Fitzsimmons. Although born in Cornwall, Fitz learned his boxing in Australia and New Zealand. Woodcock was a born-and-bred Briton.

Both of America's controlling bodies agreed to recognise the Mauriello–Woodcock fight as a final eliminator for the right to challenge Louis. Before a crowd of 14,000, Woodcock was ahead on points after four rounds when a head butt in the fifth round opened a bad cut over his left eye, with no warning from referee Arthur Donovan.

With the Britisher unable to focus properly, Mauriello landed a looping left hook that dropped Woodcock for an eight count. After Woodcock climbed somewhat groggily to his feet, Donovan intervened. It was all over, despite a protest by Woodcock's manager, Tom Hurst, that his boxer should have been allowed to continue. The victory sealed the world championship fight for Mauriello.

At the weigh-in, Louis scaled 212lb, 5lb heavier than he was for the Conn return match. Mauriello came in at 198lb. The challenger confidently boasted to newspapermen, 'Louis is ready for the taking. The two Conn fights proved that.' Louis, going for his 56th win in 57 fights, commented, 'I don't always come out with a big forecast but if you really want my opinion, I'm confident I'll still be champion when I leave Yankee Stadium tonight.'

Seconds after referee Arthur Donovan called the two boxers together for their final instructions and told them to return to their corners to await the bell, the fight burst into action. The crowd of 38,494, who had paid a total of $335,063, were taken by surprise. Normally, Louis' fights started slowly as both boxers took their time to size each other up. This one was different. The bout had been going just four or five seconds when Mauriello, warding off a Louis left jab before feinting with a right hand, started to throw a left hook but then put all his weight behind a smashing overhand right. The blow landed squarely on the champion's jaw and sent him reeling back into the ropes as the crowd roared. Was a sensational upset on the cards?

Mauriello rushed in to try and finish the job and threw another big right but Louis covered up and clinched, desperately trying to buy time. Mauriello tried another right but Louis smothered the punch by putting both arms around the New Yorker and holding him in a bear hug. Mauriello was desperately trying to shake Louis off and succeeded just as referee Donovan moved in to break the two boxers. Mauriello threw another right that almost hit Donovan.

Louis pushed the challenger away and then fired a short left hook that caught Mauriello on the side of the head and dropped him to the canvas near a neutral corner. Taking a count of five, he managed to get to his feet before Louis came in again and fired a combination consisting of a left hook, right uppercut and left hook that draped Mauriello across the bottom rope, where he was counted out. Donovan helped him to his feet as his handlers got into the ring and escorted him to his corner. Louis followed them and, smiling, shook the gallant challenger's hand. 'Hard luck, Tami,' he said, and Mauriello smiled ruefully.

In a post-fight interview, Mauriello said, 'My team had worked out before the fight that I should go straight into Louis and crack him with that right hand, just like Schmeling did before the war. I did that but Louis was ready for me. I guess I just got too damn careless.'

Louis would remember, 'When I first got the fight, I knew Mauriello had proven that he could punch, although he wasn't any great hell as a boxer. I didn't consider him any threat at all, so I was really surprised when he caught me with that right hand. He hurt me and surprised me but he was slow. He should have moved straight in when he saw I was hurt. The fight was good, the last time I felt like my old self. I had complete control, energy, power. I wonder sometimes if that wasn't my last great fight.'

Louis' earnings from the Mauriello fight came to slightly over $100,000. In three months, he had spent all but $500 of the money. When Miles confronted him and asked where all the money had gone, Joe told his manager he had invested over $400,000 in a Chicago nightclub called the Rhum Boogie Cafe. He had put a friend, Leonard Reed, a black comedian, in charge of it. The place was now losing money and suffering in a decline in the entertainment business. It eventually closed.

There had been other expenses too. Besides his debts and income tax payouts, Joe had also been playing golf for a long time, against the wishes of Mike Jacobs, and lost considerable sums on bets. The cost of gifts to his many lady friends also accounted for a high percentage of his money.

In December 1946, Jacobs suffered a stroke and business at the 20th Century Sporting Club was in the hands of his legal aide, Sol Strauss. In talks with Strauss and Miles, Louis decided on two exhibition tours. The first one took him to Mexico and Hawaii, and the second through Central and South America. The pay cheques were good, with $10,000 plus expenses per exhibition. All told, he made an estimated $157,200, although much of the money went on his large entourage. Louis also had to pay his usual debts out of it.

Louis approached Strauss to enquire if he had a title defence in mind. Strauss had provisionally pencilled in a June date at either the Yankee Stadium or the Polo Grounds but he had no particular opponent in mind. The existing heavyweight division was quite bare, with Joe having already removed the best contender Tami Mauriello. In view of Mauriello's summary defeat, a return was out of the question.

Jersey Joe Walcott, from Camden, New Jersey, was the leading contender but had done nothing remarkable to justify a title fight with Louis. True, in 1947 Walcott had won important victories over two men who had beaten him the previous year, big-hitting Elmer Ray and the classy Joey Maxim. But he was even older than Louis, if only by a few months, and hardly seemed the man to match up to the 'Brown Bomber' – a clear indication of Joe's superiority.

Maxim, from Cleveland, Ohio, was also considered but he had a spotty record against heavyweights. He was effectively a blown-up light-heavyweight and would win the world title in that division by knocking out Freddie Mills in ten rounds in London in January 1950.

Joe Baksi, the burly Pennsylvanian coalminer who had earlier destroyed both Mills and Bruce Woodcock with displays of systematic, relentless punching, was another likely challenger but he was showing no interest in coming up against Louis.

It seemed that Baksi felt that he would make more money taking on the other contenders, with a better chance of success than he would have taking a whack on the chin from Louis and then slinking off into obscurity.

Baksi also knew that Louis, at 33, was contemplating retirement after one or two more fights. Would it not be wise to stay away from Joe, and then take care of the other contenders for the vacant title? Baksi was now 27 and had time on his side. Interestingly, his name is Cockney slang for taxi, as in 'Call me a Joe Baxsi.' It is also used in parts of northern England.

The heavyweight picture changed dramatically on 6 July when Baksi journeyed to Stockholm to take on the Swedish hope Olle Tandberg, a former European amateur heavyweight champion who was on a ten-fight winning streak. The Pennsylvanian hoped to repeat his impressive performances against Woodcock and Mills, and was a 5/1 favourite entering the ring at the sprawling, open-air Rasunda Stadium.

Under a hot summer sun with a slight breeze, the fans expected a good fight but hardly believed a home win was possible. Tandberg, two inches taller than the 6ft 1in Baksi, boxed well and kept the American at a distance with sharp jabs and hooks.

Baksi's best rounds were the fifth, seventh and eighth, when he got in some solid shots to the head and body, the sort of blows that had wrecked Woodcock and Mills, and broken Woodcock's jaw. Tandberg stood his ground and boxed well, if cautiously, over the last two rounds. The verdict was a majority one in favour of the Swede, which surprised Tandberg.

'I don't believe I won,' he said in the dressing room. 'I thought I was too much on the defensive in the closing rounds.' Baksi and his manager, Nate Wolfson, were furious. 'We were robbed, no question about it,' barked Wolfson. 'The European Boxing Union will have to investigate this shameful decision.' There was no investigation.

The *New York Times* reported the fight was 'the greatest heavyweight upset in years'.

With Baksi now out of the picture, at least for the foreseeable future, Strauss called Louis to talk about an alternative challenger. 'There's really nobody interesting around just now, Joe, so we may have to wait until next summer, when the scene might change and throw up a good contender,' he said.

'I was thinking of another idea too. We might put you in at Madison Square Garden in December. But it would be an exhibition bout over ten rounds with Jersey Joe Walcott. He's your number one contender, despite a fairly spotty record, but an exhibition could draw well and stir up interest in a big outdoor fight with Walcott next summer.'

With no big-money championship fight on the immediate horizon, Louis agreed and told Strauss to work on it. But when the promoter informed the New York State Athletic Commission about the plan, they turned it down flat. Commission chairman Eddie Egan insisted that any ten-round match, exhibition or otherwise, involving Louis would have to be for the championship – and the regulations for a championship bout stipulated that the fight would have to be over 15 rounds, not ten.

Strauss decided to promote the match with Walcott as a full-blown world heavyweight championship fight and set the date for 5 December 1947 at Madison Square Garden. It would be the first all-black heavyweight title bout since Louis had knocked out John Henry Lewis in the first round, also at the Garden, in January 1939.

On that occasion, promoters and boxing people had wondered if two black heavyweights competing for the sport's major title was really a wise thing. A racial issue? America had never witnessed such a pairing previously. Jack Johnson defended his title against a black contender, Jim Johnson, in December 1913 but that fight took place in Paris. Scheduled for ten rounds, it ended in a controversial draw.

There are conflicting reports of the fight, but according to boxing authority Nat Fleischer in his 1949 book *The Heavyweight Championship*, Jack was fortunate to retain his title. Fleischer said Jack broke his left arm in the last round and was tottering on the ropes, with the arm hanging limp, when the club physician declared that the champion could not carry on under such circumstances.

In spite of screaming protests from the spectators, he ordered the referee to declare the bout a draw. Under present-day rules, or even the regulations of the day, Jack Johnson should have lost the title.

There were no racial concerns over the all-black Louis v Lewis bout in 1939, and by 1947 nobody seemed to care what colour a boxer's skin was, which was due in a large part to Louis' sportsmanship inside and outside the roped square.

* * *

Jersey Joe Walcott was born Arnold Cream in the small town of Merchantville, New Jersey on the last day of January 1914. Raised there with 11 brothers and sisters, his childhood ended abruptly at the age of 13 with the untimely death of his father, Joseph, who was born on the island of St John in the West Indies.

As the oldest member of the brood, Arnold left school and began working in a soup factory to help support his family. Forced by circumstances to grow up fast, young Arnold vowed to become a professional boxer like his father. This way, he would make some money and lift his family out of the poverty trap they were slowly sinking into.

He remembered how his father used to regale him with stories of his cousin, Jeff Clark, the old 'Joplin Ghost', a highly respected black boxer from an earlier era who had fought an epic 13-fight series with the great uncrowned champion Sam Langford. Cream senior also used to tell him about another great, Joe Walcott, the 'Barbados Demon', who was also from St John. Walcott was welterweight champion of the world around the turn of the century.

Young Arnold joined a local gym, Battling Macs, when the family moved to Camden, New Jersey and learned the rudiments of the game over the next few months from the coaches and other boxers who trained there. He also adopted Joe Walcott's name.

Arnold Cream was now Jersey Joe Walcott. Skipping the amateur ranks, he launched his professional boxing career as a light-heavyweight on 9 September 1930 with a first-round knockout win over Frank 'Cowboy' Willis at the Vineland

Arena, Camden. He was 16. In the dressing room Jersey Joe collected his $15 purse, paid off the two men who looked after him and left the arena with $7.50 in his shirt pocket. Rushing home, he handed the money to his mother, Edna, and excitedly told her the result of his first fight. 'Son,' she said, looking her boy in the eyes proudly. 'You will be champion of the world some day if they ever give you a chance.'

He won his next five bouts, each inside four rounds, before losing a decision in Philadelphia to a hard-hitting local named Henry Taylor. Walcott had his man down three times in the first round but Taylor fought back to take command of the fight and won the decision after six rounds. Shortly afterwards, back in Camden, Jersey Joe married his childhood sweetheart, Lydia Eleanor Talton.

While in Philadelphia for the Taylor fight, Jersey Joe worked out at the Arcadia gym. It was a favourite spot for visiting boxers and run by Max 'Boo Boo' Hoff, a well-known manager and bootlegger. It was one of a number of popular gyms in the City of Brotherly Love during the 1920s and 1930s, and visiting boxers from all over the world trained there when in town for a fight. If a young fighter was going to get anywhere with his boxing career, there was a good chance he would do it in Philadelphia.

It was at the Arcadia where Jersey Joe caught the eye of the legendary Jack 'Chappie' Blackburn, who was training a young contender named Joe Louis at the time. Blackburn often visited the gym to look over any potential champions he might spot, and it was Walcott who caught his eye. They arranged to meet in the gym as often as possible.

Blackburn would teach the young boxer the finer points of the game, such as how to punch correctly, how not to waste a blow, how to use defensive skills, how to slip inside and outside an opponent's punches and even how to catch punches in the air.

Walcott's confidence grew under Blackburn's teachings. The education he received from Jack was priceless. Unfortunately, Jersey Joe had little opportunity to display the skills he was learning. Black boxers were not wanted on fight cards. 'They just don't draw crowds,' said one prominent manager. 'I can get a dozen white guys. But black guys? You can keep them.'

As a result, Walcott had just one fight in 1931, none in 1932, three in 1933 and none in 1934. Throughout those years, he worked at various jobs. It was all physical work that kept him going from 7am to near midnight – tossing around bags of coal and shifting heavy ice blocks. It meant he had little time for training, let alone looking for fights.

In November 1934, Blackburn got a call in Philadelphia from a couple of people in Chicago. They had an amateur champion and were looking for one of two more boxers as well. Blackburn said he had a young heavyweight called Jersey Joe Walcott who showed potential. The caller promised he would have a look at Walcott early in the new year. A few days later, however, Jersey Joe was rushed to hospital in Camden with typhoid fever.

'Blackburn went to Chicago without me and was introduced to an amateur champion who happened to be Joe Louis,' Jersey Joe recalled in an interview. 'Who knows? If I hadn't gotten sick and been able to meet those men in Chicago, I could have been champion before Louis.'

With his temperature going up and down and at times climbing as high as 105 degrees, Walcott was bedridden for two months. His weight dropped from 190lb to 130lb. After being released from hospital, he was still unable to work and had no alternative but to apply for state assistance. An intensely proud and God-fearing man, Walcott was only accepting unemployment benefits when there was absolutely no other choice.

He was essentially a hard-working man. Years later, when he finally began to make some money in boxing, Jersey Joe paid back every cent he had received from the state. The weekly cheque was $9.50 and this was just about enough to put food on the table, and now there was also a child to feed and clothe.

The allowance was certainly not enough to pay the rent. As a result, the family fell behind financially. In no time, the landlord showed up at Walcott's door with an ultimatum to pay up or get out. Unable to come up with the money, they were evicted. Over the course of the next few months, they moved from one rundown place to another, always one step ahead of another eviction.

Although he was extremely weak and could barely lift a shovel or a rake, Jersey Joe was desperate. He got a job as a gardener in the Camden parks for $15 a week and combined with any work Lydia could get, which was mainly in kitchens, the Walcotts managed to survive. Over time, Jersey Joe gradually got his strength back.

By May 1935, he was physically fit to fight again and ran up five straight wins, including three in the first round. A heavy defeat in seven rounds against the world-ranked Al Ettore in Camden only made Jersey Joe more determined to succeed and by the end of 1936, he had lost only three and drawn two of his 21 fights.

One of his nine wins that year was a knockout in three rounds over Philadelphia's Phil Johnson. Fourteen years later, Walcott would complete a unique double by knocking out Phil's son, Harold, in the same round. In 1961, eight years after Walcott retired, Harold Johnson won the world light-heavyweight title.

Jack Blackburn came back into the Walcott picture in 1936. Remembering the young Camden boxer, he invited Jersey Joe to Pompton Lakes, New Jersey, where Jack was preparing Louis for his first fight with Max Schmeling in June. What happened next depends on the version you accept. According to Walcott, he put Louis on the canvas and was subsequently fired after being paid $25.

'I stepped around and stabbed him with jabs, moving from side to side,' he said. 'As he lunged and missed with one big, angry left hook, I came back with a right to the face. It wasn't a hard punch and couldn't have hurt him, but it was perfectly placed and enough to knock him off balance. He stumbled awkwardly across the ring.

'The rope saved him from falling flat on his face, and he landed on both knees. Blackburn and Louis' people were furious. After dinner that evening, Blackburn took me aside. "I'm sorry, Joe," he said, "but you haven't got the right style for Louis. You'll have to go. But thanks for coming." With that, he counted out $25 into my hand.'

Other versions of the sparring match have Louis knocking Walcott down and giving him such a whipping that he quit outright, climbed out of the ring and left the camp, never to return. Louis' account, not surprisingly, was somewhat different. 'Jersey Joe looked good when we had our first workout. The second workout, I must have hurt him some. The next thing I knew was that he had left the camp and never came back.'

Walcott's biographer, James Curl, explained, 'It has been accepted by some boxing historians that Walcott knocked Louis down. On the other hand, there is little doubt that Louis knocked Walcott down, since there are photographs from a newspaper that show in sequence Jersey Joe falling to the canvas during their sparring match. Quoting Walcott, "The series of photos was as much baloney as Louis' statement, and I never worked with him again."'

By 1938, Walcott's career seemed to have settled into a journeyman's role, winning some fights, losing others. He had some good wins but they were mixed in with heavy defeats and he was becoming disillusioned with the fight game. He only had two fights in 1939, two again in 1940 and just one in 1941. Jersey Joe drifted away from boxing in 1942 and was forced again to accept relief money, $9.50 a week. He even stayed away from the gym and, as a result, put on weight.

'I never knew what an extra dollar was until I was well past 30,' he remembered. 'I always had such a hard time just getting along that I could never afford any kind of luxury, not even cigarettes. As a kid, I went in for all kinds of games and I kept so busy I didn't have time to pick up any bad habits. Now take Joe Louis.

'Joe hit the top very early in his life. He did well to last as long as he did with all that easy living he went through. I was just the opposite.'

In June 1944, after being inactive for three years, Walcott made a two-fight comeback. He won both contests but no further offers came in and he began to resign himself as an ex-boxer, someone who never got the breaks.

Then, shortly before Christmas, he received a visit from a local boxing manager. Felix Bocchiccio dabbled in racketeering but was also a big fight fan and provided the money for shows run by Camden promoter Vic Marsillo.

Bocchiccio, who had a business car on which his name was spelt out phonetically as 'Bo-key-key-o', remembered Walcott boxing around Camden. He was anxious to persuade Jersey Joe to give the fight game another try, just one more. 'You can't stay in retirement,' he said. 'You've got talent and you can certainly beat a lot of the contenders around now.'

'I don't know,' said Walcott. 'Maybe I can and maybe I can't. Look at that coal bucket over there. It's practically empty and

I can hardly afford coal, just enough to keep us warm for a few hours before we go to bed.'

Despite Walcott's reluctance to return to the ring as he had gotten nowhere in the past, Bocchiccio was adamant. 'Fight for me, Joe, and that coal bucket will always be full, starting tomorrow,' he promised. 'You won't have to worry about where your next meal is coming from. I'll give you enough money to live on even if you don't fight regularly. How is that?'

'I don't know, Mr Bocchiccio,' replied Walcott. 'Maybe I can beat these guys, maybe I can't, but at the moment I'm out of condition. But maybe I'll give it one more shot.'

They shook hands on the promise and the next day a cartload of coal and a box of groceries were delivered to Walcott's home. Bocchiccio recalled, 'When I got there before the deliveries, even the chairs and beds had broken legs. I had to get a carpenter to fix doors and windows so they would stay shut. There was no coal in the cellar, no presents for the kids, no meat in the house.'

All that was about to change. Under Bocchiccio's guidance, Jersey Joe won his first fight in early January 1945 but lost his second a fortnight later. That, he assumed, would be the end of Bocchiccio's interest but the manager/benefactor had made a promise to him and planned to keep it. After two more wins, Walcott got his first big break when the formidable Joe Baksi came to Camden in August to fight him in what Baksi, a rated contender, saw as easy money and a good win.

Walcott knew this might be his last chance to crack the big time. After ten rounds, his right hand was raised as the winner on points, with the lone official, referee Paul Cavalier, scoring the fight 6-3-1. It was a huge upset and propelled Jersey Joe into the top-ten heavyweight ratings for the first time.

'Baksi's people only took me because they thought I was a washed-up old man, but I licked him,' he recalled. 'Once that happened, my whole mental condition changed. When I was coming up, my family was my responsibility and I wasn't making any money in boxing. My mind was not at rest. The win over Baksi in 1945 changed all that.'

In 1946 Walcott had five wins, including impressive victories over contenders Jimmy Bivins and Lee Oma. His two losses were to crafty Joey Maxim and the hard-hitting Elmer 'Violent' Ray. In the first three months of 1947, he defeated both Maxim and Ray in return bouts. By December, Walcott, who was at one time boxing's 'forgotten man', would climb into the ring at Madison Square Garden to fight Joe Louis for the heavyweight championship of the world.

Bookmakers were so sceptical of Jersey Joe's chances that Louis went into the fight on 5 December 1947 as a 10/1 favourite, with some reports putting the odds at 20/1. The 'Brown Bomber' was still a formidable fighter with just one loss in 58 fights and had been champion for ten years. Walcott's record was anything but impressive, with 11 losses and two draws in 57 fights. True, Louis was a veteran at 33 but he was still four months younger that Walcott. The general feeling was that Jersey Joe might last five rounds, if he was lucky.

Louis set up his training camp at Pompton Lakes, New Jersey. He had a strong team of sparring partners. When asked what he thought of Walcott, he described him as 'one of those guys that are always beating each other'. Pressed further, he said Walcott was 'a second rater'. These were uncharacteristic comments coming from somebody who had never previously expressed contempt for a challenger. Louis was criticised for his remarks but refused to soften his words. His army career had made him a more outspoken man than the Louis of the past.

Grantland Rice of the *New York Herald Tribune* was among the sportswriters who disliked this 'new' Joe Louis. He wrote a column on the morning of the fight in which he at once anticipated Louis' downfall but paid tribute to him as a boxing champion. Concluding that Louis had been one of the finest in history, in terms of performance and of character, 'he was still a champion in everyone's eyes – win, lose or draw'.

Walcott set up his training camp at Grenloch Amusement Park in New Jersey, which at the time was closed down. He rented the park and had a boxing ring and workout area set up in the grounds. During training, his team, led by manager Bocchiccio and trainer Dan Florio, insisted that no press were allowed, although the workouts were open to the public.

They had a fight plan worked out and did not want Walcott receiving any well-intentioned but confusing advice. This was Jersey Joe's long-awaited chance, the opportunity of a lifetime, and they did not want it put at risk.

At a crowded weigh-in, Louis scaled 211lb and Walcott 194lb. A crowd of 18,194 paid a Garden record of $216,477, eclipsing the previous best of $201,465 for the Jack Delaney–Jim Maloney light-heavyweight fight in February 1927. Referee Ruby Goldstein would be in charge of his first world heavyweight title bout.

Born and bred on New York's East Side, Goldstein had a distinguished career as a welterweight boxer and picked up his nickname 'The Jewel of the Ghetto', although he never reached championship standard. He would gain widespread respect and an eventual place in the International Boxing Hall of Fame in New York as one of the world's outstanding referees.

When Goldstein called the two boxers together for their preliminary instructions, anticipation was high. The action came early, and with startling suddenness. After subjecting Louis to a succession of left jabs and hooks, Walcott suddenly got through with a short, sharp right to Joe's jaw. Amid a big roar from the crowd, Louis went down for a count of two. Ever since the first Schmeling fight in 1936, Joe had shown that he was vulnerable to a right, a fault Walcott had now exploited again. On rising, Louis went on to the attack but the challenger moved around the ring, dodging the champion's follow-up punches until the bell.

Louis seemed desperate in the second and third rounds, with many of his blows thrown wildly or sailing past the shifty challenger's head. The fourth round was not a minute old when Walcott again crashed his right against Louis' jaw, toppling the 'Brown Bomber' for the second time. Was there a sensational upset on the cards?

Louis, on his hands and knees, listened as the count reached seven and when he arose, he fell into a clinch. He was still hurt but avoided Jersey Joe's follow-up attack by bobbing and weaving in a bid to avoid the eager charges of his foe.

Louis made a good recovery in the fifth as Walcott held his fire by boxing cleverly. Through the ensuing rounds, Louis pressed his challenger tirelessly as Jersey Joe fought more defensively, mainly back-pedalling. Louis' fists were poised, always ready to land a punch that would bring an end to this tricky challenger. Joe had a particularly good ninth round when he drove Walcott back against the ropes under a hail of smashing lefts and rights. Jersey Joe was in trouble but the bell came to his rescue.

The crowd sensed the finish when the tenth round started. It seemed that Louis must crash through the web of flailing arms with a decisive thrust, or at least land a punch that would expose Walcott and send him down. The roar was deafening as Louis unloaded lefts and rights to head and body but Jersey Joe not only withstood them but lashed back, although most of his blows were wild.

From the 11th to the penultimate round, Walcott was mainly on the defensive as Louis continued to pursue him.

'Jersey Joe seemed content to go on his bicycle now,' one reporter observed. But in a grandstand finish over the final three minutes, Walcott seemed full of fight and gave as good as he got against the continually advancing champion. The last bell clanged. It was all over.

Looking completely dispirited, his pride hurt and his championship in the balance, Louis hastily climbed through the ropes before reaching his corner and was out on the apron of the ring before his handlers hastily forced him back to await the announcement of the decision.

Harry Baloch walked to the centre of the ring and pulled down the overhead microphone. Reading out the scorecards, he announced, 'Judge Frank Forbes scored eight rounds to six, with one even ... Louis. Referee Ruby Goldstein scored seven rounds to six, two rounds even...Walcott.' Then came the decisive vote, 'Judge Marty Monroe scored it nine rounds to six... Louis. The winner by a split decision and still heavyweight champion of the world ... Joe Louis!'

The result not only stunned the crowd, it provoked an outburst of booing and shouts of 'robbery' that echoed through the Garden's rafters with deafening volume. Louis went to Walcott's corner and said, 'I'm sorry, Joe.' Walcott took this as an acknowledgement of defeat on Louis' part. Louis said later his apology was an admission that it had been a bad fight for the many fans who'd paid good money to see a championship contest.

In the dressing room, Louis met the press with his face puffy, his jaw swollen, a cut below his right eye and his right hand broken. When he was asked if he still thought that Walcott was a second-rate fighter, he replied, 'No, me. I was the second-rater tonight.' Would he give Walcott a return? 'He deserves one,' he answered. Asked why he tried to leave the ring before the decision was announced, he said, 'I was disgusted with myself.'

Over in his opponent's dressing room, Walcott sat on the rubbing table answering reporters' questions. 'I still can't believe it,' he said. 'I won that fight out there and everybody knows it. You heard all the booing.

'I was never hurt at any time, although he punched hard, especially in the ninth, when he had me against the ropes. But I knew all the time what I was doing.

'After the first round, I knew I could beat him. I'd like a return fight, sure I would, and as soon as possible. I'd fight him tomorrow.'

Over three decades later, Walcott was still convinced he was robbed. 'Like thousands of people who saw it, I thought I won it very big,' he said. 'But out of my respect and admiration for Louis, I never felt bad about not getting the decision. He was such an idol to the world. I think that anybody who dethroned him would be the most hated guy in the world.'

Louis recalled in 1970, 'Walcott was good but he only fought in spurts. He was on his bicycle all through and he was determined to stay the full 15 rounds. Before the decision was announced, I wanted to leave the ring but my handlers pulled me back. I knew I won, since Walcott didn't come to me. After all, I was the champion and he had to come and take the crown from me. He didn't do that.'

Out of the 33 writers at ringside, 22 had Walcott ahead at the end, ten had Louis in front and one called it a draw. This was no consolation for Jersey Joe, who felt he was cheated out of the verdict. Jimmy Cannon in the *New York Daily News* said that Louis was lucky to get the decision and retain his title. 'If the fight had been anywhere else, there would have been a full-scale investigation into the officiating,' he wrote.

James P. Dawson of the *New York Times* gave Louis eight rounds and Walcott seven. 'No longer is Louis the death-dealing, sure-fire puncher of old,' he wrote. 'He was battered, bruised and bleeding. He was outmanoeuvred, at times outboxed, always out-thought and generally made to look foolish.

'By the same token, no boxer ever won a championship by running away without attempting a defensive counter-fire. Louis made all the fighting, did most of the leading, and, his two knockdowns notwithstanding, landed the greater number of blows. Except for Louis, there would have been no fight.'

Peter Wilson, one of Britain's leading boxing writers, wrote in the *Sunday Pictorial*, 'In my opinion, this was the greatest robbery since Colonel Blood stole the crown jewels. Walcott made Louis look like a novice... he was putting up the greatest surprise of our sporting generation.' Referring to judge Marty Monroe, who voted for Louis, Wilson wrote, 'All I can conscientiously say is that I hope I never come up against a judge named Monroe if those are the sort of verdicts he'd give. I'd reckon to get a life sentence from him.'

Nat Fleischer, preparing his notes for the following month's *Ring* magazine, said, 'Louis undeniably fought the worst battle of his life. He was awkward. He looked foolish as he tried to catch up with the sprinting Jersey man. His timing was terrible and his co-ordination was lacking. He often looked bewildered as he tried to get close enough for action.

'It was a depressing exhibition for a champion. Yet it must be acknowledged that it was Walcott's sprinting that made the champion look so foolish and awkward. Though Louis missed continually, he was making the fight.'

In the days following the bout, there were rumours that Louis had fought his last fight and that he was preparing to announce his retirement. There were other rumours that he would not hang up his gloves with such a controversial decision hanging over him and, in turn, risk his legacy. Sol Strauss, still acting for the ailing Mike Jacobs, announced that the

20th Century Sporting Club would stage a return match at the Yankee Stadium on 23 June 1948.

Louis was adamant that this would be his last fight. He had no illusions about his declining skills and he was tired of the long weeks in training camps, but he had to restore his damaged pride. He wanted to go out like a champion should, an undisputed winner. Nothing else would satisfy him. He collected $80,000 for the fight but as usual he had little left after paying his debts, including a still-massive tax bill.

After boxing an exhibition in Chicago and signing for the return fight with Walcott, Louis set sail for Britain.

Louis' first official appearance on the tour was at the Health and Holiday Exposition at London's Earls Court, where he would take part in three exhibitions in as many days. Later, after several personal appearances in English cities, where he spoke of his boxing career and answered questions from the audiences, the tour moved to the continent.

Unfortunately, by the end of the tour, the organisers ran out of money and could only pay Louis half of his promised $80,000 fee. The promoter on the Swedish leg of the tour offered to pay Joe in ice skates in lieu of money. Louis cancelled the tour. Personal living expenses also soaked up his finances, although this did not stop him secretly buying expensive gifts, including bottles of perfume and fashionable clothes, for his many girlfriends back in the United States.

On their return home to Chicago, Louis left the next day for the Bear Lake resort in Michigan, where he did preliminary training such as roadwork, callisthenics and chopping logs. Seamon increased Louis' roadwork from six miles a day to eight.

Three weeks later, Joe and the team left for Greenwood Lake, New York for the second phase of his training, which included sparring.

Seamon hired several good sparring partners, ones who could imitate Walcott's shifty style. One was Richard Hagen, a 20-year-old Chicago Golden Gloves champion the previous year. Another was Roy 'Tiger' Taylor, a fast mover with a stop-and-start style similar to Jersey Joe's. 'We're leaving nothing to chance,' said Seamon. 'Joe will catch Walcott this time and knock him out.'

Louis had little to say to reporters at the camp at first, except the obligatory claim that he felt confident he would retain his title and then hang up his gloves. As the weeks went on, he talked more. 'I'll be good and strong for this one,' he promised. 'I'll be going in there to put over the knockout as early as I can. I'll catch him this time unless he jumps over the ropes and runs back home.'

Louis promised his ageing mother, who had been pleading for him to retire, that this would be his last fight and he hoped to go out in a blaze of glory. He was now 34 years of age and had fought a long and busy career.

Walcott again set up camp at Grenloch Park, New Jersey, where signs read, 'Training Camp for the Champ'. The reporters wanted to know what kind of style Jersey Joe would use this time. In the first fight, he had employed a lot of movement, counter-punching and 'walk-away' tactics to throw Louis off. Walcott was giving nothing away as he knew there were Louis spies in the camp. 'I don't know what my plan of battle is yet,' he said. 'I'm going to fight as I'm told by my team. Boxing is like a football team – there's a captain and a coach. One guy carries the signals. I'm the guy who carries the ball.'

When told of Louis' plans for a knockout victory, Jersey Joe said, 'I'm glad that Joe is in good shape because I want him in there with all his strength, so as he'll be able to go a few rounds before I take care of him.'

Regardless of what Walcott told the newspapermen, his plan was to stick with what worked in the first fight. Privately, Florio wanted Jersey Joe to again use a lot of movement and feints. He did not want him to stand flat-footed and punch it out with Louis, which would be fatal. 'Louis is the best finisher in boxing,' he told Walcott. 'To slug it out with such a dangerous puncher would be asking for trouble,' he warned.

As fight night neared, two former world heavyweight champions, Jack Sharkey and Jack Dempsey, picked Walcott by knockout, although Dempsey later changed his mind and went for Louis.

World light-heavyweight champion Gus Lesnevich, who would lose his title to Freddie Mills over 15 rounds in London a few weeks later, went for Walcott, as did former king of the heavyweights Max Baer and famed fight manager 'Dumb Dan' Morgan.

Of the 282 members of the Associated Press polled, 230 picked Louis while 52 went for Walcott. The general feeling among New York sportswriters was that Louis, already a 13/5 favourite, would win because he always did better in return bouts.

Torrential rain caused a 24-hour postponement of the fight. There were further heavy and prolonged downpours on 24 June, causing a second postponement to the following day, when the forecast was good. At the noon weigh-in, Louis scaled 213lb and Walcott 194lb.

When newsmen asked Seamon if he was worried about Louis' weight, which was one pound heavier that he'd scaled for Mauriello and five pounds more than he'd weighed for the second Conn bout, he replied, 'Look, he can weigh 210, 212, 215 or he can weigh a ton. It doesn't matter. He's in great shape and he feels good. That's more important.' Despite the two-day delay, a crowd of 42,667 fans paid over $900,000 to see the fight. Sol Strauss had anticipated a larger gate but considering the postponement, it was still a big turnout. Under a star-studded blue sky, referee Frank Fullam called the two combatants together for their final instructions. The bell rang and the big fight was on.

In the first two rounds, Walcott was on the retreat with Louis in patient pursuit. It seemed like a replica of the first fight. In the third round, the pattern of the bout changed dramatically when Jersey Joe caught the champion with a hard left hook to the head followed by a heavy right cross to the cheekbone that sent Louis to the canvas. He was up before a count could be started and nodded to his corner to indicate he was all right.

From the fourth round, it was looking as if the second fight might be similar to the first, with Walcott punching and retreating, and Louis going forward, waiting for the opening to land his big punches. The fifth and sixth rounds followed a similar pattern. Doggedly, Joe pursued the New Jersey fighter, watching and waiting for him to make a wrong move.

Heywood Hale Brown, covering the bout for the *New York Star*, wrote, 'I swore, prayed and developed a bad case of nervous indigestion waiting for Louis to spring into action.' By now, the fans were booing and hissing at the lack of action. When one newspaperman noticed the former world heavyweight champion Gene Tunney starting to doze at the slow pace in the seventh round, he nudged a colleague and said, 'Wake up Gene there, and make him suffer like the rest of us.'

In round eight, the 'Brown Bomber' caught the back-pedalling, sidestepping challenger with a solid left hook and a few stiff jabs that shook up Walcott. But the intermittent exchanges were not enough to keep the crowd satisfied.

Growing tired of Walcott's evasive tactics and Louis' tedious shuffling, referee Fullam, aware of the fans' displeasure, stopped the fight momentarily in the tenth round to tell the two boxers in stern tones, 'I want both you guys to get the lead out and let's have a fight. Remember, this is a world championship fight, not a preliminary.'

Walcott was still moving around in the 11th round, dodging Louis' left jabs and getting in some punches of his own with both hands when Louis spotted the opening he had been searching for since the first round. As Jersey Joe pulled back from a left hook, Louis followed through and connected with a tremendous right that landed flush on the side of Walcott's face.

The blow turned Jersey Joe's legs to papier mache. Sensing the kill, Louis pressed forward with a left-right combination that drove Walcott to the ropes. Jersey Joe tried to get away to the centre of the ring but Louis landed more rights and lefts to the body and head.

Walcott managed to slip away and surprisingly exchanged punches with boxing's greatest finisher. It was the same mistake that Billy Conn had made against Louis seven years earlier, and would cost him dearly. Louis connected with a blistering barrage of blows, lefts and rights to head and body, before a final right to the head sent Walcott to the canvas, landing on his back. The crowd was on its feet as Fullam waved Louis to a neutral corner and picked up the count from the timekeeper.

A stunned, glassy-eyed Walcott rolled over on to his hands and knees, shaking his head to try and clear the cobwebs that were clogging up his brain. He rose slightly but fell back down again. Bravely, he managed to force himself to his feet but it was too late. Fullam had already reached the ten count a moment before. The time was 2:56 of the 11th round. Louis had retained his title for the 25th time, more than the previous nine champions combined. He had also lived up to his reputation of doing better the second time round.

Louis was given a standing ovation from the crowd. Walcott, disappointed, made his way back to the dressing room, his face swollen and with a cut under his left eye. 'I thought I had him in the tenth round,' he told the awaiting press. 'Then the referee called for more action. I thought that he was directing his comments more at me than Louis.

'At that stage, I changed my style of fighting. I became more aggressive and then Louis tagged me. I only remember the first punch, but my corner says he hit me some more. I don't remember.' Asked if he would continue boxing now that Louis was retiring, he said, 'It's always been my ambition to win the heavyweight championship of the world, and I still think I can win it.' Three years later he did, knocking out the reigning champion Ezzard Charles in seven rounds.

A few doors down the corridor, a calm but happy Louis was being interviewed. He credited his trainer with bringing about his knockout victory. 'Mannie here deserves all the credit,' he said. 'He told me Walcott was tiring in the tenth round and that I should get him in the 11th.'

In the *New York Times* the next day, Arthur Daley reported, 'With one thunderous punch, Louis retained his title in a thrilling and heart-warming finish to as dreary a championship [fight] as ever was held.' Daley claimed that at the end of the seventh round, he heard somebody say behind him, 'If these guys are not careful, this could develop into a fight.'

Nat Fleischer, reporting for *Ring* magazine, said, 'The fight was as tedious an exhibition of fumbling and bumbling as most of the fans could remember.

The fight lacked even the bright spots of their previous encounter. It was not so much the coaxing of the referee that suddenly brought the fight to life. Instead, it was Louis' realisation that he might lose the decision if he didn't wake up. He was probably right in thinking so, for a check of the official scorecards showed that the challenger was leading on points at the end of the tenth.'

Describing the dramatic finish, Fleischer wrote, 'Nothing could save Walcott from the fury of Louis' attack. Utterly defenceless, he was spared further punishment only by collapsing in his tracks and was counted out.'

Louis was still champion of the world. As he left the ring he could hear the pleasant thunder of cheers, as he had so often in the past. He had erased the memory of his bad performance six months before. He was still the 'Brown Bomber'.

Round 11

End of a dream

Louis collected a $255,522 cheque for the Walcott fight but once again the money was reduced considerably with the various deductions, and these did not even include demands from the Internal Revenue Service, which was preparing changed tax rates for the previous year. Alongside his existing problems, more were beginning.

An ex-army champion, the Reverend Mathew Faulkner, discovered that Louis had been playing around with his wife, Carrolle, and was suing him for 'alienation of affections'. Faulkner sought a $500,000 settlement. The case was settled out of court for an undisclosed sum two years later, by which time Louis had been named in another lawsuit. Carrolle would later marry the singer Billy Eckstine.

Meanwhile, Joe was spending what money he had from several struggling businesses he was involved in, including the Joe Louis Insurance Company, the Brown Bomber Bread Company and a soft drink venture called Joe Louis Punch. Eventually, they all lost money, mainly Louis' money, and sank without trace. There were also rumours circulating that Louis had retired, although nothing official was announced.

Hints of retirement became more persistent in February 1949, when Louis and an old friend from his army days,

Truman Gibson, who was now his lawyer, announced they were setting up a boxing promotion company to rival Mike Jacobs' 20th Century Sporting Club, in association with the Hearst newspaper chain and a businessman named Harry Voiler.

Louis would give up his title officially, sign up the leading heavyweight contenders to exclusive contracts and promote a tournament to choose the next champion. Louis, in turn, would sell the exclusive contracts to Hearst and Voiler. The deal fell through when Voiler failed to arrange financing.

Harry Mendel, who had worked with Mike Jacobs and publicised some of Louis' fights, suggested they sell the deal to two wealthy businessmen, James D. Norris and Arthur Wirtz, who owned the Chicago Stadium and two leading hockey teams. They were also shareholders in Madison Square Garden.

Norris, the son of a wheat millionaire, and Wirtz, a property dealer who sponsored travelling ice skating shows, agreed to buy Louis' ambitious scheme and would pay Joe $15,000 annually as well as shares in their new organisation, the International Boxing Club (IBC).

They would also pay Louis $350,000 for the contracts of the contenders he signed up. When Mike Jacobs, still convalescing, heard about this, he was seething with anger. 'Louis is effectively selling the title to these guys, a title he fought so hard to win,' he said. The IBC would soon monopolise boxing as Jacobs' 20th Century Sporting Club had done before it. Mike's organisation had worked with Madison Square Garden for ten years. When the IBC moved into the Garden, they paid Jacobs $150,000 to step down as the Garden's promoter.

Louis' official retirement was announced on 1 March 1949 in the old airport terminal in Miami. Norris and Wirtz flanked Joe as he told an assemblage of reporters that he was hanging up his gloves. Also in attendance was Abe J. Greene, who, by his presence as commissioner of the National Boxing Association, sanctioned the departure of Louis from the ring and the official arrival of the IBC.

'So important was the announcement of Louis' departure that the usually staid *New York Times* printed it on its front page,' said Barney Nagler of the *New York Morning Telegraph*. 'Eleven years, eight months and one week after his coronation and after 25 successful defences, Joe Louis was no longer king of the heavyweights.'

Louis obtained the contracts of the four leading contenders, Jersey Joe Walcott, Ezzard Charles, Lee Savold and Gus Lesnevich. The NBA, which controlled boxing in the United States with the exception of New York, agreed to sanction a fight between the two top contenders, Walcott and Charles.

The New York State Athletic Commission refused to support the fight and would await further developments. In addition, neither the British Boxing Board of Control nor the European Boxing Union recognised the Charles–Walcott fight as being for the title.

Jack Solomons, the premier London promoter, matched British champion Bruce Woodcock with the American, Lee Savold, and had the fight endorsed by Britain and Europe as being for the world title. This was despite the fact that Charles and Walcott had demonstrated beyond any doubt that they were the logical contenders for the vacant championship.

The Woodcock–Savold fight was set for White City, London in June 1949 but the Yorkshireman was injured in a truck accident and the bout was postponed until the following June. Savold eventually stopped Woodcock in four rounds. The British Board vainly tried to pretend that Savold was the new world champion but nobody, not least the American authorities, took them seriously and Savold's claims were quietly forgotten.

Quite clearly, any legitimate heavyweight title fight would have to include either Charles or Walcott, or preferably both.

Ezzard and Jersey Joe clashed on 22 June 1949, with Charles winning on points over 15 rounds. Ironically, on the same day exactly 11 years earlier, Louis had achieved his greatest victory by defeating Max Schmeling in 204 seconds.

Charles was a competent all-round fighter, though he lacked Louis' heavy punch, explosive power and charisma. Then again, who could really follow Louis without comparisons being made? What mattered was that Charles was now the world's leading heavyweight, with a legitimate claim on Louis' old title. Universal recognition was what he wanted but that would come in time.

Born in the sprawling village of Lawrenceville, Georgia on 7 July 1921, Ezzard Mack Charles was named after Webster Pierce Ezzard, the doctor who had delivered him. When Charles was young, his mother, Alberta, who had separated from his father, William, moved to New York in search of work.

She found employment as a dressmaker and later remarried, while Charles was raised in Cincinnati, Ohio by his grandmother, Maude Foster, and great-grandfather Bell Russell. They were humble, church-going people and Charles spent his formative years in this environment, living alongside seven of Maude's own children.

After graduating from high school, Charles regularly visited the local boxing gym. He would spend hours listening to the veteran fighters, who were only too happy to pass on their wisdom to the youngster. He proved to be an exceptional student and won all his 42 amateur contests, including the National Golden Gloves middleweight title in 1938.

Ezzard's first trainer, a Welshman named Bert Williams, remembered Charles as a skinny kid who looked as if he didn't eat enough. 'He had no strength but he had the heart and the determination, not to mention the speed,' Williams said. 'He had courage and ambition. He didn't drink and he kept away from the ladies.'

After such a promising amateur career, it was no great surprise that Charles turned professional in March 1940, when still only 18. After racking up 20 straight wins in 14 months, he fought virtually a world middleweight championship eliminator against Ken Overlin in June 1941 in Cincinnati.

Overlin, a 30-year-old from Decatur, Illinois, had just lost the title in his previous bout to Billy Soose and was a bit too experienced for Charles, winning a decision over ten rounds. Later that year, having got his career back on track with two good wins, Ezzard took on another former middleweight champion in Teddy Yarosz and won a ten-round decision over the veteran, again in Cincinnati.

It was not until Charles outpointed the cagey Charley Burley in two back-to-back fights in 1942, both in Pittsburgh, that sportswriters began to take notice of him. Burley is considered the greatest middleweight never to win a world title, a smart boxer with a heavy punch in both hands.

Ray Arcel, Charles' trainer, realised he had a fine prospect in Ezzard. 'You must remember that Burley was the best fighter I ever saw who not only never won a world title but never got any glory,' remembered Arcel, who would coach a record 20 world champions in his career.

'In those days, if you were a good black fighter, nobody wanted to fight you. To get fights, Burley fought anybody who would meet him. He didn't care if the other guy weighed 180lb. Burley was 3/1 favourite in both fights but Charles outboxed and outfought him both times. That's how great a fighter Charles was.'

On an eight-fight winning streak going into 1943, which included two points wins over future world light-heavyweight champion Joey Maxim, Charles suffered two serious setbacks in his only two fights that year. He lost to crafty heavyweight Jimmy Bivins on points and was knocked out by hard-hitting light-heavyweight Lloyd Marshall in eight rounds.

His career was disrupted ever further when he got his call-up papers and signed up for the US army. He was stationed as a GI for the rest of the war, serving initially in North Africa before being shifted to Italy, where he boxed in inter-allied tournaments. Along with those of many other aspiring young athletes, Ezzard's ring career was effectively on hold until hostilities ended.

After being demobbed in late 1945, Charles linked up with the influential manager Jake Mintz. Together, they began a campaign aimed at leading them to a world title fight. Ezzard issued a challenge to world light-heavyweight champion Gus Lesnevich, but it went ignored.

Outside the ring, however, things were not going smoothly. Charles owned a sports arena in Cincinnati that had accrued an escalating $8,000 tax debt while he was away serving his country, and he was forced to sell. Even when he later became champion, Charles was still paying off the interest on the tax he owed. 'I'm about the poorest heavyweight champion, financially, the game has seen in years and years,' he used to say.

In the ring, things were far more promising, with a points win over future world light-heavyweight champion Archie Moore and two victories over his previous conquerors, Lloyd Marshall on a knockout in six rounds and Jimmy Bivins on points. With a Lesnevich title fight failing to materialise, Charles switched his campaign to the heavyweight division but returned to the 175lb weight class to beat Archie Moore on two more occasions, on points and on a knockout in eight rounds.

From the time of his return from his army duties until he defeated Walcott for the heavyweight title in June 1949, Ezzard only lost once in 31 fights against most of the best men of his day. His lone defeat was against Elmer 'Violent' Ray in 1947, a result he reversed a year later by stopping Ray in nine rounds.

Tragedy loomed when Charles was matched with Sam Baroudi in Chicago on 20 February 1948. After dominating the action for nine rounds, Ezzard floored the Akron, Ohio boxer in the tenth with three hard straight rights followed by a terrific left hook. Baroudi went down near the ropes. Referee Tommy Thomas counted him out 47 seconds into the round. Baroudi never regained consciousness.

Rushed to Columbus Hospital, he died five hours later. Ezzard was absolved of all blame and wanted to quit the ring, but Baroudi's family and friends urged him to carry on. In his next fight, the rematch with Elmer 'Violent' Ray in Chicago, Charles donated his entire purse of $5,000 to the Baroudi family.

Still campaigning for a heavyweight title shot, Charles had six more wins, including an impressive stoppage in 11 rounds against big Joe Baksi in New York and a third win over tough Joey Maxim, this time by split decision, before getting the call to meet Walcott for the vacant title in June 1949. Nat Fleischer of *Ring* magazine was not unduly impressed with Charles' victory over Walcott, making strong remarks that were criticised by many people, including several prominent newspaper columnists.

'Joe Louis left a mouldy crew to scramble for the throne when he retired,' Fleischer wrote. 'From now on, the public will be treated with heavyweight bouts in which mediocre battlers will take part in an effort to find Louis' successor. Louis left a boxing legacy of toil and brilliant action, but his heirs are about as seedy a lot as ever were assembled for world honours.'

Even though Charles was denied recognition as world champion by New York, he set about defending his NBA title against Gus Lesnevich at the Yankee Stadium in August 1949 before a disappointingly low crowd of 16,630. Ironically, when Lesnevich was world light-heavyweight champion, he did not want anything to do with Charles. Ezzard won on a stoppage in seven rounds.

Four months later, he knocked out Pat Valentino in eight rounds in San Francisco. It was the city's first heavyweight title fight in 40 years and drew state-record receipts of $167,870 from a crowd of 19,590. Charles' third bout was a win in 14 rounds against Freddie Beshore in Buffalo, New York in August 1950. It was watched by only 6,298, who paid an abysmal £28,666 at the gate, a record low in both attendance and receipts for a heavyweight championship fight at the time.

It was accepted that if Charles was to achieve anything like his due, both from the press and the public, he would have to beat Louis. It was common knowledge that such a fight was in the mind of promoter James D. Norris and his IBC. Ezzard did not want the fight. It was placing him in an awkward position.

If he didn't fight Louis, it would be said he was never the real champion. Yet if he did fight him, and win, it would be claimed that he only beat a shadow of the fabled 'Brown Bomber'. 'Joe was my boyhood idol,' Charles recalled, 'but my trainer, Ray Arcel, said that if I wanted everyone to consider me the champion, then I'd have to fight Joe.'

Louis had been hinting at a comeback only several months after beating Walcott. He had been boxing exhibitions around the United States and Jamaica but the money he earned did little to solve his escalating financial liabilities. After adding on penalties and interest, the IRS calculated Louis' tax bill at more than half a million dollars.

The government quickly slapped a lien against him, froze any revenue he was receiving and refused to allow him to sell anything unless the entire proceeds went towards paying off his back taxes. The only way to become solvent was to return to the ring.

'It was nothing but confusion,' Louis admitted. 'I had no idea what to do about all these problems. I figured I'd try to ignore them. But I couldn't forget this tax thing gnawing at my brain. My, these tax guys hang on to you. Always calling you up, showing up where they don't belong, getting on your nerves.'

But Louis himself was to blame for the soaring tax bill. The root of his financial difficulties was his own overspending. For ten years, he had outspent his income with his borrowing. Then there were his bad investments. Joe was like a spoiled kid who did not understand the full details of his financial situation. He needed good advice but never got any.

Mike Jacobs had given Louis enough rope to hang himself. Uncle Mike's loans assured Joe that he would not come to grips with his finances until it was too late. Jacobs would say to pay him first and the IRS later. Thanks to Mike, Louis would owe the government money all his life.

When IBC promoter Norris contacted Louis in August 1950 about a fight with Charles at the Yankee Stadium a month later, Joe objected. It was too soon. It would be his first fight after a lay-off of two years. He would need longer to get into condition for such an important fight, and Norris was only giving him six weeks.

Louis was 36, old as boxers go, and Charles was 29. An extra few months would allow Louis to take some easier fights and then go in with Charles, probably in December, at Madison Square Garden. Norris said he wanted a big outdoor fight in a ballpark, just like in the old days. They could do a better gate there than at the Garden in winter.

Norris then played with Louis' ego. 'You'd beat this guy Charles anywhere,' he said. 'Why, you could climb off the couch tomorrow and whip him. After all, you are Joe Louis. An older

Joe Louis but still Joe Louis.' Joe resisted as best he could but he was no match for a wealthy promoter who had all the money, all the cards and called all the shots.

Norris reminded him that no heavyweight champion had ever come out of retirement and won back the title, but that Louis could be the first. Joe eventually relented and shook hands with Norris. The big fight was on for 27 September at the Yankee Stadium.

It would be recognised universally as being for the undisputed heavyweight championship of the world, with all states, including the New York State Athletic Commission, in agreement. The European Boxing Union and the British Boxing Board of Control also fell into line. Tickets went on sale the next day.

Louis went into training, as short as it was, at Pompton Lakes. He got into good shape but no amount of training could restore the reflexes of his youth. Charles had no such worries. He was already in good condition, having had four fights, combining a total of 44 rounds, since Louis had stepped down after beating Walcott in June 1948. Charles' team, led by managers Jake Mintz and Tom Tannis, set up camp at the grounds of the Nemerson Hotel in South Fallsburg, a summer resort high in the Catskill mountains.

By the afternoon of the weigh-in, both boxers expressed satisfaction with their preparations. Louis was first on the scales, and the bar balanced at 218lb, the heaviest of his career. Charles weighed 184lb, the lightest heavyweight champion since Tommy Burns in the first decade of the 1900s. Louis was not at all happy with his weight. Then again, he'd had only six weeks to train, and had not been in a competitive fight for 27 months. What could he expect?

Nevertheless, he expressed full confidence in his ability to win back the title. No other heavyweight champion in boxing history had ever done that. James J. Corbett had tried and failed. So had Bob Fitzsimmons. James J. Jeffries came out of a six-year retirement to be trounced by Jack Johnson. Jack Dempsey had tried it and so had Max Schmeling, both without success.

Could Louis be the lucky one and break the jinx? The bookmakers thought so and installed him as a 2/1 favourite. So did most of the writers, including Grantland Rice of the *New York Herald Tribune* and Arthur Daley of the *New York Times*. A poll by the United Press found that 30 of 49 reporters picked Louis to win.

On fight night, the tension was high as a crowd of 22,357 filed into the Yankee Stadium, producing a live gate of $205,370. They were not the figures the IBC were hoping for. Three weeks earlier, Willie Pep and Sandy Saddler had drawn a live gate of $262,000 for their world featherweight title fight at the same venue – and attracted a crowd of 38,781.

Norris put the disappointing attendance and gate receipts for Louis–Charles down to national television. The Pep–Saddler fight was not televised. Thousands of potential paying customers in New York would see the Louis–Charles fight in the comfort of their living rooms or visit their favourite neighbourhood bar to watch the action.

Figures released later showed that the fight drew an unprecedented audience of 25 million viewers, thanks to a cable that linked the eastern part of the country to many stations in the west. It cost the CBS network $146,000, including radio rights. A new era had begun, the television era. Boxing's live attendances and gate receipts would never be the same again.

Still, Louis had good reason to be pleased. He would collect $193,529, though not nearly enough to pay off his rising debt to the government, not to mention his team. But it helped. Charles would clear just $57,404 before expenses. It was one of those rare occasions when the challenger got more than the champion.

As Louis had his hands taped in the dressing room by his trainer, Mannie Seamon, his mind drifted back to the old days. He used to love that last hour before a fight, when his opponent's dressing room seemed almost to work in concert with him. He would relax in the room, mindful that his reputation across the hall was wreaking havoc on his opponent's mind, feeding on his fears and insecurities, filling him with dread. There had never been a boxer better than Louis at using the dressing room before a fight to reduce his opponent to a ball of anxiety.

Hadn't King Levinsky, a competent heavyweight contender, been so frozen with terror before his fight with Louis in 1935 that promoter Mike Jacobs had to move the time of the fight forward by an hour to keep him from fleeing the venue, Comiskey Park in Chicago? Levinsky had locked himself in the toilet.

A month later, former champion Max Baer was so jittery before his fight with Louis that when Max's close friend and mentor Jack Dempsey stopped by the dressing room to wish him luck, Baer pleaded with the former champion to get the fight called off. Dempsey responded by threatening to lay Baer out on the floor there and then with one blow if he did not get into the ring.

Even former world light-heavyweight champion John Henry Lewis, a personal friend of Louis, was terrified as he went out to meet Joe in 1939. Heavyweight contender Lou Nova resorted to kicking everybody in sight in the dressing room and doing yoga in an attempt to calm his nerves before he faced Louis in 1941.

Now, after all these years of scaring his opponents silly, the great Joe Louis himself, the epitome of a stone-cold killer with gloves, the man who never went into a fight thinking he could lose, was doubting himself against Ezzard Charles, a man whose punching ability did not match his own. But he had a job to do and he would do it.

Louis' confidence increased as the days went by. He told Red Smith of the *New York Herald Tribune*, 'Charles is the best man around today but he lacks good opposition. I feel I can whip him. I don't mean that in the cockiest sort of way but I'm confident I can win.' Would Charles be the toughest man he had ever met? 'He'll be the toughest I ever met at my age,' Louis retorted.

Louis left the dressing room for his walk down the aisle to the ring in that frame of mind. As he looked over the crowd, it was just like old times. The ringside was filled with beautiful people. The high and the mighty were there. So were the kings and queens of society and business. So too were the political leaders, as well as showbusiness celebrities such as Frank Sinatra and his beautiful girl friend, Ava Gardner. Sinatra was a devoted Louis supporter, and would remain so until the end.

Sport was well represented and among the boxing stars present was Sugar Ray Robinson, the world welterweight champion who was destined for the middleweight title. Luis Firpo, the Argentinian who had once sent Jack Dempsey tumbling through the ropes, was there too. Newspapermen looked over their programmes. The two contestants had impressive records, Charles 66-5-1 and Louis 58-1. When they met in the ring centre, Louis looked like the heavyweight champion of the world. Charles had the appearance of a middleweight.

Referee Mark Conn called the two boxers together for their final instructions. Soon the bell rang and they were on their way. The moment of truth had finally arrived. Louis started off by stalking his prey, seeking an opening, but his quicker, lighter and younger opponent darted in and out of harm's way. Charles peppered the veteran with sharp hooks and jabs, driving him back all over the ring, a pathetic sight for those who had followed the former champion's illustrious career.

As the rounds went by, it became painfully clear that the advancing years had robbed Louis of his reflexes. In the past, he had been a great boxer because he was fundamentally sound and his hands were quicker and stronger than anyone else's. He was still strong but his co-ordination had deserted him. Louis was fighting on pride alone.

Sugar Ray Robinson, a long-time Louis supporter, was sitting alongside acting New York Mayor Vincent R. Impellitteri. At the bell ending the fifth round, Robinson left his seat and came along the aisle to tell Louis' handlers, 'Joe's got to keep sticking with that left hand. He's got to take the play away from Charles and keep him off balance.'

Charles was now almost dancing around the old 'Brown Bomber' and was not afraid to trade punches in close. He constantly beat Louis to the punch. Most of Joe's punches were not finding their target but he connected with strong rights on several occasions. Charles sustained a bruised left eye in the seventh and at the bell Arcel applied ice to Ezzard's bruised face.

The eye was closing rapidly but he was still able to slam left jabs into Louis' battered features. 'Charles was proving tougher than I had visualised,' Joe would remember in his retirement years. 'He was hooking and jabbing, and often concentrated on the body. Whenever I saw openings, I couldn't respond fast enough. My reflexes and co-ordination were all mixed up.'

Whenever Louis connected with heavy punches, Charles was able to slip out of danger because of his greater speed. Ezzard was peppering him with jabs, hooks and uppercuts, and Louis found he could do little about it. In the tenth, he managed to rock the Ohio fighter with a solid right to the head followed by a sharp left hook, but Ezzard moved into a clinch and was able to smother any further attack. 'The dominant image of Louis,' wrote Tim Cohane in *Look* magazine, 'was of a raked, swollen hulk, wearily, if gallantly and proudly, groping for the top ring rope.'

Charles was always sniping away with an assortment of hard shots and there was very little the old 'Brown Bomber' could do about it. 'I knew after the tenth, I was all over,' said Louis later. In the 14th round, Charles landed a smashing right to the jaw and while Louis countered, most of his punches were slow and Ezzard had little trouble avoiding them. Bruised, bleeding and bone-tired, Louis had to be lifted off his stool by his manager and trainer before the start of the last round.

The barrage from Charles continued for the full three minutes until the bell mercifully sounded, with Joe backed against the ropes as Charles delivered the final blows of the night. It was the worst beating Louis had suffered since the first Schmeling fight 14 years earlier. The decision was unanimous. Referee Mark Conn scored it 10-5 for Charles. Judge Frank Forbes had it 13-2 and judge Joe Agnello 12-3, both for Ezzard. The consensus around the ringside was that Louis had won just three rounds.

Louis was gracious in defeat when he met the gathering of newspapermen in his dressing room. 'Ezzard is a good fighter and I want to wish him well,' he said. 'He's the real champion now.' As to his own performance, he said, 'After the third or fourth round, I knew I was washed up. Certainly by the seventh round, I knew I couldn't do it. It wasn't a case of reflexes or anything. I just didn't have it. I did the best I could but I'll never fight again. Thank you all for coming.'

Charles said, 'Joe was always dangerous and I did not want to take any unnecessary risks. Why, when I felt his left jab in the early rounds, I could understand why he became heavyweight champion of the world. He was always my idol and always will be.'

Robinson was one of the first to enter Louis' dressing room. 'It was a sad occasion,' remembered the former world welterweight and middleweight champion. 'Blood seeped from cuts above each of his eyes. One of his eyes was swollen shut. I was in there with him but it was like to console an old blind man. Squinting in pain and embarrassment, he was unable to put on his pants or locate his shoes. I bent down and worked his feet into his big shoes and tied the laces. I helped him out of the ball park.'

Arthur Daley wrote in the *New York Times* the following day, 'There were several rushes of hope, including the tenth round when the Jolter's dreaded jab repeatedly rocked Charles. Maybe sentiment has no place in sports. Perhaps there is something in the ancient but stern admonition, "No cheering in the press box, please." But a guy wouldn't be human if he remained neutral in this fight. The one-time cotton picker from Alabama saved boxing and gave it some of his own nobility, innate decency, integrity and class. No sir, I rooted for Louis, unashamedly.'

Ring magazine's Nat Fleischer, a noted critic of Charles in the past, wrote, 'From the forgotten man in pugilism, and the most ridiculed, Charles emerged the proud possessor of the heavyweight crown worn in the past by many illustrious fighters. He proved his mastery in every branch of the sport to gain the universal recognition he sought.

'Yet it was a sad exit for a great champion, a defeat that carried with it a sadness such as I never have witnessed in a heavyweight title bout.

'Louis injured the knuckle of his left hand in the third round but said nothing about it to his handlers until the fight was over. A sportsman to the end.' Louis officially announced his second retirement the following day.

It had been a long journey, but an illustrious one. The $193,529 cheque he received from the IBC for the Charles fight raised nowhere near enough money to clear his mounting debts, as he had expected, though it helped. Federal taxes would be deducted by the patience and hunger of officials from the Internal Revenue Service. The old champion, now 36, had no option but to continue his comeback, with the aim of a return fight with Ezzard. He felt that a longer period than six weeks in training camp might make a big difference.

Cesar Brion was the first opponent selected. An ambitious and skilful heavyweight from Cordoba, Argentina, he had quit his job in the diplomatic service and headed for the United States in the summer of 1949 with the hope of making it big in boxing. Brion was not the aggressive, powerful boxer that his countryman Luis Firpo had been in the 1920s but he was skilful, tough and had a good punch.

Norris matched him with Louis over ten rounds at the Chicago Stadium on 29 November 1950. Conveniently, Norris now owned the stadium where the 'Brown Bomber' won the title in 1937. The Brion fight was even through the first seven rounds before the Argentinian abandoned his crouching style and changed to a more upright offensive in a bid to get more leverage into his punches. It was a mistake. The former champion both outjabbed and outpunched him to win a unanimous decision.

Louis said it was as hard a ten-rounder as he had ever been in. There was criticism from ringside writers that Louis had not used his right hand often enough. They estimated that in 30 minutes of combat, Joe only threw ten rights. Arthur Daley of the *New York Times* observed, 'It was as if his right hand never knew what his left was doing.' Seven months later, Brion travelled to London and outpointed the British and European champion Jack Gardner at the White City Stadium.

Fight number two of Louis' comeback went ahead on 3 January 1951, when he stopped Freddie Beshore at the Olympia

Arena, Detroit in four rounds. An ex-sailor from Harrisburg, Pennsylvania, Beshore had gone 14 rounds with Charles five months earlier before being stopped on cuts. Against Louis, he took a methodical beating. He was bleeding from the first round, his left eye was cut in the second and his mouthpiece was knocked flying in the third before the fight was stopped with 12 seconds left in the fourth round.

Louis, who said he had trained harder than at any time since the second Conn fight five years earlier, was unmarked and hardly out of breath. He asked his manager, Marshall Miles, to send a telegram to John DaGrosa, chairman of the Pennsylvania State Athletic Commission, who had recently stated that he should be compulsorily retired 'for the good of boxing'. 'Ask him how he feels now,' laughed Joe.

The dramatic return to form of Louis was prompting Norris to seriously think of a rematch with Charles. 'Louis is obviously not the Louis of old,' said the promoter, 'but his impressive showing against Brion, and Beshore in particular, make a rematch with Charles a real possibility.'

The Louis rollercoaster continued at the Miami Stadium a month later when the ex-champ climbed between the ropes to meet Omelio Agramonte, a rugged Cuban with a 44-10 record. Agramonte seemed more determined to last the full ten rounds than win, and stayed away from Louis' big punches by jabbing and hooking, mainly at long range. Joe managed to cut Agramonte's eye, bloody his mouth and stagger him on several occasions but failed to catch him with enough solid punches to bring about a stoppage. At the final bell, Louis won a unanimous decision. 'He ran and ran like Billy Conn,' he said in the dressing room.

On 23 February, Louis was in San Francisco for a scheduled ten-rounder against Andy Walker. Born in Louisiana and based in 'Frisco, Walker was little match for the rejuvenated

'Brown Bomber'. Louis opened up Walker's defence with sharp combinations of left hooks and right uppercuts before the one-sided affair was stopped after 1:49 of the last round.

Omelio Agramonte was telling anybody who would listen that he deserved another chance at Louis, and that he had not been fully prepared for their first fight two weeks earlier, when Joe won a unanimous decision. 'I know his style now, and I feel I can send him back into retirement,' he told sportswriters. The return fight was held at the Olympia Arena, Detroit on 2 May. The result was no different.

Though the Cuban did not run this time, Louis landed enough solid punches with both hands to win a unanimous decision again. He had Agramonte on the canvas from a long right in the second round – Joe's first knockdown success since starting his comeback – but Omelio was up at nine and managed to keep out of trouble for the rest of the fight. It was the first time in his career that Louis had failed to do better in a return fight, but he expressed satisfaction with his performance.

There was a step up in class for Joe's next fight. Norris matched him with Lee Savold, the number four contender, at the Polo Grounds on 13 June. From Canby, Minnesota and whose farming parents were of Norwegian ancestry, Savold had looked impressive in stopping the British and European champion Bruce Woodcock in four rounds a year earlier.

Lee boasted 98 wins and three draws in 140 fights going back to 1933. A hard puncher with both hands, he had knocked out contender Lou Nova in eight rounds in 1941 in a fight that was later named Upset of the Year by *Ring* magazine. At 36, Savold was ten months younger than Louis. The IBC promised the winner a world title fight with Charles, who was expected to retain his title against Jersey Joe Walcott on 18 July in Pittsburgh. Charles against the winner of the Louis–Savold bout would be held at either the Polo Grounds or the Yankee Stadium in September.

Heavy rain caused the postponement of the Louis–Savold fight to 15 June but a big baseball game was scheduled for the Polo Grounds that night, so Norris shifted the venue to Madison Square Garden. So many fans stormed the Garden box office that the IBC moved the 10pm starting time back 15 minutes. When IBC officials counted the takings, the figure came to $94,684, paid by a crowd 18,179. At the weigh-in, Louis scaled 211lb against Savold's 190lb.

Louis started fast, jabbing the oncoming Minnesota boxer and hooking him hard to the body, which made Savold blink. Lee moved around, trying to get a good shot at the former champion's head, but Louis was a moving target. Amazingly, the 'Brown Bomber' was showing much of his old form from his championship days, hooking, jabbing and uppercutting, which Savold seemed unable to avoid.

Lee looked indecisive and uncertain, and he was certainly being hurt by Louis' heavy blows. Only on rare occasions was he able to land with his vaunted right hand. From the second round to the fourth, Louis dominated the action and was able to fend off Savold's dangerous hooks both at long and short range. Louis had a solid lead after five rounds with his consistent attacks. It seemed that only a knockout could save Savold at this stage – and that seemed as likely as a snowstorm in July.

It was all over in the sixth. Beckoning Savold to 'Come on in', Lee obliged by jabbing and hooking Louis, but Joe responded with a barrage of left hooks and right uppercuts that drove Savold back to the ropes. Dizzy, his face covered in blood and his nose damaged, Lee was caught by a powerful left hook thrown with all Louis' power and crashed to the canvas on the seat of his trunks.

Referee Ruby Goldstein, who had voted for Jersey Joe Walcott against Louis in 1947, counted him out at 2:29 of the sixth round. It was the round in which Louis had predicted he would end it. Goldstein had given five straight rounds to Louis, as had judge Frank Forbes. Judge Harold Barnes gave Louis four rounds and Savold one, the fifth.

In the dressing room, a beaming Louis said, 'I was never hurt, not even by Savold's much-publicised right hand. He hit me hard in the fifth round, almost on the break, and my feet were together. It might have looked like he rocked me. He hadn't. Those three fights which went the distance on my comeback were wonderful tune-ups for me. I feel better now than I have in five years, since the second Conn fight.' He added with a laugh, 'Good luck to Charles.'

Reporters could not praise Louis highly enough. Nat Fleischer of *Ring* magazine wrote, 'Louis' terrific punches in the sixth round, especially that finishing right hander, were reminiscent of the Joe of yore. His general demeanour was remarkable. He fairly oozed confidence from the outset. He was the man in charge and he never relinquished that position. Savold did some fine jabbing but Louis was in great condition and cut him down. Lee underrated Louis and was sure he had lost his skill and punch.'

Sitting near Fleischer, the *Ring*'s associate editor Daniel M. Daniel reported, 'The summary ending of the fight reminded boxing aficionados of Louis' disposal of Paulino Uzcudun in 1935. The youthful Louis tore into the Basque. The fading Louis ripped Savold. The win gave the boxing business the greatest shot in the arm it has enjoyed since the Bomber's heyday. It shoots Louis back into the limelight, and will give him a second chance against Charles to regain the heavyweight title.'

Unfortunately, the Louis–Charles return fight never happened. On 18 July, four weeks after Joe beat Savold,

Charles took on Walcott at Forbes Field, Pittsburgh. Ezzard had previously beaten Jersey Joe on two occasions. In the third meeting, Charles, a 6/1 favourite, lost his title in a stunning upset when he was sensationally knocked out in the seventh round.

The result threw the heavyweight scene into turmoil as Jersey Joe would show no great interest in defending his hard-won title against a rejuvenated Louis, having already lost twice to the 'Brown Bomber'.

All Louis could do was continue his comeback and see what developments unfolded. He was back at the Cow Palace, San Francisco on 1 August for a return match with Cesar Brion. Joe had outpointed the Cuban over ten rounds the previous November and knew his style. He also hoped to beat him inside the distance this time.

It was not to be. Brion, a 12/1 underdog, was tough and once again survived Louis' attacks to finish on his feet, but he lost a unanimous decision.

Two weeks later it was on to Maryland, where Joe was matched over ten rounds with Jimmy Bivins at the Memorial Stadium, Baltimore. Born in Dry Branch, Georgia and boxing out of Cleveland, Ohio, Bivins was never given the opportunity of competing for a world title in his prime, despite at one stage being the number one contender for both the light-heavyweight and heavyweight championships.

In a busy career, Bivins fought and beat many of the best men in the two top divisions and was the 'duration' champion at both weights during World War Two. This was a notable achievement considering that, at 5ft 9in, he was often significantly smaller than his opponents.

When Louis stepped on to the scales at the weigh-in he scaled 203lb, his lightest weight for ten years. Turning to Bivins, 23lb lighter and essentially a light-heavyweight, he said, 'I'm going to knock you out in four rounds.' The Clevelander retorted, 'You'll have to hit me first, Joe.'

Bivins elected to keep moving and refrained from getting into any close-quarter exchanges with the power-hitting former champion. This resulted in an unexciting bout, with Louis unable to land any significant punches on his shifty opponent. Joe won a unanimous decision and claimed after the fight that he had injured his right hand, though he did not offer that as an excuse.

The eight-fight comeback since his defeat by Charles had netted him less than $200,000, out of which had come his expenses. The tax bill now stood at $1 million and it was estimated that every day Louis woke up, he owed the government an additional $270 in interest, or $100,000 a year. He had no choice but to continue fighting. He was now ranked number two by *Ring* magazine among the contenders for new champion Walcott. Jersey Joe was already committed to giving Charles, the number one contender, a return match.

While Louis still retained the affection of fans and the press, the long-sought messiah for boxing promoters had appeared on the scene, a genuine white hope. His name was Rocky Marciano, the number three contender. Short for a heavyweight at 5ft 9in and light, generally weighing around 184lb, Rocky was also limited in skill. He did not turn professional until he was nearly 24, a relatively late age to join the paid ranks.

But Marciano made up for any deficiencies with a killing punch in both gloves and a frame of iron that allowed him to absorb powerful blows to the head and body. He had won every one of his 37 fights, all but five inside the distance, and was known as the 'Brockton Blockbuster'.

Marciano was born Rocco Francis Marchegiano in the American shoe-making capital of Brockton, Massachusetts on 1 September 1923. His parents had met in Brockton after emigrating from Italy. Rocky's father, Pierno, was a small man of around 150lb who, for the rest of his life, suffered breathing difficulties that were not helped by his work on the production line of the shoe factory where he earned his living. Pasqualena, on the other hand, was a large, strong woman. Rocky was to say that he got his physical strength from his mother and his inner strength from his father.

As a baby, Marciano weighed in at a hefty 12lb, perhaps the only time in his life that he would be viewed as much bigger than normal. After an ordinary spell in high school, he dropped out and got a job working alongside his father at the shoe factory.

Meanwhile, he had developed a passion for baseball but a potential career in the sport was derailed when he 'threw his arm out', a permanent injury that future ring opponents could have been forgiven for wishing was much more serious. Then health problems due to factory conditions meant Marciano had no future in the shoe-making industry.

Rocky was now 16 and worked various jobs, including on a coal truck, in a confectionery shop and even for a few weeks in the dreaded shoe factory before developing his back, arm and leg muscles on a construction site. In March 1943, he was drafted into the army. Rocky was stationed in Wales for a while and legend has it that he first discovered the power in his fists when he knocked out a big Australian with one right hand after a disagreement in a pub.

Back in civvies after the war, Rocky began seriously considering a boxing career and in 1946 he pulled on the gloves for the first time as an amateur. His aim was to represent America as a heavyweight in the Olympic Games in London two years later. An injury to the knuckles on his left hand ended that dream, and while the injury cleared up he decided, having had 12 contests with four defeats, to leave the amateurs and turn professional.

Rocky joined up with Allie Columbo, a boyhood chum and army buddy, and headed for New York after writing to Al Weill, one of the most influential managers in the country. Weill sent them to see a well-known and respected trainer in the city, Polish-born Charley Goldman. After watching Rocky in a sparring session, Goldman said that while the Brockton fighter lacked any semblance of skill and finesse, he had tremendous power. 'Rocky was crude and awkward and was consistently off balance, but he had a hell of a wallop,' remembered Goldman.

Born in Warsaw, his parents emigrated to the United States while Goldman was very young and he became a street fighter in Brooklyn before turning professional. He never won a title but by his own estimate had around 400 fights as a bantamweight before retiring to become a trainer.

Based in New York, Goldman worked successfully with many boxers at Stillman's famous gym, including four world champions – middleweight Al McCoy, welterweight Marty Servo, lightweight Lou Ambers and featherweight Joey Archibald. But he would always be associated with Marciano.

Employing his philosophy of improving upon but not changing a boxer's natural style, Goldman tightened Marciano's defence and showed him how to get more power into his left hook. Goldman worked tirelessly with Rocky and was convinced that the 24-year-old Brockton fighter could well go to the top. The development of the left jab and the left hook became the centrepiece in the Goldman–Marciano programme of improvement. In the gym, Goldman tied Rocky's right hand behind his back so he would become more accustomed to using his left.

Famed sportswriter and *Ring* magazine contributor W. C. Heinz remembered running into Goldman on Broadway one afternoon. 'How are you getting on with the new kid you're training?' asked Heinz.

'There are things that I could do but I'm afraid to do very much,' he replied. 'Because if I changed him too much and changed around his stance and his style so that he doesn't get hit with many punches, I might take something away from his punch. His punch is his greatest asset. You don't fix something if it ain't broke.'

Slowly but surely, Marciano began to develop his left, which became one of his most potent weapons. There were never any problems with his right. From the start, Rocky possessed a looping overhand right that was lethal. His team nicknamed the punch the Suzy Q.

Under Goldman's daily tuition, with Weill as manager and Colombo as an odd-job man, Marciano made his professional debut in Holyoke, Massachusetts on 17 March 1947. He knocked out Lee Epperson in the third round. Rocky kept on winning and moving up the ratings. By the time he went in against Louis, he had compiled 37 straight wins without a single loss or draw.

The IBC offered Louis $300,000 to fight Marciano at Madison Square Garden on 26 October. It was an offer too good to turn down. Joe felt in his heart, even at 37, that he could outbox Rocky. Even though Marciano had youth, stamina, power and hunger, Louis had a nine-inch advantage in reach and far more experience than the Brockton fighter – and the prospect of a big purse was not bad either. After all, he had been making around $15,000 in the comeback bouts since the Charles loss.

Louis went into training at his familiar camp, Pompton Lakes. He was balding and puffy, and while his left jab had lost much of its speed and sting, he was still able to bang his sparring partners around the ring with power and authority. In the closing week of camp, the ageing 'Brown Bomber' knocked sparring partner Holly Smith down with a smashing left hook.

It was a critical match for both boxers and one that would surely determine who would be the top contender for the world heavyweight championship. An indication of the esteem in which Louis was held by the boxing public was seen when he was installed as a 6/5 favourite with the bookmakers, and 8/5 in some quarters, although most writers were picking Rocky to win. At the weigh-in, Louis scaled 212lb, the heaviest he had been since defeating Cesar Brion in their first bout 11 months earlier. Marciano balanced the bar at 187lb.

On fight night, a crowd of 17,241 paid $152,845 to see the highly publicised fight. Marciano was first into the ring, accompanied by his handlers, including trainer Goldman. Louis followed soon afterwards with his coach, Mannie Seamon. Mannie knew this was going to be a tough one and advised Joe to keep the fight at long range, picking up points with his better boxing. The referee was Ruby Goldstein.

For the first time in his career, Louis was not the aggressor. From the opening bell, with Rocky pursuing him, the 'Brown Bomber' followed Seamon's advice and relied on his famed left jab to keep his younger, stronger opponent at a distance. But it was never easy. Marciano was relentless and, fighting from a crouch, a looping right shortly before the end of the first round staggered Louis, an indication of Rocky's immense power.

Louis was boxing well, repeatedly catching his man with left jabs and hooks, but the 'Brockton Blockbuster' kept storming forward like a tank, seeking openings for his heavy bombs. Rocky missed as often as he landed but when he connected, it was noticeable that Joe backed off and reverted to his sharper boxing. 'Keep it up, Rocky,' advised Goldman in the corner between the third and fourth rounds. 'He won't stand too much of that.'

For five rounds it was fairly even but while Louis' long-range work was impressive, there was always the lurking danger of Marciano's powerful punching bringing the bout to a sudden end. Rocky had to take punches to enable him to deliver his own punishment. Joe's left cheek was raw and swollen and there was a nick under his left eye. A trickle of blood came from Rocky's nose and there was a slight cut in the corner of his right eye.

Louis' superior experience showed when the two fought at close range but although he landed well with uppercuts and used his left jab frequently, he seemed to conserve his once-deadly left hook. This was possibly out of respect for Rocky's looping overhand right, which had accounted for most of his wins and could be delivered over an opponent's left.

By round seven, Louis appeared weary under Marciano's relentless pressure. He became slow-footed but he was still in with a chance. Rocky slammed two heavy rights to the chin but Joe came back with a savage left hook that crashed into the right side of Marciano's jaw. Yet Rocky was winning. Referee Goldstein had it four rounds to two for Rocky and one even. Judge Joe Agnello had Marciano ahead 5-2 and judge Harold Barnes favoured Rocky 4-3.

In the eighth round, Marciano continued to get in close with body attacks, his plan of action from the start. Suddenly, he caught Louis with a sweeping left hook and Joe went down on his back with his legs crossed. He took a count of eight on one knee as the fans leapt from their seats, roaring.

Louis' eyes were cloudy and his head was spinning as Marciano came at him like a shark that had tasted blood. Most of his blows missed before he steadied himself and aimed his punches directly at Louis' jaw. One struck with such power that it knocked Louis against the ropes, his hands hanging loosely by his sides. The old champion began to sag, alone and helpless, unable to prevent his own annihilation.

Rocky's eyes were wild with frenzy. In a split second, he aimed a devastating right that rang against the bone of Joe's jaw, like a bell declaring a moment in history. Louis fell backwards through the ropes and sprawled awkwardly on to the ring apron, with one leg still inside the ring.

Goldstein began the count but when he reached three he waved his arms, signalling that the fight was over. Then he hurried on to the apron to assist his old friend Joe, who appeared as if he might roll off it into the press rows. The time of the stoppage was 2:36 of round eight. It was a poignant moment in boxing history. One era had ended and another had begun. The king was dead. Long live the king.

Sugar Ray Robinson, who had won back his world middleweight title a month earlier, climbed up on to the apron and cradled his idol's head in his arms, fighting back tears, oblivious to the roar of the crowd. 'Joe, Joe, you'll be all right, Joe,' he said. 'You'll be all right, man.'

In Louis' dressing room, which was a melodrama of emotion, Joe gave Rocky full credit for his win. 'I think he hits harder than Max Schmeling,' he said. 'This kid finished me off with two punches. Schmeling knocked me out with maybe a hundred punches.

'The better man won tonight, and this kid is tough enough to beat anyone around. What's the use of crying? I'm not too disappointed and I hope everybody feels the same way I do about it. I'm not looking for sympathy from anybody. I guess everything happens for the best.'

In the winner's dressing room, Marciano took time out from his victory celebration to write a note to Louis. He had tremendous respect for the former champion's fighting ability, and he envisioned how Joe must have been feeling. 'It was a good fight, a very good fight,' he told reporters. 'He kept hitting me with those jabs and I just had to take them.'

John Roxborough, Louis' former manager, claimed he overheard Marciano's mentor, Al Weill, bragging at ringside about Rocky's great victory and claiming he always knew his boxer would beat the 'Brown Bomber'. 'Al,' said Roxborough, 'Your boy didn't beat the great Joe Louis. All he did was beat Joe Louis' shadow.'

Louis remembered in later years, 'Marciano came into the dressing room and he was crying. "I'm sorry, Joe," he said. I understood him but my needs and interests had changed. I was just as sorry seeing him there crying as I was sorry about myself.

'When I was on the rubbing table, Dr Vincent Nardiello, the medical officer of the New York Commission, said to me, "Joe, you can't fight for at least three months." I turned my head and said, "Doc, do you mind if I don't fight no more at all?" He smiled at me and said, "That's good."

'Right then, I knew I wasn't going to take part in another professional fight. I was 37 years old. I thought, like many fighters before and after me, that I'd always be some kind of superman. That's the dream, not the reality. I just didn't have it any more.'

'For many people, it was a sad affair,' recalled referee Goldstein, who had been on tour with Louis during the war and refereed Joe's controversial first fight with Jersey Joe Walcott. 'People idolised Louis. They didn't want to see him when he wasn't himself. It wasn't easy for me. We were friends, still are. But when you are a referee, you've got to steel yourself. You've got to be a little hard.

'You've got to realise there are two men in the ring, and they are both trying very hard to win the fight because it means a lot of money to them. I couldn't bring myself to count Louis out so I stopped the fight,' Goldstein continued, once again capturing the supreme status that Louis had in boxing. 'I noticed early in the bout that Louis' jab was not the same any more. I figured Joe might find himself but he never did.

'Was Marciano ever in trouble during the fight? It would be hard to tell if Rocky was ever in trouble, because hitting him was like hitting a stone wall. If he was ever hurt, he didn't show it. He was a rough, tough, game guy who came to fight and came to win.'

A. J. Liebling told his readers in the *New Yorker*, 'Louis' punches didn't sicken Marciano as they had sickened Joe's opponents from 1935 to 1940. In the sixth round, things started to go sour for him. It wasn't that Marciano grew better or stronger. It was that Louis seemed to get slower and weaker. The spring had gone from his legs, and it had been only a slight spring in the beginning.

'In the clinches Marciano was shoving him around. A right-hand specialist, Marciano knocked Louis down with a left hook. When he got up, Marciano hit him with two more left hooks, which set him up for the right and the pitiful finish.'

Sitting next to Liebling was a tall, blonde woman who had come to the fight with a Marciano supporter. As the fight began, she yelled, 'I hate Marciano! I hate him! I think he's the most horrible thing I've ever seen.' When Louis was sent crashing through the ropes, she began to boo. 'Rocky didn't do anything wrong,' said her male companion. 'He didn't foul Louis. Why are you booing him?' She turned to him and replied, 'You're so cold, I hate you too.'

Arthur Daley of the *New York Times* said the fight had been 'a strange, unpleasant, nasty sort of dream'. He wrote, 'Joe Louis, the symbol of invincibility, of dignity, of class and of compelling majesty had suddenly vanished.' Daley lamented that he should write more about Marciano and latch on to the rising star. But the dream of what Louis had been, back before the war and television, lingered. 'This reporter has been carrying the torch for Joe much too long to start any new flirtation. It's still love. In this corner, Louis losing is more important than Marciano winning.'

In the days following the fight, attention remained squarely on Louis. 'An old man's dream ended,' said Red Smith in the *New York Herald Tribune*. 'A young man's vision of the future opened wide. Young men have visions, old men have dreams. But the place for old men to dream is beside the fire.'

Louis never officially announced his retirement but his competitive career in the ring was over. An exhibition tour followed, his last. It was in the Far East. At the end of the tour, Joe realised it had netted him only $20,000, and the IRS back in the United States would be waiting for him. What would a man do next? He looked in the mirror one morning and asked himself that very question. He did not have an immediate answer.

Invisible enemy

Louis' comeback earnings, estimated at around $400,000 less expenses, made little more than a dent in his tax liability. A biopic, *The Joe Louis Story*, with the promising heavyweight Coley Wallace, a former Golden Gloves champion, playing Joe, opened in 1953. Wallace's chief claim to fame was that as an amateur in the 1948 New York Golden Gloves, he defeated future world champion Rocky Marciano.

It cost $400,000 to make, with investments by several interests, including the car magnate Walter Chrysler, a public relations company and Louis himself. The movie did little business. The *New York Times* treated it kindly with an eight-paragraph review. Leonard Maltin in his annual *Movie Guide* said, 'The film is interesting historically but dramatically hokey. Wallace looks the part of Louis but is no actor.'

'It was distributed by one of Hollywood's biggest studios, 20th Century Fox,' recalled Louis. 'It wasn't a bad movie but it wasn't a good one, either. The producers said they ran out of money part of the way through.

'Maybe, but it was fun hanging around Hollywood again, being a consultant on the picture and meeting new friends. Plus, of course seeing some of my old friends, men and women.'

Insofar as Louis was concerned, it added up to just another financial flop. It now seemed impossible for Joe to earn enough money to pay off his tax bills. He even harboured fears that he would end up in prison. During the next few years, he was constantly met with demands from the IRS. When his mother died in December 1953, she left a modest estate of $5,500. Joe's share amounted to $667, and the IRS took that too.

A few months earlier, Louis' old promoter, Mike Jacobs, died of a heart attack in Florida after returning from the races in Hialeah Park. He was 73. The news saddened Joe. He had lost an old friend. 'If it weren't for Mike willing to take a chance on a black boxer, I would have never gotten to be champion,' Louis recalled. 'Mike opened the door so that many other black fighters could get a better chance. He helped break down a lot of prejudice in the fight game, and he was the one who got rid of the crookedness in the heavyweight division.'

Louis managed to put a bit of light back into his life on Christmas Day 1955, when he married a long-time friend, Rose Morgan, who ran a chain of hairdressing salons. The wedding was held at her beautiful house in St Albans, Long Island, and among the many guests was the great musician and bandleader Count Basie.

Joe had too much pride to live off his wife and he soon turned to wrestling to make a living. Newsreel cameras recorded the staged spectacle of the former great boxing champion in his first match, his belly sagging over the waistband of his trunks, receiving dirty blows from a bad-guy opponent before ending the bout with a well-choreographed forearm or right cross. Rose Morgan said with a deep sadness that was felt across the United States, 'It's like seeing President Eisenhower washing dishes.'

Louis was wrestling 'Cowboy' Rocky Lee in 1956 when his 320lb opponent sat on him and broke a rib that pierced his heart muscles. That brought an end to Joe's wrestling career. His two-year marriage was also in trouble after Rose discovered he was seeing other women on a regular basis. Louis denied this but they parted in the summer of 1957. The break-up affected Joe so much that he blindly got himself involved with a promiscuous half-Oriental woman who started to supply him with drugs. Louis would claim that she got him hooked on drugs by injecting him while he was asleep.

The FBI tipped him off that the woman had Mafia connections and was a star of pornographic movies. He had the sense to get away from her and headed for Los Angeles where, in late 1959, he renewed acquaintances with a lawyer friend, Martha Jefferson, a Texan and the first black woman to be admitted to the Bar in California.

His marriage to Rose Morgan at an end, Louis married Jefferson in a civil ceremony in Winterhaven, California in 1959. They lived in Martha's ten-room Spanish-style house in Los Angeles. For Joe's viewing convenience, she had eight televisions placed throughout the house, including one in the bathroom. When not watching television, which was often, Louis played a lot of golf. While he never became a great golfer, he was a very good amateur who shot in the low 70s. He had already invested most of his ego in boxing and because of his success in the ring, he could accept his limitations in his second sport.

Louis still travelled frequently, making commercial personal appearances and refereeing wrestling matches. Boxing promoters paid him small fees to appear at training camps and talk to the press. Martha even set him up as a boxing promoter but Louis lost money on the venture because he insisted on paying his boxers more than the going rate. When Martha complained, he said, 'I was a boxer, and I know how tough it is. That's why I pay them good.'

In 1960, the couple set off for Hawaii, where Martha watched her husband perform in a new nightclub act put together by an old friend, Leonard Reed. The highlight of the act was when the short, pencil-slim Reed knocked down his much larger buddy, much to the amusement of onlookers. Martha could not decide whether the routine was dumb or degrading, or both. A local reviewer tried to be kind. 'The consensus was that as a comic, Joe was a great boxer,' he wrote. Much the same thing had been said about Sugar Ray Robinson when he became a song and dance man several years earlier.

Louis never made any money from his sporadic attempts at enterprise, and the IRS still took $20,000 a year in back taxes on top of the normal tax rate. Martha got so fed up with their relentless pursuit of her husband that she contacted IRS commissioner Dana Latham asking him to forget about Louis' back taxes and tax him only on his current income. Though the IRS never officially wrote off his massive debt, they agreed to tax him on his current earnings only. In 1961, these amounted to no more than $10,000.

Around this time, Louis got news that his elder brother, Lonnie, had been found dead in a room above his shoeshine shop. Police suspected that he had gassed himself but a distraught Louis always vehemently denied their findings. 'There is no way Lonnie would have taken his own life,' he said.

Louis' next problem was self-inflicted. On a business trip to New York in 1964, he got involved with yet another pretty girl who dragged him back into the world of drugs. To further complicate his life, she claimed he had got her pregnant. He finally summoned up the courage to confess all to the remarkably patient and understanding Martha, who immediately went to New York to confront the girl.

A few days later, she returned to their home in Los Angeles carrying a baby boy in her arms. He was the image of Louis and they officially adopted him and gave him the name Joseph. About the time of the adoption, Martha noticed that Louis, who had always been a sharp dresser, had begun to go several days without changing his clothes. He just sat around the house some days. Other days, he played golf with friends.

With growing frequency, he told Martha that somebody out there, probably a woman he knew as Annie Mitchell, who was attached to the Mafia, was trying to kill him. Louis went into hospital for gall-bladder surgery early in 1969 and on being released he slipped back into the habit of sniffing cocaine. He was soon back in hospital to have his stomach pumped after collapsing following a drug session. Martha stood by him and encouraged him to beat the habit.

Louis was now refusing to eat outside his home and Martha had to constantly travel with him, packing a hot plate and soups so she could cook for her husband in their hotel room. His most persistent fear was that Annie's Mafia friends were now trying to gas him. Louis was being imprisoned by insecurity.

'It was pitiful, really,' recalled Martha. 'He would tape up all the outlets. He would take a piece of paper and fold it neatly and paste it over the grilles. That wasn't anything new. What was new was the way he tried to sleep. In our place, he would build a cover for the bed. Then he would take the shade from the window and use it as a backdrop, like the top of a tent. Then he'd crawl up under it in his clothes and lay under it. Here he was with his shoes and everything lying under this tent. It was the most pathetic thing in the world.

'Like when Jesse Owens, the Olympic runner, was honoured at a Hall of Fame dinner in Birmingham, Alabama. We went down there for it. We stayed in this hotel and there was Joe working on his air-conditioning tent, which was quite large. It was so large that Joe could get the upper part of his shoulder up into it after he removed the grille. He had this paper twisted up against the light to make it shine into the vent so he could see. He said, "Yeah, that's where they put the stuff in, up there. This is where the gas is coming from." I could have cried.

'Another time when we were in Florida – I guess it would have been in February 1970 – I left Joe and went to Nassau on business. When I got back the next day, there were grease spots on the ceiling. I said to him, "Joe, what on earth is that on the ceiling?" I knew I hadn't seen the spots when I left.

'It was a brand-new hotel and we were the first ones to occupy the apartment we were in. Joe said, "I was stopping up the outlets and cracks. The poison gas is coming through them." When I asked him what he meant, he said, "I got this mayonnaise out of the fridge and smeared it over the cracks. They can't get the gas through there." You know, if it wasn't so tragic I would have laughed.

'The worst thing is that Joe wanted to stay in bed all day. He didn't have any physical fitness programme. At least it would have been more satisfying than what he did. He just ate and slept during the day, and what he ate, I had to push it on him. I had to believe there was some solution to all this.'

Martha took him to several doctors, including a long-time family friend. Neither the doctors nor Martha could convince Joe to seek medical treatment. Desperate, Martha, with the help of the former champion's eldest son, Joseph Louis Barrow Junior, who was now a practicing lawyer in Denver, signed the commitment order to have Joe admitted to Colorado Psychiatric Hospital, where he would have intensive treatment to cure him of his phobia.

When deputies arrived at his house in Los Angeles, Louis told them he was not going anywhere. Picking up the phone, he put in a call to the White House and asked to speak to President Nixon. The operator said the president was not available but that Louis could speak to one of his aides. He then hung up and instead called the local newspapers to schedule an impromptu press conference. It never happened.

When news of Louis' mental illness got into the newspapers, hundreds of letters not only from the United States but all over the world flooded into his hospital ward. Doctors determined that his condition had nothing to do with his years in the ring. They felt it was a hereditary link. His father, who never boxed, had been confined to a mental institution in Alabama.

'People were nice to me and I really appreciated what they did,' Joe remembered years later. 'I know at first I didn't want to go into hospital and when I had to go, I just wanted to get the hell out of it. But after a while, I sort of relaxed there. I was tired. Tired of all the running and the hustling and I figured I might as well stay there and rest and get better.

'The thing that had me almost crying was when I found out my friends were putting on a big "Salute the Champ – Joe Louis" party at the Cobo Hall arena in Detroit. Can you imagine? People were going to try and raise $100,000 for me – to honour me, and to help pay those hospital bills. Martha went and represented me. Billy Conn was there too.'

Louis spent five months in hospital. He was released on condition that he returned twice weekly for therapy on an outpatient basis. He obeyed instructions for a while but stopped going when his physician, Dr Martin, became ill. He never returned to Colorado.

Early in 1971, a visitor called at Louis' home in Los Angeles. It was Ash Resnick, a former army buddy and boxing promoter who was now running the casino at Caesars Palace in Las Vegas.

When they first met around ten years earlier, Resnick was putting on world championship fights at the nearby Thunderbird Hotel and regularly had Louis as his special guest at the gambling tables.

'Back then, we knew Joe couldn't win anyhow because he didn't push hard with big bets when he was winning,' Resnick said. 'I'd see Joe with as much as $6,000 in front of him and I would tell him, "Quit, Joe. Save the money. Put it away." But he wouldn't walk away from the table with the money. He would keep on playing until he didn't have any more. Just as long as he had a dime to get his newspaper and go to sleep, he was happy.'

At Caesars Palace, Resnick put Louis on a permanent payroll as 'official greeter' on a salary of $50,000 a year. His duties included playing golf, gambling with house money, posing for photographs and rehashing just one more time his fights with the likes of Billy Conn and Max Schmeling, who were often guest celebrities. Hollywood movie stars would turn up too, including Oscar winner Gregory Peck. Frank Sinatra, 'Ol' Blue Eyes' himself and a long-time Louis supporter, was also a regular visitor.

George Puscas of the *Detroit Free Press* recalled Louis' duties. 'He would sit by the blackjack table opposite the number one crap table for three or four hours, signing autographs and chatting to whoever came up to him,' said Puscas. 'Everybody knew him, of course, and so it was always "Hello, champ" or "I remember when you knocked out Schmeling." Other times it would be someone recalling the Braddock fight or the Conn fight or whichever. He liked the attention.'

Puscas told of one evening when Joe had slipped some chips to a nearby friend and turned to Bill Weinberger, a long-time friend who now ran Caesars Palace. 'I need some more chips,' said Louis. 'But you've already gone through your allotment today,' said Weinberger. 'I know what you are doing, Joe. You're giving the chips away to people when they come to your table.'

Louis mumbled something that sounded like a denial but Weinberger could only smile helplessly. Joe got another $5,000 and he was happy.

Visitors walked away from Louis after a brief chat as if they were old friends. Some were secretly saddened. What was a national hero doing on the tacky Las Vegas Strip, lurching along on the fumes of his fame, wearing a cowboy hat? 'It was degrading,' said one visitor from Arkansas who had seen the 'Brown Bomber' in action several times, including his great win over Billy Conn in 1941. 'I would prefer to remember him as he was, not what he is now.'

Joe's son said any criticism was unfair. Although aware that his famous father was also drinking and smoking, Joseph Louis Barrow felt he was in his element again. 'Dad was earning a salary, travelling and meeting people,' he said. 'He was loved by Caesars Palace and the people who visited there.

'They wanted him to retire in some quieter place but that's not the way he lived his life. He'd always had an exciting, worldly life, and Las Vegas was just an extension of that life. It might not be what you or I would do but it clearly makes him happy. Las Vegas didn't take away anything that he had accomplished before.'

Louis took a short break in 1974 to visit New York and got his three wives together – Marva, Rose and Martha – to talk about old times. *New York Post* gossip columnist Earl Wilson tracked down Joe later and asked him how they all got on. 'Fine, just fine,' said Louis. 'My second wife fixed the hair and make-up for my first and third wives, and they all looked just beautiful. We had a grand old time, just grand.'

By the summer of 1977, Louis had a heart condition and his coronary problems reached the crisis stage in October. He had flown to Houston, Texas for an operation. Heart specialist Dr Michael Debakey performed an arterial graft to correct what is known in medical terms as a dissecting aneurysm. The prognosis was grim. He also had high blood pressure and soon after he suffered a stroke. The toll it took on him was terrible, damaging his legs with near paralysis and badly affecting his speech. He was confined to a wheelchair from then on.

'The legs that once stalked opponents in the ring and carried him through nearly 12 unforgettable years as heavyweight champion of the world were rendered limp and useless,' said the *National Enquirer*. They published an appeal to readers, telling them how much Joe needed a boost to his general morale, which was low. Over 25,000 responded with get-well cards and letters. Each day, the Paradise Valley post office in Las Vegas was at its busiest ever delivering the mail. 'Just knowing that people care about him has given Joe a real mental lift,' said Martha.

Louis and Martha were now living at a ranch-style house in a cul-de-sac just a mile from the Las Vegas Strip. They shared living space with a housekeeper and a nurse. The housekeeper, Pilar Aldana, said, 'I've been reading the cards and letters to him but he's been opening some of the mail himself. A lot of it has brought a smile to his face – something we hadn't seen for a while.

'People wrote about the old times and how great he used to be. Many said he was even greater than Muhammad Ali, the current champion. Some wrote how they remembered listening to his fights on the radio. Many said they were praying for him to get well. A lot of schoolchildren have also been writing to him. Some have been making their own get-well cards with little hearts and gloves on them. It's beautiful. It really is.'

On 9 November 1978, Frank Sinatra hosted a benefit for Louis at Caesars Palace, with 1,500 people paying $500 a plate. The event was designed to benefit the Joe Louis International Sports Federation. The tax-exempt charity was based in Houston, Texas and had been formed earlier in the year to develop sports programmes and scholarships for youngsters.

Among the guests at the benefit were many leading figures from the world of entertainment, sport and public life, including

Los Angeles mayor Tom Bradley, Hollywood great Cary Grant, Muhammad Ali and two of Joe's former opponents, Billy Conn and Max Schmeling.

Max, who had flown over from Germany for the occasion, recalled, 'It was the last time I saw Joe. He was brought in by wheelchair. I spoke to him and he recognised me. He said, "Max." But he was in very bad condition.'

On 11 April 1981, Louis was wheeled to the ringside at Caesars Palace to watch Larry Holmes defend his world heavyweight title against Trevor Berbick. Holmes won on points. Though too ill to enjoy the fight and wearing a big cowboy hat, he waved in appreciation of the standing ovation from the crowd.

Had Louis looked around, he would have realised how much attendance figures for championship fights had changed. There were just 4,000 on hand. Back in 1935, a crowd of 88,150 came to see him fight Max Baer and 70,043 watched his return with Max Schmeling in 1938. There were 45,266 on hand for his second match with Billy Conn in 1946.

The boxing scene had moved with the times. This was the age when big crowds at important boxing matches did not count. Shows were held in casinos and hotel car parks, with the revenue coming in from television.

Early the next morning at home, Louis collapsed while walking to the bathroom and was rushed to Desert Springs Hospital. Within half an hour of being admitted, he died of cardiac arrest. He was four weeks short of his 67th birthday.

The funeral service was held in front of the Caesars Palace Sports Pavilion, where the Reverend Jesse Jackson, the civil rights activist and politician, delivered a touching eulogy. He reminded the attendance, estimated at 3,000, that Louis had outlived other powerful black figures such as Martin Luther King and Malcolm X.

'We could have lost Joe too,' he said, 'when we were so vulnerable ... when the stench of oppression and the lynch mobs filled our nostrils. He was our Samson, our David who slew Goliath, but he did it with kindness, with tenderness. He soothed our wounds.'

Jackson ended with a prompt to mourners, 'Let's hear it for the champ.'

Frank Sinatra said a few words. The singer had become a huge Louis fan in the late 1940s, when a boxing tournament Frank was promoting was poorly attended for several reasons. Joe was a paid guest but he waived his fee in view of the circumstances. Sinatra never forgot that. It was Frank's money that helped cover Louis' medical bills and other expenses in his final years. With Max Schmeling, he also paid for the funeral and burial expenses.

On Sunday 19 April, Louis' body was flown on an Air Force jet to Washington DC. The casket lay in state for two days at the 19th Street Baptist Church, whose pastor, Reverend Jerry Moore, had grown up in Louisiana, inspired by Joe's exploits in the ring.

Two days later, Louis was finally laid to rest at Arlington National Cemetery with full military honours before around 800 mourners. The cemetery is normally reserved for heroes of war dating back to 1864 but President Ronald Reagan waived the regulations. 'Arlington is a fitting place for a man whose instinctive patriotism and extraordinary accomplishments have made him one of the most unforgettable Americans of our time,' he said.

'It is hard to re-create for a new generation the world in which Joe Louis first appeared, or his role in changing that world for blacks in general,' wrote Thomas Sowell in the *Los Angeles Times*. 'What made Louis a unique figure was not simply his great talent as an athlete. He appeared at a time in

American history when blacks were not only at a low economic level, but were also the butt of ridicule.

'What Joe Louis did as a man could reinforce or counteract stereotypes that hurt and held back millions of people of his race. He was a continuing lesson to whites that to be black did not mean to be a clown or a lout, regardless of what the image-makers said. It was a lesson that helped open doors that had been closed for too long.'

Louis received many honours during his lifetime but perhaps the finest accolade was to come when he was posthumously inducted into the International Boxing Hall of Fame in Canastota, New York in 1990, nine years after his death. 'Joe Louis dominated the sport of boxing from the 1930s into the 1950s,' said chief executive Edward Brophy.

'He was arguably the best world heavyweight champion ever and in an era when blacks were still riding in the back of the bus, he was widely respected as an individual. Fans just didn't like Louis, they loved him. He was also a hero to a generation of younger boxers, some of whom faced him in his post-championship years.'

In many ways, it was the end of an era. Despite his disastrous business ventures and his notorious womanising, which led to a complicated love life, Louis, in his own quiet, undemonstrative way, had knocked down racial barriers the way his fists had knocked out opponents.

Holder of the world heavyweight title for nearly 12 years, which is still a record, he showed the world that dignity was as much a strength as his jabs, hooks, uppercuts and crosses. A champion inside and outside the roped square. Perhaps Jimmy Cannon of the *New York Daily News* summed it up best. 'Joe Louis was a credit to his race,' said Cannon, 'the human race.'

Joe Louis' professional record

Total contests: 67
Won 64, Lost three

Key: W = won
L = Lost
ko = knockout
tko = technical knockout, either stopped or retirement
Disq = disqualified
* denotes world title fight

1934

4 July	Jack Kracken	W tko 1	Chicago
12 July	Willie Davis	W tko 3	Chicago
30 July	Larry Udell	W tko 2	Chicago
13 August	Jack Kranz	W pts 8	Chicago
27 August	Buck Everett	W ko 2	Chicago
11 September	Al Delaney	W tko 4	Detroit
26 September	Adolph Waiter	W pts 10	Chicago
24 October	Art Sykes	W ko 8	Chicago
31 October	Jack O'Dowd	W ko 2	Detroit
14 November	Stanley Poreda	W ko 1	Chicago
30 November	Charlie Massera	W ko 3	Chicago
14 December	Lee Ramage	W tko 8	Chicago

1935

4 January	Patsy Perroni	W pts 10	Detroit
11 January	Hans Birkie	W tko 10	Pittsburgh

21 February	Lee Ramage	W tko 2	Los Angeles
8 March	Don 'Red' Barry	W tko 3	San Francisco
29 March	Natie Brown	W pts 10	Detroit
12 April	Roy Lazer	W tko 3	Chicago
25 June	Primo Carnera	W tko 6	New York
7 August	King Levinsky	W tko 1	Chicago
24 September	Max Baer	W tko 4	New York
13 December	Paulino Uzcudun	W tko 4	New York

1936

17 January	Charley Retzlaff	W ko 1	Chicago
19 June	Max Schmeling	L ko 12	New York
18 August	Jack Sharkey	W ko 3	New York
22 September	Al Ettore	W ko 5	Philadelphia
9 October	Jorge Brescia	W tko 3	New York
14 December	Eddie Simms	W tko 1	Cleveland

1937

11 January	Young Stanley Ketchel	W ko 2	New York
29 January	Bob Pastor	W pts 10	New York
17 February	Natie Brown	W tko 4	Kansas City
*22 June	James J. Braddock	W ko 8	Chicago
*30 August	Tommy Farr	W pts 15	New York

1938

*23 February	Nathan Mann	W ko 3	New York
*1 April	Harry Thomas	W ko 5	Chicago
*22 June	Max Schmeling	W ko 1	New York

1939

*25 January	John Henry Lewis	W ko 1	New York
*17 April	Jack Roper	W ko 1	Los Angeles
*28 June	Tony Galento	W tko 4	New York
*20 September	Bob Pastor	W ko 11	Detroit

1940

| *9 February | Arturo Godoy | W pts 15 | New York |
| *29 March | Johnny Paychek | W ko 2 | New York |

*20 June	Arturo Godoy	W tko 8	New York
*16 December	Al McCoy	W tko 6	Boston

1941

*31 January	Clarence 'Red' Burman	W ko 5	New York
*17 February	Gus Dorazio	W ko 2	Philadelphia
*21 March	Abe Simon	W tko 13	Detroit
*8 April	Tony Musto	W tko 9	St Louis
*23 May	Buddy Baer	W disq 7	Washington
*18 June	Billy Conn	W ko 13	New York
*29 September	Lou Nova	W tko 6	New York

1942

*9 January	Buddy Baer	W ko 1	New York
*27 March	Abe Simon	W ko 6	New York

1943–1945
Inactive

1946

*19 June	Billy Conn	W ko 8	New York
*18 September	Tami Mauriello	W ko 1	New York

1947

*5 December	Jersey Joe Walcott	W pts 15	New York

1948

*25 June	Jersey Joe Walcott	W ko 11	New York

1949
1 March
Announced retirement as world heavyweight champion

1950

*27 September	Ezzard Charles	L pts 15	New York
29 November	Cesar Brion	W pts 10	Chicago

1951

3 January	Freddie Beshore	W tko 4	Detroit
7 February	Omelio Agramonte	W pts 10	Miami
23 February	Andy Walker	W tko 10	San Francisco
2 May	Omelio Agramonte	W pts 10	Detroit
15 June	Lee Savold	W ko 6	New York
1 August	Cesar Brion	W pts 10	San Francisco
15 August	Jimmy Bivins	W pts 10	Baltimore
26 October	Rocky Marciano	L tko 8	New York

Selected bibliography

Astor, Gerald, *Gloves Off*, Pelham Books, 1974

Bak, Richard, *Joe Louis, The Great Black Hope,* Da Capo Publishing, 1998

Fleischer, Nat, *The Ring Record Book*, The Ring Book Shop, 1957

Kent, Graeme, *A Welshman in the Bronx*, Gomer, 2009

Louis, Joe, *My Life,* Angus and Robertson, 1978

Mead, Chris, *Champion Joe Louis*, Robson Books, 1986

Monninger, Joseph, *Two Ton*, Steerforth Press, 2007

Myler, Patrick, *Ring of Hate*, Mainstream Publishing, 2005

Myler, Thomas, *Close Encounters with the Gloves Off*, Pitch Publishing, 2016

Nagler, Barney, *The Pilgrimage of Joe Louis*, World Publishing, 1972

Roberts, James B, Skutt, Alexander G, *The Boxing Register*, McBooks Press, 2006

Roberts, Randy, *Joe Louis*, Yale University Press, 2010

Von Der Lippe, George, *Max Schmeling: An Autobiography,* Bonus Books, 1998

Other sources

Boxing News

Boxing News's 100 Greatest Boxers of All Time

Joe Louis: The Rise and Fall of the Brown Bomber

Ring
Boxing and Wrestling
The Fights, The Facts, The Action Videos
DeAgostini's Boxers, The Undisputed DVD Collection

Index